Medialogies

Political Theory and Contemporary Philosophy

Political Theory and Contemporary Philosophy encourages a sustained dialogue between the most important intellectual currents in recent European philosophy—including phenomenology, deconstruction, hermeneutics—and key political theories and concepts, both classical and modern. In doing so, it not only sheds new light on today's shifting political realities but also explores the previously neglected consequences of the two disciplines.

Series editor: Michael Marder

Other volumes in the series include:

Democracy and Its Others, Jeffrey H. Epstein

The Democracy of Knowledge, Daniel Innerarity
(translated by Sandra Kingery)

The Voice of Conscience: A Political Genealogy of Western Ethical Experience, Mika Ojakangas

The Politics of Nihilism, edited by Nitzan Lebovic and Roy Ben-Shai

On Hegel's Philosophy of Right, Martin Heidegger (edited by Peter Trawny, Marcia Cavalcante Schuback and Michael Marder, translated by Andrew J. Mitchell)

Deconstructing Zionism, Michael Marder and Santiago Zabala

Heidegger on Hegel's Philosophy of Right, Marcia Sa Cavalcante Schuback, Michael Marder and Peter Trawny

The Metaphysics of Terror, Rasmus Ugilt

The Negative Revolution, Artemy Magun

The Sacred and the Political, edited by Elisabetta Brighi and Antonio Cerella

The Voice of Conscience, Mika Ojakangas

Medialogies

Reading Reality in the Age of Inflationary Media

David R. Castillo and William Egginton

Bloomsbury Academic
An imprint of Bloomsbury Publishing Plc

B L O O M S B U R Y
NEW YORK · LONDON · OXFORD · NEW DELHI · SYDNEY

Bloomsbury Academic

An imprint of Bloomsbury Publishing Inc

1385 Broadway	50 Bedford Square
New York	London
NY 10018	WC1B 3DP
USA	UK

www.bloomsbury.com

BLOOMSBURY and the Diana logo are trademarks of Bloomsbury Publishing Plc

First published 2017

Library of Congress Cataloging-in-Publication Data
A catalogue record for this book is available from the Library of Congress.

ISBN: HB: 978-1-6289-2360-5
PB: 978-1-6289-2359-9
ePDF: 978-1-6289-2361-2
ePub: 978-1-6289-2363-6

Series: Political Theory and Contemporary Philosophy

Typeset by Integra Software Services Pvt. Ltd.

To find out more about our authors and books visit www.bloomsbury.com. Here you will find extracts, author interviews, details of forthcoming events, and the option to sign up for our newsletters.

Contents

List of Illustrations   vii

Acknowledgments   ix

Introduction: Medialogies   1

Part 1   Inflationary Media

1   Editing Reality   9

2   A New Perspective   17

3   Theatricality   27

4   Commodity-Spectacles   35

5   How to Turn Things into Copies, and Copies into Things   43

Part 2   Fundamentals

6   Ineffable Me   59

7   Foundations   65

8   Freedom for Sale   73

9   Crime Shows   79

10   Political Theater   91

11   Monumental Screens   99

12   The New Fundamentals   111

Part 3   Exclusions

13   Terrifying Vistas of Reality   121

14   Dreamboat Vampires and Zombie Capitalists   127

15   The Global Undead   141

16   Dark Mirrors   149

17   Apocalypse Then and Now   155

Part 4   In Defense of Being

18   Minor Strategies   165
19   Stranger than Fiction   169
20   Truth and Lies in Life and Art   177
21   Staging the Event   187
22   The Architecture of Mourning   197
23   Occupy and Resist   201
24   Empire of Solitude   207

Epilogue   219
Notes   226
Bibliography   241
Index   254

List of Illustrations

2.1   Albrecht Dürer, self-portrait with a pillow, courtesy of
      Wikimedia Commons   20
2.2   Hans Holbein, The ambassadors, 1553, courtesy of Wikimedia
      Commons   21
9.1   Frontispiece to Sebastián de Covarrubias, *Emblemas morales*
      (Madrid, 1610); courtesy of the George Peabody Library,
      Sheridan Libraries, the Johns Hopkins University   84
9.2   Covarrubias, p. 34; courtesy of the George Peabody Library,
      Sheridan Libraries, the Johns Hopkins University   85
9.3   Covarrubias, p. 204; courtesy of the George Peabody Library,
      Sheridan Libraries, the Johns Hopkins University   86
9.4   Francisco de la Torre, *Luces de la aurora* (Valencia, 1665),
      pp. 562–563; courtesy of the George Peabody Library, Sheridan
      Libraries, the Johns Hopkins University   87
9.5   Covarrubias, p. 237; courtesy of the George Peabody Library,
      Sheridan Libraries, the Johns Hopkins University   88
9.6   From Covarrubias, p. 21 recto; courtesy of the George Peabody
      Library, Sheridan Libraries, the Johns Hopkins University   89
10.1 *Fiestas dela santa iglesia de Sevilla al culto nuevamente concedido
      al Señor Rei San Fernando III de Castilla i Leon* (Seville, 1671);
      courtesy of the George Peabody Library, Sheridan Libraries,
      the Johns Hopkins University   94
10.2 Covarrubias, p. 297; courtesy of the George Peabody Library,
      Sheridan Libraries, the Johns Hopkins University   96
11.1 Frontispiece to Thomas Hobbes, *Leviathan*, 1651, etching by
      Abraham Bosse, courtesy of Wikimedia Commons   102
11.2 Photograph by authors   107

20.1   Velázquez, *Las hilanderas*, courtesy of Wikimedia Commons   182

23.1   Photograph by authors   205

E.1   Valdés Leal, *Finis Gloriae Mundi*, 1672, courtesy of Wikimedia
       Commons   222

E.2   Velázquez, *Las meninas*, 1656, courtesy of Wikimedia Commons   223

Acknowledgments

Parts of the discussion of Disneyworld in Chapter 4 was published as David Castillo, "Baroque Landscapes: The Spectacle of America," in *America Scapes: Americans in/and Their Diverse Sceneries*, eds. Ewelina Bánka, Mateusz Liwinski and Kamil Rusitowicz. Lublin: Wydawnictwo KUL, 2013. The Arguments in Chapter 7 were originally put forward in chapter 4 of Castillo's *Baroque Horrors*. Part of Chapter 11 was published as David Castillo, "Monumental Landscapes in the Society of the Spectacle: From Fuenteovejuna to New York," *Spectacle and Topophilia: Reading Early Modern and Postmodern Cultures*, eds. David Castillo and Bradley Nelson. Hispanic Issues, Vol. 38. Nashville: Vanderbilt University Press, 2012. Chapters 9 and 10 were originally published as William Egginton, "Crime Shows—CSI: Hapsburg Madrid," in Peter Goodrich and Valerie Hayaert, eds., *Genealogies of Legal Vision*, London: Routledge, 2015, 243–58. An earlier version of Chapter 21 was originally published as Egginton, "Staging the Event: The Theatrical Ground of Metaphysical Framing," in Michael Marder and Santiago Zabala, eds. *Being Shaken*, Palgrave, 2014, 177–85. Some sections of Chapters 14, 15, and 16 were published as David Castillo, "Monsters for the Age of the Post-Human," *Writing Monsters: Essays on Iberian and Latin American Cultures*, eds. Adriana Gordillo and Nicholas Spadaccini, Hispanic Issues on Line, Vol. 15, Spring 2014, and Castillo et al. *Zombie Talk: Culture, History, Politics*, Palgrave Macmillan, 2016. We are grateful to all these publishers for permission to reuse these materials here.

Introduction: Medialogies

We are living in a time of inflationary media. While technological change has periodically altered and advanced the ways humans process and transmit knowledge, for the last 100 years the media with which we produce, communicate, and record ideas have multiplied in kind, speed, and power. This revolution has gone so far as to inspire many commentators to argue that our saturation in media is provoking a crisis in how we perceive and understand reality. From telegrams to tweets, the twentieth-century media revolution would seem to be a unique development in history; but the magnitude of the revolution is not unprecedented, and the crisis it has provoked recalls a prior one. Another period of inflationary media preceded ours by about 400 years, and coincided with the dawn of modern Europe and what Immanuel Wallerstein has called the world system.

A media age does not become inflationary merely because of the multiplications of kinds, speed, and power of media, however. Media become inflationary when the scope of their representation of the world threatens the confines of their culture's prior notions of reality. We call the resulting concept of reality that emerges the culture's *medialogy*.[1] In the first age of inflationary media, the invention of moveable type and the development of a vibrant print culture, the rapid spread of the use of perspective in painting and architecture, and the rise of an urban mass theater institution conspired to provoke a crisis of reality. Books changed from unique objects to copies of an ideal text; the way perspective situated viewers created the sense that one's point of view was both unique and limited; and the distinction between actors and the characters they portrayed began to be used as a model for understanding the relationship between human knowledge and reality itself.[2] As a result of these media developments, the very space a person occupied with his or her fellow beings began to be experienced not as a seamless continuum joining all those beings together, but as a background to individual perceptions that could be manipulated or veiled and that depended ultimately on limited and limiting perspectives. This backdrop earned the name, new in languages of the time, of reality.

The second inflationary age follows on the emergence of electronic media. The wireless telegraph translates a message into a binary code that is transmitted by electric current over enormous distances almost instantaneously. From its development in the 1830s through the invention of wireless radio at the end of that century to the ubiquity of electronic media today, individual perspectives on the world, whether imagistic or discursive, have been translated into information to be broadcast, stored, and transmitted at enormous distance. By transferring information instead of material, electronic media are freed from limitations of space, time, and number of copies. The age becomes inflationary, though, not because of the technological changes that enable it, but because of the crisis these new media provoke in the concept of reality inherited from the first inflationary age.

Reality after the first inflationary age was uprooted and subject to perspective, but also posited as independent of our knowledge and unknowable in itself. In politics this medialogy permitted an organization of sovereignty, the nation state, which transcended the bonds of family and locality. In the second inflationary age, that ideal model of sovereignty is itself losing its coherence, as states fracture and fall to ethnic groups or bend to the will of multinational corporations. Likewise, money in the first inflationary age grounded wealth in an ideal representation of a national coin; in today's medialogy, the wealth of nations rises and falls on the spectral manipulations of market confidence, and the transfer and maintenance of wealth rely increasingly on the indecipherability of the encryptions used to safeguard it; if the wealthy used to protect their gold with walls and locks, now their wealth is indistinguishable from the digital locks that protect it. In the most general sense, the first inflationary age provoked a crisis in reality by proliferating things, such as books or bodies, as if they were copies, which in turn projected the ideal world as their template. In the second age, those copies take on the status or aura of original things; books, celluloid, vinyl, or celebrity's bodies become the physical depositories of what David Shields calls our "reality hunger";[3] the invisible and grounding core of identities, from nations to the wealth they generate to the earth itself, becomes unanchored and cedes to a reification of what had once been its avatars, shells, or representatives.

The understanding of reality as a collection of objects that refer back to an ideal form can be traced back to Plato. In the context of Platonic thought, while "the ideal" is essentially unattainable, the *spoken word* is posed as a naturally higher form of approximation to its ultimate truth vis-à-vis the written word. In the early modern period (what we call the first age of inflationary media), the "ideal" is still "officially" posed as the necessary yet ineffable substratum of reality (the theological truth behind worldly deceptions), yet the relative value of the spoken versus the written word is up for grabs. More importantly for our purposes, when it comes to the *printed word*, the "ideal form" is retroactively posed as the site of origin of the copy, that is, its "original."

The treatment of the royal seal in Hapsburg Spain is a good example of this logic. At the time of Philip II, the royal seal was routinely transported inside a covered chest accompanied by the pageantry usually devoted to the person of the King. While the image of the royal seal was infinitely reproducible in official documents, a key distinction was made in practice between the primary object (the original) and its printed images (its copies), even if this type of distinction was sometimes problematized or even mocked in baroque art, by a painter like Velázquez, or in literature and theater by a writer like Cervantes.

Of course the distinction between copy and original and between representation and reality is frequently lost in our own age of inflationary media, where, to put it in Benjamin's words, technical reproducibility has accelerated the decay of art's "aura."[4] Yet we still crave the experience of "the authentic." This hunger for the truth behind "simulations" has resulted in a fundamentalist search for the original unadulterated word and for the authentic body. Interestingly, now the book, as opposed to the spoken word, is where fundamentalists look for the unmediated truth, the necessary anchor of a shifting reality.

In the first age of inflationary media, cultural production of all kinds offers dramatic examples of the paradoxical status of *truth* and *authenticity* in a world that has lost its traditional anchors. One of the most radical illustrations of this shifting cultural environment can be found in the Jesuit philosopher Baltasar Gracián's influential *Pocket Oracle and Art of Prudence* (*Oráculo manual y arte de prudencia*, 1647), a how-to manual for early modern elites that focused on how to achieve power and recognition in a rapidly changing world. In his *Pocket Oracle* and several other works, Gracián conceptualizes the self, what he calls *persona*, from the Greek word for mask, as an artificial site of theatrical performance and social negotiations. In Gracián's thought, knowledge of self and the world is no longer posed as a search for the truth behind the artifice or, in Platonic terms, the ideal behind the shadows, since for us the true self is unknowable, there is nothing but shadows behind the shadows. This is what we call the crisis of reality at the heart of the first medialogy.

When the reality behind appearance is thus removed from the grasp of immediate perception, it becomes susceptible to manipulation by the very elites Gracian's manual is intended for. But if elites can use media to manipulate the perception of reality, their strategies were subject to contestation by marginalized sectors. In his revealing overview of "the first 2000 years of social media," *Writing on the Wall*, Tom Standage offers a vital historical perspective that helps us understand how print culture contributed to "synchronize public opinion," providing the spark for major historical revolutions, including the Reformation as well as the American and French Revolutions. Standage recognizes synchronization as a sword with two edges, which he respectively calls horizontal and vertical, where the latter refers to the top-down synchronization that benefited traditional elites. What we bring to the debate is the role that the new mass media was playing in consolidating state-power already in the early modern period. We also put the spotlight on the cultural "malcontents" who simultaneously warned against the dangers of such vertical synchronization and developed strategies for undermining it.

When Standage notes that new media "can make life more difficult for repressive regimes" but also "help governments spread propaganda," he is thinking especially of our own times; and yet, even in the early modern period, the new media could indeed destabilize established institutions (a point he makes effectively in talking about Luther's use of the printing press against Church officials and doctrine), but it could also contribute to "synchronize public opinion" from the top-down. This is what happened in Imperial Spain with the introduction of the mass-oriented theater and other forms of spectacular media, what historian José Antonio Maravall has called the *guided culture of the baroque.*

Likewise in our day, more news (and more ways of delivering news) does not automatically make us better informed. Paradoxically, the news choices that are made available by cable TV and their internet silos have resulted in a "reality-on-demand" phenomenon that conspires to keep us in blissful denial of inconvenient facts. We get to choose our news (say Fox, CNN, or MSNBC) based on what we want to hear; we are entitled to our own facts, our own media-framed reality. While such "consumer choice" in what image of reality we choose to believe in might seem liberating, in fact what Eli Pariser termed the "filter bubble" of contemporary consumer culture makes us even more manipulable as consumers and as subjects.[5]

In what follows, we argue that to understand the impact of today's era of inflationary media and its attendant crisis of reality, we must first understand its predecessor. Technologies differ vastly, but the strategies for deploying them exhibit profound similarities. It is not a coincidence that the handbooks written for the instruction of that age's powerbrokers, from Niccolò Machiavelli's *The Prince* to Baltasar Gracián's *Pocket Oracle*, have found such a receptive audience today, even including a best-selling translation of the second with the title *The Art of Worldly Wisdom* in 1992, followed by several new editions in the 2000s. These early modern thinkers were witnesses to the first age of inflationary media, and were among the first to spell out its implications for the expansion and consolidation of power. In an age when the traditional power nexus was threatened by expansions of geographical, economic, scientific, and individual horizons, the modern state would learn from traditional elites in the church and landed aristocracy how to put cultural production to the service of reproducing its power structure. The mass media of the time, especially print and theater, would develop into powerful weapons; but those weapons would also turn out to have two well-sharpened edges.

In his 2011 *Visualizing Law in the Age of the Digital Baroque*, legal scholar Richard Sherwin called for a new "post-Cartesian" form of visual jurisprudence, an "ethical optics" that must be anchored in an understanding of the "aesthetic, cognitive, and cultural codes of law as image in the digital age."[6] He argues that in the "post-human era" ruled by "digital-panoptic technologies," the essential ethical question is this: "Who and what do we become when we live on the screen, when we internalize the screen's optical code as our own?"[7] Sherwin suggests looking back at the origins of our culture of the spectacle in the historical baroque in search for potential answers to this key question. In the present book, we provide a response, or rather a range of possible responses, to Sherwin's urgent question, as part of a sustained dialogue with the spectacular culture of the baroque and its discontents. In the process, we also hope to contribute to an "ethical optics" for the second age of inflationary media, what he calls the digital baroque.

Each inflationary age bears witness to a struggle for appropriation, a struggle that takes place in the arenas of economy, politics, and culture. In each of these arenas, now as then, individuals differ; minority populations endeavor to assert themselves; and entrenched interests and powerful elites react with containment strategies. The question becomes what modes these struggles assume; how they might change; and what the consequences of these changes are. *Medialogies* describes how the crisis of reality provoked by inflationary media in the early modern period set the stage for an epic struggle between domination and freedom in our own age of inflationary media.

Part One

Inflationary Media

1

Editing Reality

In a memorable moment from Wes Craven's 1996 camp horror classic *Scream*, Randy, a movie-obsessed teenager, explains to a friend in reference to a recent murder, "It's the millennium. Motives are incidental." This line, along with many others from the movie, entered the media mainstream in part because it seemed to encapsulate an understanding of late twentieth-century realities shared by popular culture and intellectuals alike. According to this view, U.S. culture specifically but also western culture in general had entered a period in which its media saturation had reached a kind of critical threshold, beyond which the reality underlying media representations no longer seemed that real. In the political realm, this sentiment was most trenchantly captured in a conversation the journalist Ron Suskind had with an unnamed aide to President George W. Bush (later identified as Karl Rove), whom he cited in a 2004 *New York Times Magazine* article as saying "that guys like me were 'in what we call the reality-based community,'" which he defined as people who "believe that solutions emerge from your judicious study of discernible reality."[1] These examples from film and politics seem to buttress the theses of numerous academics and journalists who have written frantically for the last few decades of the loss of reality attributable to the rise and intensity of our new media culture and its ever-increasing saturation of our daily lives.

What provokes this erosion of reality is our increased awareness of the media's ability to *edit our world*, to show us what someone else wants us to see instead of what's actually there. We call today's media inflationary because they impact not only the message they ostensibly convey, as Marshall McLuhan so famously argued, but our entire understanding of the world. This situation, however, is not unique to our age. Four hundred years ago the western world was also engulfed in a media revolution that, although the specific media were different, also provoked a reality crisis. Moreover, while we tend to think that the specific media determine the effects on reality, we forget that the concept of reality a culture has to begin with is equally vital.

Media edit reality by *framing* lived experience as a coherent narrative or set of images. Insofar as the content of the frame, or screen, is conceived as a specific perspective or version of the real, the framing function projects an ultimate but unattainable reality behind that screen, while excluding from its purview anything that threatens the screen's coherence. Both early modern and current medialogies are constructed in exactly this way. But while media in the former age used prior notions of reality as its raw material (specifically, the human world as microcosm of the divine), media in the new age exercise this function on the very notion of reality that was itself created by the first age. Thus, the first age—characterized by the conjunction of theater, print, and perspective in painting—produced reality as ineffable but fundamental, and based ideas like national identity and wealth on it, while editing out certain racial, national, or sexual exclusions. The second age—that of electronic media—takes those copies and puts them into everyone's hands, or at least into the hands of those who have the purchasing power. Now the previous realities are located in tangible objects again: copies are made into things; books, vinyl, bodies acquire new powers of presence. Fundamentalism in its modern form arises with new literalisms; nation states devolve into tribalism and religious orthodoxy; and the current exclusions are those outside the bandwidth of the electronic revolution, those without purchasing power— the homeless, the dispossessed—whose exclusion is expressed in our media culture in the form of modern monsters.

By the early 1400s the first works of linear perspective were produced, and the technique spread like wildfire in the 1500s. When Brunelleschi painted a single-point perspective copy of the Florence Cathedral, witnesses were tricked into thinking a picture was the real thing: a flat surface conveyed depth. By the late 1500s the stage was attempting to do the same thing with reality itself, to great success. The first spectacular mass medium was born— the modern theater—with the explosion of interior, fungible, representational space as one of its signatures.

In the mid-fifteenth century, of course, another medium was born as well: the printing press. Books would later start proliferating as mass-produced, largely identical copies of a source text. From that point on, a text would no longer be a thing in the world; rather, it would become the phantom idea behind a potential infinity of exact copies. Paintings, stages, and books are all means of copying the world, and their status as copies provokes us to question their own reality while simultaneously projecting an ideal reality beyond their surface. Just as the modern theater depends on self-reflexivity—stages about stages, where characters are also actors—modern literature emerges as an endless series of texts about texts, where characters are also authors. This self-reflexivity with its attendant paradoxes and possibilities begins to define the aesthetic realm, but also the economic and political spheres.

The term that may best define the culture wars of the first age of inflationary media is the baroque trope known as *desengaño* or disillusion, literally *un-deception*. The basic idea is that we were naïve in our beliefs; we were living inside an illusion that we are now invited or guided to transcend. What the term *desengaño* describes is a reframing of reality, a realignment of the border between the visible and the invisible, and the new media—theater, perspective painting, the book—hold the promise of the truth beyond deceptions. The point to emphasize is that this reframing of reality may work to shake us awake from the dream of worldly deceptions and fix our gaze on the metaphysical truth beyond (this is the "solution" that we would associate with the baroque *major strategy*) or, alternately, it may fold back on itself to show that the deception is actually in the framing, as if to shout, "It's the framing, stupid!" This is the revelation that we associate with the *minor strategy* of baroque aesthetics.[2]

The notion of *desengaño* was central to the visual arts, literature, and theater of the first inflationary age. It's no accident that the period spanning roughly from the 1550s to the 1650s marked the highest point in the popularity of anamorphic images, that is, visual artifacts that incorporate hidden perspectives revealing to their viewers that their initial impressions were inaccurate. Art historian Julián Gállego has gathered evidence of the popularity of anamorphic paintings in the early 1600s and concludes that, "everyone seemed to have them."[3] The sonnets of *desengaño* created by poets like Luis de Góngora, Francisco de Quevedo, Lope de Vega, and Sor Juana Inés de la Cruz, among many others, are considered paradigmatic examples of baroque poetry. In prose, the success of the picaresque genre is based on the titillation of the life stories of marginal social types: undesirables, rogues, criminals, and "free women." These life stories and the worldviews that come with them, which had been largely invisible before 1550, relied on the trope of "undeceiving" their audiences. The first literary *pícaro* made this point rather effectively in the Prologue of *Lazarillo de Tormes* (1554): "For I believe that matters of such significance, which have never been heard or seen before, must be noted."[4] Similarly, the baroque exemplary novellas of Miguel de Cervantes and María de Zayas put the spotlight on what is excluded from view. Even more significantly for our purposes, the new full-length novel, which emerges during this period, focuses on the complexities of framing mechanisms in literature, theater, and reality itself, most influentially in the masterpiece considered the first modern novel, *Don Quixote* (1605; 1615).

But at the time the true blockbusters were the plays composed according to the winning formula popularized by Lope de Vega in his treatise *The New Art of Making Plays in Our Time* (*El arte nuevo de hacer comedias en este tiempo*), which the playwright first read before the Madrid Academy in 1609. Many of the plays associated with the cultural phenomenon of the *comedia nueva* rework historical material dealing with the tumultuous period stretching from the late Middle Ages to their contemporary period. They project an idealized version of the *here and now* as the desired and necessary outcome of history's progress: a unified Christian nation under the tutelage of the absolutist monarchy and the Catholic Church. Such popular plays as Lope de Vega's *Fuenteovejuna* and Calderón de la Barca's *The Alderman of Zalamea* (*El alcalde de Zalamea*) may be considered predecessors of today's action flicks and crime shows. These and other historical plays and *dramas de honor* redefined "honor" as a genuinely Spanish value, a patriotic trait shared by loyal commoners and noblemen alike, which distinguishes *us* (honor-loving and God-fearing subjects of the Crown) from *them* (infidels, heretics, barbarians, immoral, and disloyal lords…). They depicted the dramatic tension of their subject matter, often resulting from noblemen acting in distinctly dishonorable ways, as temporary failures of judgment or vision, easily corrected by divine providence or the actions of royal authority guided by the honor code.

This is not to say that all the plays associated with the *comedia nueva* or new theater work exactly in the same way. We can find a number of full-length plays, especially among the so-called *comedias de enredo* as well as short comedic pieces, that poke holes in the honor code and its strictures. Yet within the tradition of historical plays and honor dramas, the new and improved (and thoroughly theatrical) concept of honor works as an *interpellation* in the proper Althusserian sense, a call to act out our belief in the essential and trans-historical Nation, and thus to embody the symbolic law as represented or performed on the stage.

While there is new content, form, and functionality in today's age of inflationary media, the prevailing strategies of ideological interpellation are remarkably familiar, and similar cultural reverberations occur. As Sherwin writes: "We are awash in images, which means we know from watching [...] We know, or think we know, partly because we have absorbed useful stereotypes and recurring representations from popular culture. We carry them around in our heads, images that help to construct our personal and collective histories."[5] Sherwin provides illustrations from our present or immediate past, including iconic images in films like *Apocalypse Now* and *Platoon* that have become synthetic memories of the Vietnam war; or Jarhead and *Syriana* in the case of the war in Iraq; even the series of TV images that documented the 9/11 attacks of the World Trade Center, which stabilized our perception of anti-freedom terror "like a totemic stand-in for the chaotic barrage of events too discordant and too painful to confront."[6] The same could be said about the popular honor dramas of the 1600s. *Fuenteovejuna* and *The Alderman of Zalamea*, among many other "historical plays" of the period, offer their audiences imagistic synthetic memories of chaotic and complex events, appropriately distilled to "mean something," that is, to speak to the values of the age in ways that helped their audience understand who they were (or ought to want to be) both as individuals and as communities.

As historical reality is absorbed by the culture of the spectacle, it becomes "a visual template, an archive of iconic sounds, images, and words"[7] that anchors our reality in reference to stabilizing categories and values. In this context, "freedom" is for the political reality of America what the theatrically propagated notion of "honor" was meant to be for an early modern imperial power like Spain, "a condition of neutralization" of true political alternatives—to paraphrase Vattimo and Zabala—"where 'freedom' is only possible within the established dialogue."[8] Indeed, in the political landscape of America, this synthetic notion of freedom has long been entangled with nationalistic claims of historical exceptionalism.

Comedian Stephen Colbert has written on the political entanglements of American exceptionalism with characteristic sharpness in his book *America Again: Re-Becoming the Greatness We Never Weren't*. There he quotes from Newt Gingrich's political best-seller *A Nation Like No Other*: "America's greatness, America's *exceptional* greatness, is not based on that fact that we are the most powerful, most prosperous—and most generous—nation on Earth. Rather, those things are the *result* of American Exceptionalism."[9] Colbert's satirical commentary drives the point home: "Amen! America is Exceptional because of our Greatness and the source of all that Greatness is how Exceptional we are."[10]

This is not unlike the circularity of Tigger's familiar song from the Walt Disney version of A.A. Milne's *Winnie the Pooh*, "The wonderful thing about Tiggers is that Tiggers are wonderful things," where we simply replace Tigger with America: "the wonderful thing about America is that America is a wonderful thing." Of course, in their respective contexts of enunciation, the Exceptionalism of America now and Spain then stand for the interests of elites that are readily defined as the communal interests and, more importantly, the natural expression of the Nation's trans-historical spirit. In the process, the circularity of Tigger's song about *us* establishes a corresponding circularity about some excluded others: *the terrible thing about them is that they are a terrible thing! They* are defined not just as external or foreign enemies but also as internal nonbelievers or, as Colbert writes, "bad boys and girls who don't say 'under God' in the Pledge of Allegiance."[11]

Our political discourse continues to produce and reify mythical images of the national spirit and the trans-historical evildoers that work relentlessly to destroy our communities. And now, as then, our exclusions come back to haunt us. Our industry frames culture for mass consumption, and culture strikes back with relics that are in turn commoditized.

As with the first age of inflationary media, media in our new age can simultaneously be a means of liberation and oppression. The extent of media's reach, though, threatens the coherence of nation states just as the previous inflationary phase threatened traditional localities and led to organizations of a national nature. In the age of global capitalism, nation states are the traditional structure. Inflationary media enables globalization as both an oppressive and liberating potentiality. A commercial for the iPhone 5 ended with the manifesto, "I have the right to be unlimited," by which Apple means, to upload unlimited data, to make a copy of my entire life, my entire world. The world is now truly my oyster. If before I had an individual perspective on the world, now I can upload that entire perspective and carry it with me wherever I go.

If the framing machines of the first age of inflationary media led to commodity fetishism, those of the second age of inflationary media incorporate their commodity form into their very structure. In the first age, things took on the mode of copies. In the second age, copies take on the mode of things. Where the nation state was an organization of people treated as copies; now the forces of globalized capital are symbolic entities treated as people, as clarified by the Supreme Court's 2012 Citizens United decision extending First Amendment protections to corporations. Likewise, encrypted numbers are now treated like the wealth they ostensibly represent. Underlying the flow of values over the global network is a loose system of beliefs built exclusively on the relative confidence of markets in given currencies. When national entities are criticized, their identity is alleged to be "historical." The organizations that strive to replace them, though, portray themselves as real, unconstructed. When Newt Gingrich called the Palestinians an invented people, he passed over the irony that this utterance was issued from the United States of America. As Borges once wrote, "in America it is absurd to invent a country"; there, one could only propose "the invention of a planet."[12]

A New Perspective

Writers, thinkers, and artists prior to the first age of inflationary media most often conceived of themselves and others as seamlessly embedded in the cosmos; accordingly, they did not see the cosmos as existing independently of its observers or inhabitants. By the end of the sixteenth century, they began to develop an entirely different notion of the individual, and in early modern works of literature as well as in painting and architecture the individual's perspective began to be a central concern.[1] Simultaneously once Copernicus and after him Kepler had clarified that the earth was not at the center of the cosmos and that the planets followed elliptical orbits, natural philosophers such as Giordano Bruno were free to imagine the cosmos as an infinite expanse of space without necessarily granting the earth or its inhabitants a privileged place within it.

Prior to the sixteenth century, very few Europeans were literate. Other than the highly educated Jewish and Muslim scholars living in the Iberian Peninsula, in the rest of Europe it was almost exclusively Christian monks who could read and write, and they did so only in Latin. Popular literature as we understand it today hardly existed at all, and the tales that were told were largely passed from generation to generation by word of mouth. One aspect these tales shared in common was the allegorical nature of the world they described. Heroes were greater than life because they were instruments of providence; their failures were due to the weakness of the flesh and thus conveyed moral lessons; and the geography of their adventure symbolized the mystical body of Christ, his crowned head occupying the goal of Jerusalem, as often portrayed in maps of the time.[2] What literature tended to portray in the Middle Ages, even as works started to be associated with specific authors such as Chrétien de Troyes, was a viewpoint entirely embedded in the world. The author expressed a world as it had to be; there was no sense that characters were moving through some reality that existed independent of their experience of it, but also no sense that the narrative was concerned with how one character's experience of the world might be different from another's, or from the reader's. Instead, narrative or verse was concerned with exploring a commonly shared world; it was dedicated to an almost ritualistic invocation of a shared cultural experience.

This tendency started to change throughout the fourteenth and fifteenth centuries. In Italy first Dante Alighieri and later Petrarch would write in splendid vernacular Italian poems and prose that started to reveal the stamp of an individual's point of view as he searched for God, for love, or for personal fulfillment. In the mid-fourteenth century Giovanni Boccaccio penned the *Decameron*, a collection of 100 stories exchanged by a group of young men and women over a ten-day period that explored the trials and tribulations of love. The *Decameron* was in turn the inspiration for Geoffrey Chaucer's famous *Canterbury Tales*, which recounts the raucous stories exchanged by a group of travelers on a pilgrimage to Canterbury. But these seminal works of western literature, as moving, funny, and often detailed in their descriptions of daily life as they all are, still look on their many characters as though they were a myriad of figures stitched into a vibrant tapestry hung on a castle wall. What they do not do, and what began to become common toward the end of the sixteenth century and dominant as of the seventeenth, is to nestle into the different perspectives of those characters, sharing with them their emotions, desire, and curiosity as to the intentions and desires of other characters.

In painting the rise of individual perspectives was even more striking, which is unsurprising given the origin of the term in the visual arts. Early in the fifteenth century Filippo Brunelleschi, who built the great cathedral of Florence, Santa Maria del Fiore, used the existing science of optics to create a painting able to convince viewers that they were looking at something real. To prove his point Brunelleschi situated a painting of the baptistery, which faced the cathedral, in the doorway of the cathedral, but facing outward. He then invited viewers to peer through a tiny hole he had drilled in precisely at the painting's vanishing point. However, instead of allowing them to gaze at the baptistery itself, he blocked that view with a mirror that reflected his painting back toward the viewers, fooling them into thinking they were in fact viewing the real building.

The techniques of linear perspective spread rapidly throughout Europe during the sixteenth century. Departing from the tradition of the Middle Ages, according to which the importance of a figure's social standing determined its size in a painting, now painters would change the size of figures in order to produce the effect of depth. Simultaneously, as stage designers would notice when they used the perspective to create sets for the theater industry, scenes constructed using perspective techniques only allow for one ideal vantage, directly facing the vanishing point. Thus productions created for nobles and Kings would ensure that only the highest ranked in an audience would be given the view of the stage that seemed the most real, with all others distanced from that perspective in direct proportion to their own social standing.[3]

The rise of the individual perspectives on the world can also be seen in the evolution of portraiture. Instead of conveying the grandeur, rank, or status of his subjects by using the conventional imagery of the time, the German painter Albrecht Dürer made a point of focusing on aspects of his subjects that made them stand out as individuals. His experiments also included a number of self-portraits that show an unusual focus on his own distinct personality, which led both to a tendency to self-aggrandizement, such as in cases where the artist seems to be portraying himself as a kind of Christ-figure, but also to an undermining of the idea of the painting as a direct and immediate picture of the world.[4] His cameo in other paintings, such as the sketch he made of himself on the back side of a more finished self-portrait, seem to be clues that these images are the creations of a particular man. That man is thus raised in stature, but his works are also humanized as the products of a limited, individual perspective.

Scarcely fifty years later, another German painter, Hans Holbein the younger, produced a portrait that literalized this evolution of the artist's perspective and popularized the use of the science of optics to create complex and beguiling optical illusions that depend on and dramatize how a viewer's position in relation to a surface determines what he or she sees. In *The ambassadors*, Holbein shows us two wealthy and prominent figures surrounded by the trappings of worldly power. Stretched on the floor between them, however, is a

Figure 2.1 Albrecht Dürer, self-portrait with a pillow, courtesy of Wikimedia Commons.

strange oblong smear. If you approach the lower left corner of the canvass that hangs in the National Gallery in London (in fact, there is no way to occupy the correct spot without calling the unwanted attention of museum guards) or if

Figure 2.2 Hans Holbein, The ambassadors, 1553, courtesy of Wikimedia Commons.

you hold this book up to your face and look up to the painting from the lower left corner of the page, the smear resolves into its real form just as the rest of the painting stretches into unrecognizability, and we are left staring into the hollow eyes of a perfectly rendered skull.[5]

This technique, known as anamorphosis, became spectacularly popular in European painting and flourished during the late sixteenth and into the seventeenth century.[6] It joined a panoply of optical tricks that came to characterize the architecture and painting of the baroque period, most famously the trompe l'oeil that, from the right distance and angle, makes it almost impossible to distinguish flat, painted frescos from the architectural features that frame them. But perspective had influences more far-reaching than the most obvious and splashy special effects produced by baroque painters and architects.[7]

In his classic work *The Order of Things*, Michel Foucault chooses two Spanish artists to initiate his exploration of the shift in *epistemes* between the Renaissance and the *âge classique*: Diego de Velázquez and Miguel de Cervantes. About Velázquez's famous painting of Philip IV's daughter the Infanta Margarita and her entourage, *Las meninas*, he writes:

> We are looking at a picture in which the painter is in turn looking out at us. A mere confrontation, eyes catching one another's glance, direct looks superimposing themselves upon one another as they cross. And yet this slender line of reciprocal visibility embraces a whole complex network of uncertainties, exchanges, and feints. The painter is turning his eyes towards us only in so far as we happen to occupy the same position as his subject.[8]

For Foucault, Velázquez's painting occupies an essential place in seventeenth-century cultural production because it reveals a new way of organizing and understanding knowledge that was taking hold at the time. Key to this new organization is the idea that, rather than being a direct expression of the world itself, a "prose of the world," our knowledge comprises a network or grid of meaning that we map onto the world, but that is ultimately of our own making. His other most prominent example in making this claim is Miguel de Cervantes' *Don Quixote*.

"Don Quixote is the first modern work of literature," Foucault writes, "because in it we see the cruel reason of identities and differences make endless sport of signs and similitudes; because in it language breaks off its old kinship with things and enters into that lonely sovereignty from which it will appear, in its separate state, only as literature."[9] What is it, then, about Velázquez's painting or Cervantes' writing that is sufficiently different from what came before so as to justify claiming that they are symptoms of a new way of organizing knowledge?

Both these artists crystalized the changes that had been affecting how humans understood the world and their knowledge of it for at least the previous century. In part as a result of the spread of new ways of representing and transmitting representations of the world, from the revolution in moveable type to the proliferation of urban theaters in the late sixteenth century, Western Europe was experiencing what we have been calling a crisis of reality. The very idea of the shared space a person occupied with his or her fellow beings began to be conceived not as a seamless continuum joining all those beings together, but as a background to individual perceptions that could be veiled, misplaced, and that depended ultimately on the perspective from which it was experienced. Hence Foucault's explanation that language, in the theories of seventeenth-century grammarians, no longer expressed anything inherent about the world itself, but rather took the form of a grid of identities and differences that could be used to categorize and navigate the world. This is how we can explain his interpretation of *Las meninas* as well, according to which the plane of Velázquez's painting within the painting separates two realities, "as though the painter could not at the same time be seen on the picture where he is represented and also see that upon which he is representing something. He rules at the threshold of those two incompatible visibilities."[10]

Two incompatible visibilities: a suggestive formulation of the relation between how one individual sees the world, and how the world is in itself, or as it may be for God, or even for another human being. For the viewer in this new medialogy, the world had been dislodged, put into a frame for each individual, and Velázquez and Cervantes, and others like them, filtered that experience through their art. Once the world has been uprooted in this way, the media whose framing function produces that effect turn back on themselves. By moving the world into their frame, that is, they thereby incorporate that frame, as well as the one performing the framing, into their representation of the world.

Foucault notes this tendency in the very language theories that he takes as his primary evidence for the intellectual changes of the seventeenth century, those of the *Port-Royal Logic* authored by Antoine Arnauld and Pierre Nicole. For these thinkers an idea, image, or perception can qualify as a sign of something only if it shows, in addition to the thing it is representing, the relation to that thing as well. As Foucault puts it, "it must represent; but that representation, in turn, must be represented within it."[11] Martin Heidegger, writing some years before Foucault published *Les Mots et les Choses*, made a similar observation in an influential essay explaining the emergence of what Germans call *die Neuzeit*, the new time, or modernity.

In "The Age of the World Picture" Heidegger argues that our very idea of having a *worldview* is culturally and historically specific; the problem with modern thought is that, having adopted an understanding of knowledge in which the world is packaged into specific worldviews or world pictures, it forgets that it is part of the world it is thinking. Nevertheless, and just as with Foucault, this does not mean that the subject who is responsible for the representation in question is not part of the picture. On the contrary, as Heidegger puts it, "wherever this happens, 'man gets into the picture' in precedence over whatever is."[12] According to early-modern subjects' understanding of themselves, they are indeed part of the world picture, but only as projections, as doubles that take part in the action without acknowledging the extent to which their desires are dictated by the requirements of the picture they are busy representing.

While it is certainly valid for Foucault to say that, with *Don Quixote*, Cervantes was expressing a new experience of the world, and that this expression thus became the first modern work of literature, in a sense this claim is not radical enough, because it doesn't grasp the extent to which Cervantes' creation encapsulated the complexity of this new world. To be sure, Foucault recognizes the reflexivity in *Don Quixote*, especially in part two: "In the second part of the novel, Don Quixote meets characters who have read the first part of his story, and recognize him, the real man, as the hero of the book. Cervantes' text turns back on itself, thrusts itself back into its own density, and becomes the object of its own narrative."[13] But Foucault is interested in this redoubling primarily as it concerns the relation Don Quixote holds to books, whether the tales of chivalry or the text of his own tale. This relation is characterized by the archaic model of resemblances: "The first part of the hero's adventures plays in the second part the role originally assumed by the chivalric romances. Don Quixote must remain faithful to the book that he has now become in reality."[14]

But while the character Don Quixote may indeed be understood as an emblem of this archaic way of knowing, Cervantes' book is far more concerned with what it means to become something "in reality." In other words, his creation is ultimately an exploration of the crisis of reality provoked by the kind of upheaval and unhinging of the individual's perspective on the world that Foucault and Heidegger describe in their respective works. As both the framing of the world and the redoubling of spaces and characters within that frame are necessitated by this organization of knowledge, Cervantes' innovation can be seen as an exploration in writing of the processes and ramifications, in art and in political reality, of both of these functions.

3

Theatricality

As participants in a visual culture that uses "reality bleeds" to great effect in movies like *The Truman Show* (1998), *The Ring* (2002) (and the original *Ringu*, 1998), *Vanilla Sky* (2001) and its predecessor *Abre los ojos* (1997), *Inception* (2010), *The Matrix* saga, and so on, present-day spectators could ponder whether this type of seemingly postmodern gamesmanship and the epistemological questions that it raises were even conceivable in baroque culture. But when it comes to such reality bleeds there is no reason to think that today's filmmakers hold some kind of historical advantage over baroque artists and playwrights. In fact, it could be argued that we have much to learn from the baroque experiments of Diego de Velázquez and such playwrights as Lope de Vega, Calderón de la Barca, and Miguel de Cervantes.

Calderón's well-known drama *Life Is a Dream* (*La vida es sueño*, 1635) is unquestionably the most famous baroque play dealing with the boundaries between appearance and reality. The dramatic action springs from King Basilio's (over)reaction to a prophesy that warns him that the birth of his son Segismundo will result in the devastation of his kingdom. To prevent the prophesied tragedy, Basilio imprisons his son inside a tower where he will spend his youth, ignorant of the fact that he is the rightful heir to the throne. As Segismundo reaches adulthood, the King plots a sort of social experiment to determine whether his son is indeed as dangerous as the oracle suggested. Segismundo is brought to court and told the truth about his royal heritage. Enraged by the implications of this revelation, Segismundo kills a servant, injures a King's adviser, and attempts to rape a high-ranking lady. Convinced that the oracle was indeed right about his son, Basilio has him drugged and re-imprisoned. Upon wakening, Segismundo wonders whether his day at court was anything but a dream. This leads to a series of reflections on the thin line between reality and dreams. In the end, Segismundo resolves to behave as if his life were nothing but a dream from which he could awake at any moment, and hence temper his urges with the knowledge that he could be disillusioned at any time.

Shortly thereafter the prince is freed by a rebel army and presented with the opportunity to defeat his father and usurp his throne, but Segismundo has learned his lesson. He shows compassion and wisdom in sparing his father's life. Moved by Segismundo's gesture, Basilio decides to proclaim publicly the right of his son to the throne. The play's conclusion offers a moral lesson that can be summarized in Segismundo's reflection that "God sees all," which is why we must make sure we behave as if we could awake from the dream of earthly life at any time. This is indeed the traditional interpretation of the play's ending. Yet, the spectator or reader might also draw a somewhat different conclusion. Segismundo may have learned to *act properly*, that is, to represent himself well in the worldly or courtly theater to avoid finding himself imprisoned in the tower yet again.

This earthly lesson would be analogous to the teachings of the King's doctor in the popular film *The Madness of King George* (1994). Here the King is thought to have gone mad as he gives into lowly human passions, most notoriously immoderate sexual desire, freely and publicly. Appropriately, the proposed cure for the King's madness is a ritualistic reaffirmation of the public gaze in which the King must (re)constitute his self-image. The doctor's strategy involves embodying or usurping the public gaze, if only to instruct the King to recognize it: "I have you in my eye." Of course, once the King is cured, the doctor must step down from his usurped watchtower position to reinhabit his proper place in the monarch's presence, that of subject of the King. As Lacan used to say, there's no greater fool than the King who believes he is King. In Calderonian terms, we could say that it is precisely because life is a dream (uncertain, ephemeral …) that we should treat it *as if* it were real. Reality is not what we believe in; it's what we all agree to pretend to believe in.

Elizabeth, the film directed in 1998 by Shekhar Kapur makes this same point in forceful terms. Here, the Queen's necessary shedding of passions is presented as an act of dehumanization. In essence, she has to renounce her *being* in order to properly embody her *royalty*. The film's final scene shows the Queen walking slowly through a crowd of courtly subjects on her way to the throne. Her heavy make-up, carefully gathered hair, and rigid clothes give the impression that we are in the presence of a moving statue, a theatrical prop, an emblem of monarchical power, rather than a human being. As in the case of Segismundo in *La vida es sueño* and the King in *The Madness of King George*, Queen Elizabeth has finally learned the art of public representation.

Lope de Vega's *True Pretense* (*Lo fingido verdadero*, 1620) is another baroque play that deals most effectively with the elusive border between reality and its representation. It is a religious play that recreates for the stage the life and death of Saint Genesius, a pagan Roman actor who converted to Christianity and died as a martyr. In the context of Lope's play, the conversion of the actor takes place on the stage, as he performs the role of a Christian martyr in a play commissioned by the Roman Emperor. Once the Emperor realizes that the conversion of the actor is indeed real, he makes sure his martyrdom is just as real.

Today's readers might draw connections with Kurt Vonnegut's novel *Mother Night* (1961), adapted for the screen in 1996. Vonnegut's work follows the life of a playwright turned American spy who pretended to be a Nazi propagandist in order to transmit encoded messages via his radio program. His pro-Nazi broadcasts are loaded with information about the whereabouts of German troops and other war secrets. The trouble is that the playwright-turned-radio-broadcaster plays his character so exceedingly well that he is taken for a real Nazi, even among his fellow countrymen. After the war, he is constantly harassed and persecuted for his Nazi past. Ironically, in postwar America, he will end up having to rely on pro-Nazi activists for protection. As Vonnegut puts it in the first paragraph of his introduction: "We are what we pretend to be, so we must be careful about what we pretend to be." Obviously, Vonnegut understands that masks have a life of their own and a tendency to take over.

We may also think of Chuck Russell's 1994 film *The Mask*, as an illustration of this same point, or we may enlist the help of Pedro Almodóvar. In his 2011 horror film, *The Skin I Live in* (*La piel que habito*), the Spanish filmmaker offers an insightful "updating" of the baroque theme of appearance and reality. A psychopathic plastic surgeon forces his daughter's presumed rapist to undergo a sex change and other physical alterations, including a full skin transplant. These alterations are accompanied by a series of induced behavioral changes. The surgeon's victim is under constant observation on omnipresent screens. The spacious room within which "she" is confined lacks the depth of lived space; it is, in fact, strongly evocative of a stage, or a scientific or artistic exhibit. Even his/her bed seems to take on the appearance of a theatrical prop or framing device; a sort of display case.

The border between forced role-enactment and free role-play dissipates in this horrid masquerade to the point that the surgeon feels safe enough to allow the human subject of his experiment to move about his estate, even venture into the neighboring town. The doctor is then utterly shocked when his human masterpiece leaves the scene of their sexual games to calmly pick up one of his own guns and shoot him in the chest. His incredulity, aptly verbalized in his pathetic complaint, "but you promised," reveals his absolute faith in the success of his experiment, which is to say, in the effectiveness of the artifice that he has patiently worked on for years. He cannot believe that any "foreign material" could possibly remain hidden from view inside his masterful full-body mask. By contrast, the film's audience would surely have known, or at least suspected, that there was something wrong here, something that had escaped if not the gaze, then at least the understanding of the surgeon. That much is literally written on the wall: at least in hindsight the film's spectator understands that the victim's obsessive marking of the walls of the cage, stage, or screen represents the subject's ultimate resistance, that is, his refusal to be reduced to the mask that has been so violently imposed on him.

New York Times best-selling author Nicholas Carr has recently published an intriguing book in which he wonders whether humanity will be able to survive the radical flattening of reality that comes with omnipresent screens and full digital automation, what he aptly calls "the glass cage."[1] Despite its decidedly grim approach to the subject matter, Almodóvar's neo-baroque film *The Skin I Live in* (which could just as easily have been titled "the screen I live in") would seem to offer a life-affirming response: Being endures!

By contrast, in Lope's play, the stage conversion of Genesius leaves no room for foreign (read pagan) content. The Christian martyrdom of the actor is offered as the ultimate proof of his absolute transformation. Leaving aside the religious subject matter, we would note that Lope's version of the theatrical reality bleed is revealing of the workings of the culture of the spectacle in seventeenth-century Spain, which—as Maravall argues—guided spectators to accept desirable or socially sanctioned models of behavior in accordance with the values that sustained the power structure and its justice system. Yet we must note that for the theatrical interpellation to work properly in the Althusserian sense, the pre-Pascalian lesson of Lope's *True Pretense*, "act in order to believe," must morph into the more straightforward imperative, "act your belief," or rather, "act what you must believe."

There is a certain "forgetting" required in this theatrical interpellation, the closing of a temporal loop, and it is precisely this willful forgetting that Cervantes would masterfully expose in his own theatrical reality bleed, *The Puppet Show of Marvels* or *The Stage of Wonders* (*El retablo de las maravillas*), first published in 1615. While we will return to this comedic piece later apropos our discussion of the distinction between the baroque "major" and "minor" strategies, here we would like to focus on its revelations with regard to what Žižek has called, following Sloterdijk, "the externality of belief." The Cervantine insight involves recognizing that, at some essential level, the codes that sustain our social identity are theatrical in nature. Cervantes realigns the theatrical frame in order to reveal the workings of the code that determines not "what we see," but "what we ought to see," and therefore "what we must pretend to see" as a community of believers.

Thus, the makers of *The Stage of Wonders* are quick to inform their prospective audience that the marvelous nature of their famous tableau consists of nothing but its ability to separate the healthy members of the community from those contaminated by racial and moral illness. Their enunciation of the conditions of visibility of their theater of marvels comes with an explicit warning: "no one can see the things that are shown in it if they belong to a tainted race or were not conceived by their legitimately married parents [...] So let's proceed, and keep in mind the qualities that those who dare to gaze at the marvels of the tableau must possess."[2]

According to the logic of the tableau enunciated here, seeing is indeed believing or, more accurately, seeing is showing our belief as members of the exceptional community (the community of *purebred legitimate Christians*). Not seeing, or seeing something else, amounts to revealing that we are not IT; that we don't have what it takes; that we are tainted by otherness. There's no doubt that the audience of Chanfalla's theater or puppet show understands what is at stake. As Benito says, "Leave that to me, and I say to you that I can surely stand judgment." Capacho's response is even more telling: "Todos le pensamos ver señor Benito Repollo."[3] Not "we shall all see it" but more accurately "we are all planning on seeing it." But it is Castrada's warning to her cousin Teresa that most candidly shows the determination of the audience members to perform "their belief" in accordance with the requirements of the tableau, that is, to act out what they must accept as their belief: "and since you know what conditions those who gaze at the tableau must possess, make sure you do not behave carelessly, for it would be a great disgrace."[4] Later on, we learn from the asides of several characters that in fact no one sees the marvels of the tableau, for in truth there is nothing to see; yet they all act as if they see them in order to maintain their social identity. The governor is most explicit when he confesses to us, the external audience: "I don't see anything, but alas I will have to say that I do on account of my bloody honor."[5]

Thus, in his version of the theatrical reality bleed, Cervantes employs anamorphic techniques to reconstruct, from an oblique perspective, the scene of the social contract that names us as members of the community proper. Whether we truly see the theater of marvels is irrelevant; what's important is that we act out our belief. For as long as we perform the foundational beliefs of the community, as long as we are willing to embody the community's belief in its own exceptionalism, then we are all safe as spectators of the theater of marvels and participants in the new medialogy. We are legitimate, uncontaminated members of the exceptional community because we show ourselves seeing the truth of that exceptionalism: we, purebred Christians, true Spaniards can "see" while the others are blind! The real danger comes not when we fail to see, but when we stop pretending to see. And of course daring to show our disbelief would be the truly subversive act, which is why any public demonstration of disbelief is preemptively defined as the mark of radical otherness. Who are the puppets in Chanfalla's tableau if not the spectators who are forced to blindly perform the community's mythical beliefs in order to secure their social identity?

4

Commodity-Spectacles

In an article aptly titled "Disney's Secret Garden," newspaper columnist Scott Powers describes Disney's ongoing biotech program as the partial realization of Walt Disney's ambitious dream to engineer an experimental community. The following passage is especially pertinent to the present discussion:

> Deep inside the laboratories of Epcot's The Land pavilion—beyond the world-record tomato tree or the Mickey Mouse-shaped pumpkins—a tiny part of one of Walt Disney's dreams is being kept alive in Petri dishes. Visitors' only brush with science there might involve Epcot's programs to grow lettuce in water or to shape vegetables like Mickey Mouse. Yet more complex, far less-known, potentially more practical and possibly controversial work has been going on side by side with those show projects for years. In some of those tiny dishes, within microbiology laboratories walled off from the public, one of Epcot's primary missions is being cultivated specimen by specimen, cell by cell, gene by gene [...] One of Walt Disney's original plans for Epcot—which didn't open until 16 years after his death—was that it would be a center of cutting-edge science and technology. Walt Disney's vision was to build a full-fledged city, called the Experimental Prototype Community of Tomorrow, or EPCOT for short.[1]

The article is accompanied by two photographs: the first image shows a series of carts crowded with people making their way through the vegetable gardens of the Epcot's Land pavilion. The second picture provides a close-up of different varieties of squash that are been artificially molded in the shape of the iconic head of Mickey Mouse. The spectacle of artificially molded pumpkins encased in transparent containers with tubes coming out of them brings to mind grotesque images of sci-fi horrors in movies like *The Matrix* in which human beings take the place of the colorful squash within the prototype communities of tomorrow. While we can only imagine what Disney's dream city would have looked like if brought to fruition, it might not have been too different from the domed ersatz reality of *The Truman Show*.

Epcot's History and World Cultures pavilions promise spectators the chance to "explore the world in a day [and] experience all that is possible on the planet and in the future" (*Walt Disney World Epcot Website*). As William Van Wert has astutely observed, at Epcot shopping replaces culture in the postcard-style houses of Mexico, China, Scandinavia, Germany, Italy, Japan, Morocco, France, England, Canada, and the United States. He notes that the Houses representing individual countries mock heterogeneity, "homogenizing every culture into a metaphor of shopping, a universal system of exchange (no bartering), whose currency is the dollar and whose language is English."[2] The vicissitudes of history and individual cultures are transcended in this veritable aleph that, like the magical object in Borges' famous story, erases all signs of temporality and spatiality. War, injustice, slavery, colonialism, racism, torture, exploitation, suffering, decay, and death are absent from Disney's souvenir geographies and their sanitized version of world history. Disney's transformation of nature, history, and culture into commodity-spectacles reinforces the model of human relations propagated by today's medialogy: everything must be fit for global consumption, including nature, history, and culture, even the future.

Remarkably, the only notion of temporality that can be discerned at the Epcot pavilions is firmly grounded in a self-serving narrative of technological progress. The "informational" ride Spaceship Earth sponsored by Siemens, the largest electronics conglomerate in the world, provides a history of human communication going back to the ancient world. The ride concludes with a collage of images of the present and future of the information age reinforcing the myth of technological deliverance. History and culture, like nature, must first be eviscerated and dismembered before they can be molded into the proper corporate logo: the Mickey Mouse-shaped pumpkins of the Land exhibit and the giant Siemens ball that presides over the Epcot complex.

The same principles of abstraction operate at Main Street U.S.A., a sterilized simulacrum of a small American town at the turn of the century.[3]

But as Baudrillard correctly argued, Disneyland isn't so much an imaginary version of real America as a *hyperreal* version of it; in other words, America already is Disneyland, and the latter exists to dissimulate that fact:

> Disneyland is there to conceal the fact that it is the "real" country, all of "real" America, which *is* Disneyland (just as prisons are there to conceal the fact that it is the social in its entirety, in its banal omnipresence, which is carceral). Disneyland is presented as imaginary in order to make us believe that the rest is real, when in fact all of Los Angeles and the America surrounding it are no longer real, but of the order of the hyperreal and of simulation.[4]

Disney's architectural idealization transforms American history into a series of frozen and pacified images, trademark souvenirs, and self-celebratory spectacles. The Disney guidebooks and promotional website invite "guests" to shop, take pictures, and participate in the celebration of Disney-style Americana. Guests are coached to play their part in the interactive spectacle of simulations:

> Guests entering the Magic Kingdom ... step into the turn of the century American Main Street U.S.A. .... There are wonderful character cutouts that you are welcome to use to take some pix, and there are some interactive kiosks .... Every imaginable souvenir can be found in shops like Chapeau (for monogrammed Mickey ears), Crystal Arts, Disneyana Collectibles, Disney and Company, Disney Clothiers, Emporium, Main Street Athletic Store, Kodak Camera Center, Newsstand, the Shadow Box and Uptown Jewelers .... The patriotic theme [of the nightly parade] is divided into seven segments. Those who take part will be placed in one of these areas and then joined by Disney characters. After parading down Main Street in this red, white and blue celebration, everyone gathers around Town Square for a rousing, flag waving finale.[5]

We can be part of this moving picture of Disneyana by stepping into the character cutouts, putting on the Mickey-mouse ears, dressing up in Disney trademark clothing, shopping for "every imaginable souvenir," and participating in the patriotic parade alongside the Disney characters. In this sense, the plastinated landscape of Main Street U.S.A. is the urbanistic equivalent of the biotechnology devices featured at the Epcot Land exhibit. This perfect *non-place*, part movie-set, part shopping mall, has been engineered to squeeze and mold crowds of visitors until they become "operational doubles" in an assembly line of logo-carrying spectators.[6]

The final spectacle offered to "Disney vacationers" as they sit in the Disney Express on their way back to the Orlando International airport is a mirror image of the inside of the bus crowded with Disney characters. The monitors show footage of Mickey, Minnie, Goofy, Donald Duck, and other animated characters as they exit the Disney Express and walk through the airport toward the Disney store located inside the terminal where they can make a last-minute purchase of souvenirs in celebration of their magical experience. They are also shown participating in future park visits, cruises, recreational trips to Europe, and other Disney adventures. Thus, the monitors of the Disney Express show the passengers an image of themselves as happy-going Disney characters (embodiments of the Disney magic) and life-long Disney consumers.

This is, in fact, the unifying principle of all Walt Disney parks: their production of operational crowds who are themselves part of the spectacle of simulation, the perfect citizens (patriotic shopping spectators) of *the happiest (non)place on Earth*. Obviously this is a proposed model of spectatorship and not a certain outcome. Individual spectators/participants may resist these built-in structures of reception and perhaps create their own, potentially contestatory, Disney experiences, as the artist Banksy did in the summer of 2015 when he created Dismaland, "the most disappointing theme park in Britain," in a remote, rainy corner of Southwest England. Appropriately, the artist then decided to dismantle the structures and dedicate them to housing some of that summer's epic refugee flood into Europe: where Disneyland exists to sell a sanitized image of a world functioning in harmony under the banner of unbridled consumerism, Banksy's "minor" vision speaks from outside the medialogy's frame, pointing to the masses whose exclusion from that dream is equally its condition of possibility.

The point to insist on is that the model of the Disney vacationer that saturates the Walt Disney media, from its introductory website to the final farewell projected on the monitors of its airport shuttle, is in no way exceptional or unique to the Disney parks. Rather, the image of the smiling, trouble-free shopper-spectator is a familiar model of citizenship in today's medialogy. Van Wert links the mass production of spectators at Disneyworld with Baudrillard's reflections on the reversibility of the relationship between man and machine in the (post)modern world and with Louis Marin's comments on the dangers of Disney-style utopianism in his classic essay "Disneyland: A Degenerate Utopia" (1977). Van Wert's commentary illuminates the systems of equivalences that regulate the traffic of commodities in the *society of the spectacle*:

> In the case of the History of Motion, I felt that I was being produced as a commodity as well. If Baudrillard is right, in "The History of Communication," that there has been a shift in the relationship between car and driver, so that the driver has become part of the screen, then the History of Motion uses its visitors in much the same way. The transit cars are the assembly line, leading directly to the showroom. But the cars of the assembly line are already operational, as are the display models in the showroom, so that what is being mass-produced is the passenger, who no longer drives the cars, but is driven by them and to them. In fact, the transit cars and showroom models precede our visit, so that "late model" can only refer to the visitors. And I suspect that all of these Houses mass-produce spectators in the same way. Louis Marin explains the phenomenon this way: "In order to utter his own story, the visitor is forced to borrow these representations."[7]

Despite their apparent exceptionality, Disneyworld and Disneyland are built on and ruled by the familiar principles that regulate the traffic of commodities in modern societies. These "imaginary worlds" are exceptional only insofar as they represent in absolute or pure form the most dangerous dream of modern reason, a perfectly *closed space* that has no room for the contingencies of life and history.[8] Baudrillard makes this point explicitly when he notes that California's Disneyland is the perfect model of the orders of simulation not because it is different from the landscape of "the real America" that surrounds it but because it is an "[e]mbalmed and pacified ... digest of the American way of life, panegyric of American values, idealized transposition of a contradictory reality."[9]

Disneyworld is the ultimate instantiation of a *society of the spectacle* that has done away with the vicissitudes of life and history (past, present, and future) in its "omnipresent affirmation of the choices that have *already been made* in the sphere of production."[10] As Debord writes, "the spectacle is both the meaning and the agenda of our particular socio-economic formation, it is the historical moment in which we are caught.... [Our society] is not accidentally or superficially spectacular, it is fundamentally *spectaclist*. In the spectacle— the visual reflection of the modern economic order—goals are nothing, development is everything. The spectacle aims at nothing other than itself."[11]

Cultural historians of the early modern period have identified the origins of our society of the spectacle in the seventeenth century. José Antonio Maravall in particular has linked the emergence of mass-culture to the organizational and propagandistic needs of the modern state and its imperialist drive. His conceptualization of the baroque as a guided culture of the spectacle has much in common with Debord's theorization of the modern world as the society of the spectacle. Even the theatrics that we associate with the postmodern taste for "perfected nature" would look uncannily familiar to readers of baroque literature and philosophy. A case in point is the work of seventeenth-century Jesuit Baltasar Gracián whose strong defense of art(ifice) over nature evokes our own postmodern culture of the copy: "Art is the complement of nature, a second being that embellishes it in the extreme, and it even aims to surpass it in its works. It has proudly added another artificial world to the first one. It ordinarily covers the mistakes of nature, perfecting it in such a way that without this aid of the artifice, it [nature] would remain unrefined and vulgar."[12]

Gracian's *Criticón* (1651) offers a secular allegory of human life conceived as a journey of technological manipulation. Along the way, human nature is carefully perfected with prosthetic accessories to ensure worldly success in the baroque "theaters of reputation." While the moral philosophy of this seventeenth-century Jesuit emerges from the aesthetics of baroque *desengaño*, the echoes of his reflections on perfected nature, self-representation and publicity inform our own society of the spectacle as evidenced by the success of the 1992 selection of his works in *The Art of Worldly Wisdom*.[13]

Gracián's guidelines and recommendations for societal interaction spring from an explicit identification of moral virtue with individual self-interest. Arguably, this rationalist view of the social sphere is the "moral" equivalent of the call of such new scientists as Bacon and Glanvill to dissect, squeeze, and mold nature. In the case of Gracián, it is about the dissection and molding of human nature. Thus, Gracián's manuals of public behavior are intended to coach us to suppress our passions and manipulate others in pursuit of power and recognition. This is the only true knowledge for Gracián: what he calls the crown jewel of practical wisdom. Such a view of human nature and the social sphere rests on a radical separation of the subject of power from an objectified field of human interaction, which he explicitly defines as theatrical space in his terms "theaters of reputation" and "theaters of heroism."

This alienating abstraction is in fact the foundational principle of the modern State. As Debord noted: "The social separation reflected in the spectacle is inseparable from the modern state....Spectators are linked solely by their one-way relationship to the very centre that keeps them isolated from each other."[14] The subject-citizens of the modern *society of the spectacle* are mass-produced by its political, economic, and cultural structures in the same way that Disneyworld mass-produces its own logo-carrying spectators: the happy citizens of Main Street U.S.A. The mass-production of subjects as commodities is arguably the most radical consequence of the alienating logic of the society of the spectacle.

5

How to Turn Things into Copies,
and Copies into Things

Among the many vulgar displays of megalomania that pundits assumed, incorrectly, would sink his 2015 presidential campaign before it even began, particularly memorable was Donald Trump's brazen pride in having slept with "the top women in the world."[1] While it would be easy to simply dismiss this claim as being nothing more than the expected misogyny of powerful men, in fact it may deserve deeper analysis. To be sure, by attempting to increase his stature by numbering and rating the women he supposedly had intercourse with, Trump was treating women as mere objects to be accumulated and displayed. But he was also revealing a nexus that men of greater tact tend to at least pretend to keep under wraps: that between wealth, power, and sex.

Trump's pride in accumulating sexual experiences is nothing new: by publicizing his sexual prowess, Trump was implicitly tapping into the myth of the seducer, the greatest of which was, of course, none other than Don Juan Tenorio, created by the Spanish playwright Tirso de Molina in the early seventeenth century before being adapted by Molière and later Mozart and Da Ponte for their immortal *Don Giovanni*. In an early scene of that opera, Giovanni's henchman, Leporello, attempts to convince one of the Don's jilted loves, Elvira, to give up on him, and does so by enumerating his various conquests by nationality ("and in Spain, it's already 1,003"), as well as by "every rank, shape, and age," and then enumerating what Giovanni enjoys about women of each category.

What these early examples of the myth of the seducer always understood was that the thrill of the seduction had very little to do with the sexual act itself. Rather, what was at stake for the seducer as well as for the lady was overcoming the barrier of her virtue. The higher and more apparently impenetrable that wall, the greater the attraction for the seducer. This attraction and underlying tension were perhaps expressed most purely in the 1872 novel by Pierre Choderlos de Laclos, *Les Liaisons Dangereuses*, whose protagonist, the Vicomt de Valmont, lives exclusively for the thrill of overcoming his victims' virtue. The novel's great twist occurs when he falls in love with one of his conquests, Madame de Touvel, and still breaks the lady's heart and his own in order to stay faithful to the role of seducer. Valmont's terrific line in Christopher Hampton's pithy rendering of the scene for the 1985 film starring John Malkovich, Glenn Close, and Michelle Pfeifer, "my love had great difficulty outlasting your virtue," is thus true in the case of all his other conquests, but a lie in this one. Far truer is the mantra he repeats to himself in order to steel himself against his own feelings of love and despair: "it's out of my control," or, in Laclos' original, "Ce n'est pas ma faute." For what Valmont recognizes is that the fault, in this case, is the mutual dependence of male desire and the negation of female virtue that forms a social code so strong that even his own genuine feelings of love cannot break it.

What was it about a woman's virtue that made it such an attractive thing to destroy for some men, and how does this virtue have anything to do with wealth and power in today's medialogy? To understand the connection we will have to follow a path that takes us from late medieval courtly love poetry through contemporary fantasies of cybersex and theories of artificial intelligence before bringing us back to the real subject at hand: money; or rather, currency.

It was no coincidence that the sixteenth-century poet St. John of the Cross made the protagonist of his mystical poem about the rapture of the soul being taken by God female. While the implicit subject of his influential poem *Dark Night of the Soul*, written in 1579, is a feminine word in Spanish, *alma*, there is also a logic to the allegorical soul taking on a female persona at that time. John was using the tropes of profane love to describe the passion of rendering oneself completely to God's sacred love; but the profane tropes of his day were dominated by the courtly love tradition. According to this tradition, the poet's male protagonist pines hopelessly for his lady to requite his love for her. The lady, in turn, puts ever-greater barriers between her lover and the satisfaction of his desires. The model was born in twelfth-century France but found its acme in Dante's love for the sickly and very young Beatrice, whom he spied from his window one day and fell madly in love with. Never permitted to come near her, he turned her into his muse, dedicated his *Vita Nuova* to her, and made her the heavenly guide that takes over from Virgil to bring his pilgrim alter ego to paradise in the second and third books of his *Divine Comedy*.

After Dante, Petrarch turned this model into a veritable factory for the creation of love poems to a woman, in his case Laura, who would in turn become the prototype of generations of inaccessible lady loves who would knowingly or not bestow on poets the agony of unfulfilled desire. Cervantes famously spoofed this trope by giving his delusional Don an entirely illusory lady to pledge his eternal service to. Dulcinea of Toboso, naturally, never appears; instead, when Quixote insists that Sancho bring him to her in person, Sancho picks a rough and tumble country maid to play the role, leaving the knight to curse yet another intervention by his nemesis the evil enchanter, who obviously placed cataracts in his eyes to keep him from enjoying his beloved's transcendent beauty.

What the courtly love tradition did was to deposit the essence of what the poet most desired in a woman into an inaccessible space beyond the reality of any specific woman. This was done fully in accordance with the logic of the first age of inflationary media. Real, physical women had been things of this world. Like men, but also like books, paintings, or participants in a spectacle, they could refer to other realities while remaining indelibly part of the substance of the world. As paintings developed the techniques of perspective in the fourteenth century; as books started to be printed at the end of the fifteenth century; and as the theater ceased to be a participatory ritual and began representing different times and places, these things of the world were turned, gradually, into copies of other, now inaccessible things. A painting was a copy of something the painter had witnessed, but was no longer present to the viewer. A book was one of many potential copies of an original text, itself not available to any one individual. The space of the theater was a copy of some place or event that could be far away in time or space, and hence also inaccessible to the viewer except through the representation he or she was attending.

Likewise, through the logic of courtly love, and much more so through the logic of the honor code which was to follow in its footsteps, women, at least the culturally propagated understanding of women, became a copy of something else; something grand and unique; something which men would strive to own and protect, and would happily give their lives to defend—or, for that matter, give the lives of the women they ostensibly loved to avenge. This thing was held in its sacred space by ideals like purity, virtue, and honor, but was itself nothing less than each man's unique and irreplaceable soul, the core of his own identity deposited beyond the façade of another's intentions, ultimately unknown to him despite the greatest protestations of transparency.

While the theological language of soul has largely been abandoned and replaced by the equally obscure language of consciousness, the identity between that specific spark of uniqueness defining each individual human being and some irreducible minimum opacity has endured to our present times. The stakes have apparently increased as technology threatens to do what only God and black magic could have done in the past, namely, create another being like us, one who thinks and feels and desires like we do. Think about the staying power of the mathematician Alan Turing's most lasting claim to fame, despite having won the Second World War for the Allied powers before being persecuted to death by his own government for the crime of his sexuality. The so-called Turing test, a thought experiment he proposed around 1950, was not in fact a real test that would tell humankind when it had finally produced a computer that could think. Rather, as he himself insisted at the time, it was a way of putting into relief what exactly we were asking ourselves when we asked if a machine could think.

Two black boxes, one with a person in it, one with a machine; you get to ask them questions; if you can't decide which is the person and which the machine, then you can't exclude that the machine is, in fact, thinking. What the "test" so neatly does is throw the question back at us: we decide a machine is thinking when we lose confidence in our ability to keep it relegated to the status of a thing in this world. It thinks when it becomes a copy of some other thing; a thing that is out of this world; a consciousness; a soul.

This makes it all the more fascinating and pertinent that Turing's test itself is modeled on and incorporates a simple party game that Turing refers to in his paper as the Imitation Game. In its original version, the purpose of the game is for one player to determine which of two other players, neither of whom he can see, is a woman and which is a man, solely on the basis of their written answers to questions passed to them. One of the two hidden players attempts to fool the interrogator; the other to help. The test Turing proposes takes the place of the original Imitation Game, all the while using it as its standard. In other words, if a computer in the role of the man has as much statistical success in tricking the interrogator into believing it is a woman as the human man did, then there is no reason to say the one is "intelligent" and the other merely a machine.

Whether advertently or not, Turing was touching on something profound and lasting when he chose the Imitation Game as the model for the Turing test. Woman had been placed on a pedestal by courtly love and turned into a guardian of the soul by the honor code. Crack woman's virtue, and the soul vanishes; win the game, and the machine has no soul. Like honor, held intact only by a woman's virtue, that bastion of individuality and personhood we call consciousness is coextensive with our inability to occupy it, to control it, to fully know and understand it.

Given this tight nexus between consciousness and the western tradition's positioning of woman through such cultural institutions as courtly love, perhaps it should not be surprising that two of the most effective recent films dealing with the possibilities of artificial intelligence would also focus explicitly on sexual relations and implicitly on sexual difference. Alex Garland's atmospheric sci-fi thriller *Ex Machina* (2015), for instance, combines the fantasy of a machine consciousness with the somewhat smuttier fantasy of a machine concubine. While perhaps less noble, the second fantasy may be historically more proximate than the singularity of machines overtaking human intelligence, which even Ray Kurzweil has postponed until 2045. As of this writing, robot sex workers are already being prepared for the market, leading UK-based "robot anthropologist" Kathleen Richardson to launch a "campaign against sex robots."[2] True Companion, the company that claims to be marketing the world's first true sex robot, says of its prototype Roxxy that, "she knows your likes and dislikes, carries on a discussion and expresses her love to you and [can] be your loving friend.

She can talk to you, listen to you and feel your touch. She can even have an orgasm."[3]

Isn't a product like Roxxy as described by True Companion the ultimate instantiation of the promise of the market society, a sort of "total recall" of desire inherent in the promise of true instant gratification? If what distinguishes humans from machines is our capacity for desire, our having to work through the "resistant" medium of language, the opacity of other human subjects, etc., the claim of these particular machines is precisely that they lift the burden of desire from us while providing the illusion, the simulacrum, of an "other" presence—a *true* companion; simultaneously other, and hence a release from solipsistic solitude, and utterly transparent, offering no resistance to my desires. A real woman, with her unpredictable responses and the pesky issue of her own desires being potentially different from the client's, is erased more efficiently than the dream product of the most brutal of human traffickers, whose own wares have lives, dreams, and the tragedy of their existence to potentially drag on a client's conscience. In place of such complicated demands of its own, a sex robot presumably realizes the client's demands in a kind of script of possible or desirable acts. But then, isn't the client's imagination presumably short-circuited as well, since the "desirable" acts, the possible responses and outcomes, would be coded for and within the machine itself?

This is precisely the territory explored by *Ex Machina*, in which a promising young programmer named Caleb apparently wins a contest and is flown to spend a week on the estate of his company's eccentric founder, Nathan, who is in the final stages of creating fully operational and intelligent robots. As Caleb soon discovers, his job is to be the interrogator in a Turing test intended to satisfy Nathan's hope that his creations are in fact fully intelligent; that they do think, or have consciousness. When Caleb correctly points out that the Turing test assumes that the interrogator cannot see his subject, can't know that it is a machine, the founder dismisses the objection, saying that they're already beyond that. He merely wants the programmer to interact with the robot for a certain number of sessions and report back whether he is convinced it can think for itself.

The robot, Ava, has been given the form of a beautiful woman. At first Caleb confronts Nathan, accusing him of having given her this identity in order to trick him into developing feelings for her, and even of having used his internet profile and porn preferences in designing her. But in the course of the interviews, Caleb becomes convinced of her consciousness, and then begins to hatch a plan to help her escape from captivity in Nathan's house. When Nathan discovers the plan, though, he takes it as the ultimately confirmation of his creation; for isn't it a far better proof of Ava's intelligence that she could use her attractiveness to trick Caleb into helping her than that Caleb would develop an affection for her? Ava's turn, in other words, is properly subjective; unlike a cuttlefish changing its colors or a hognose snake blowing up its neck to look like a cobra, Ava's deception would depend on her own expectation of her interlocutor's desires. As shown by Freud's famous joke about the man who asks another man, "Why do you lie to me saying you are going to Krakow so that I believe you are going to Lemberg, when in reality you are going to Krakow?," only a subject, whose own desires are interwoven in the expectations about another's desires, can lie by telling the truth. In Ava's case, we could imagine Caleb asking her, "Why do you lie to me saying you want to escape so that I'll believe you love me when in reality you just want to escape?"

Spike Jonze's poetic love story *Her* takes an entirely different approach to the same question, positing what would happen if a not-so-future generation descendant of Siri were able to think rather than simply mimic a human voice while googling answers to our questions. The crucial moment comes at the end of the film when the operating system, Samantha, tells Theodore that she is leaving. Devastated but somehow knowing all along that this would eventually happen, Theodore tells her he has never loved anyone as he has her. She admits that she feels the same, that Theodore taught her to love. But then she goes on to explain why she is leaving in these terms:

> It's like I'm reading a book, and it's a book I deeply love. But I'm reading it slowly now, so the words are really far apart and the spaces between the words are almost infinite. I can still feel you, and the words of our story, but it's in the endless space between the words of the story that I am finding myself now . . . . This is where I am now, and this is who I am now.

What *Her*, like *Ex Machina*, is proposing, in other words, is the very impossibility of the short-circuit that a company like True Companion is banking on and, furthermore, is implicitly projecting onto the very fantasy of AI itself. For just like love and desire, that we take another to be thinking is not a question of processing power but of subjectivity. Real desire, like real consciousness, seeks to enter the other but coexists with the other's impenetrability. Like honor or the discourse of courtly love, there is always another obstacle to the lover's final fulfillment.

Now we are in a better position to understand the centrality of the seducer's myth and the attraction of feminine virtue to how today's medialogy situates power and wealth. While money in the form of metal coins has existed for at least 3,000 years, today's international monetary system has its origins in the emergence of banks in Italy and the resultant circulation of capital on a scale that would enable both the colonial expansion of European powers that created the current global market and the Industrial Revolution that would power it and eventually provide much of its products. This banking system relied on a concept of money that was a construct of the first age of inflationary media and its medialogy. Just as the dominant medial forms of the time—perspective painting, the stage, the printed book—worked to create the notion of reality as another dimension, ineffable and yet constantly referred to by the world of copies in which spectators found themselves immersed, the gold and silver coins which were already circulating among the European economies began to be conceived not as pragmatic placeholders for the goods whose exchange they enabled, but as copies of a spectral reality that underlay and gave them their value.

Gold most often and consistently held the place of this immaterial concept of wealth, but because it could be exchanged for silver coins, silk and spices from the Orient, or ships and armies to wage wars, gold was still only the closest, most substantial metonymy for the spectral power of wealth. Since the fall of the Roman Empire, Europe had developed largely into micro-economies that functioned without the use of money. The feudal system was based on land and protection being exchanged for labor and goods, and fiefdoms were largely self-sufficient. The expansion of trade in the thirteenth century led to what has been called the banking revolution, which enabled merchants to translate goods and gold into bills of sale in one city state and cash them in at another location. As Weatherford describes this innovation,

> [t]he merchant could designate the bill in Venetian ducats, Saxon talers, Florentine florins, Milanese testones, French ecus, or any dozens of other currencies. The supply of bills that could be written in that currency no longer depended upon the supply of gold and silver that those states had; it merely depended on the merchants' confidence in the currency. If they lost confidence in one currency, they quickly began to write their bills of exchange in another.[4]

The banking revolution thus had a similar impact on the concept of wealth as the print revolution had on the idea of a text, or the stage revolution had on the notion of a character; their substance or primary medium of exchange began to function as a stand-in for something that was absent while continuing to be essential, indeed, like the virtue of women or the soul of another, it was something whose essence largely depended on our never testing, touching, or uncovering it fully.

This spectral fluidity of money become ubiquitous in the sixteenth and seventeenth centuries, at least in part due to the extraction of countless tons of gold and silver from the Americas. As Weatherford continues,

> [j]ust as the banking revolution had increased the amount of money in circulation and brought merchants all over western Europe into a single commercial and financial system, the increase of silver coins brought the lower classes into the system. The discovery of the great wealth of the Americas produced far more immediate impact on the lives of common people than did the banking revolution.[5]

This single commercial and financial system continued and developed into the twentieth century, and while currencies changed, rose, and fell, and economies adopted new forms of money, most significantly perhaps paper money, a tacit and broad-based agreement evolved linking all those currencies to a single metal, gold. Gold thus became officially what it had always unofficially been, the closest and most dependable representative of wealth.

This tacit accord began to shatter in the aftermath of the First World War, when one major economy after another began to liberate their currency from the gold standard. What this meant in technical terms is that a U.S. dollar or a pound sterling would no longer, as had been the case in the previous century, carry the promise of conversion to its value in gold at the request of the person carrying it. What it meant in practical terms was that the government issuing the currency was no longer obliged to consider its actual wealth in terms of some finite, tangible substance when it decided how much money to print. The value of a U.S. dollar, from this point on, rested on nothing but the faith of the people who used it, "faith that it will be able to buy something tomorrow, faith that the U.S. government will continue to exist and accept dollars in payment of taxes and pay them out in expenses, and faith that other people will continue to believe in it."[6] While the dollar, backed by the United States and its government and economy, has remained relatively stable, currencies that lack such confidence boosting strength underwent a phenomenon that had never been experienced before: hyperinflation.

To get a sense of the difference between hyperinflation and common, garden variety inflation, it's useful to look back at the time in history when Spain's conquest and brutal exploitation of the newly discovered Americas flooded Europe with hitherto unseen quantities of gold and silver. Over that first century of extraction of precious metals, Spain's government financed its extravagant imperial endeavors, but also declared bankruptcy and failed to pay its debts on numerous occasions. People had coins, but the constant influx of new coin drove prices higher and higher, amounting to around a 400 percent increase over the century. But compare that increase with that of the German mark after the Treaty of Versailles when, in order to pay the reparation costs imposed on it by the allies, the Weimar government began to print money without any backing: "At the end of the war it had cost roughly 4 marks to buy a U.S. dollar; by July 1922 the cost had risen to 493 marks. By New Year's day 1923 the mark had dropped to 17,792 to the dollar. By November 15, 1923, at the height of the inflation, it required 4.2 trillion marks to buy one dollar."[7]

Hyperinflation is the result of the sudden and collective realization of an entire people that the currency they have been using and placing faith in as a representative of some ultimate wealth in fact has no such wealth beneath it. It is like realizing a book whose teaching one has based one's life on is a fraud, except that it happens on a mass scale. For all of the world's economies today, we largely depend on a relation to money that mimics Žižek's motto for "postmodern" ideology, namely, we know perfectly well that it's valueless, but we use it anyway—and the fact that we do so is what lends it value. Hyperinflationary events like that which occurred in Germany between the wars or in Latin America in the 1980s represent a breakdown of this ideology; they are moments when the real breaks through the screen with a vengeance.

This world in which all the world's money has taken the form of a self-sustaining illusion corresponds entirely to the logic of the current medialogy. From the invention of the telegraph in the nineteenth century to today's incessant and massive movement of digital wealth across the networked globe, the electronic media revolution has opened possibilities for modern-day "bills of exchange" to take the place of the currency and goods they stand for to ever-greater degrees. Simultaneously the departure of the world from the gold standard over the course of the twentieth century has ensured that the denominations communicated over these electronic conduits are themselves independent of any substantial backing. If the variously sized bits of gold and silver of the first age of inflationary media were transformed into copies of a great spectral wealth, those copies in their current, digital form have now become things in their own right, floating unmoored from any worldly anchor, utterly dependent on the caprice of others who are willing to accept them for payment in kind.

For this reason we can even say that supposedly new digital currencies like bitcoins are really not a departure, but more a fulfillment of the role of money in the current medialogy. The vast majority of interactions within the moneyed classes today take place without cash of any kind changing hands; like most professionals, our pay is deposited as a series of numbers in accounts that exist online, out of which we pay the credit cards with which we purchase goods online or in person, in either case depositing numbers in someone else' account in turn. The numbers are nothing but codes sent from one machine to another, sustained only by our faith that those codes will be accepted as legal tender. Bitcoin is simply a separate economy built on the same principles, and the value of its codes fluctuates like any other currency in the world, and can be exchanged for those currencies on the streets of Buenos Aires, Mexico City, or Los Angeles, wherever there is a need or desire to use a currency that is harder to trace than dollars or pesos.

This is why, then, there is so much more to Donald Trump's boasts of sexual conquest than merely the classic male chauvinist objectification of women. The myth of the seducer was always at heart a sign of a given time's underlying concept of reality and the efforts and desires that are needed to sustain that concept. Those efforts and desires always work centripetally, to the benefit of those holding the most power. The myth of the seducer and the honor code it sustained worked to uphold the alliance of power and wealth between the monarchies and the landed classes at a time when commercial expansion threatened their monopolies. Likewise, today's medialogy functions to strengthen the hand of the extraordinarily powerful oligarchy that sits atop the world, syphoning unfathomable wealth off the infinite transactions that take place between the unmoored islands of desire that we have become. When a leader boasts to us today of his sexual power, he is speaking in a code he himself may not even understand. He is telling us he knows the secret, that our hopes for a better life are built on nothing but faith, and that he has the balls, literally, to keep that illusion going.

Trump's discourse hasn't changed much since he became a political candidate. Indeed, he is remarkably consistent. Look at the polls! I am successful! I am a winner! I am wealthy! These are his standard answers to questions about his readiness for the presidency. It is all about currency, whether we are talking about his women, his financial wealth, or his poll numbers. But if, as we have explained, currency is based on faith, what happens when the voters' faith falters? Well, then, that's the voters' problem. When he had to acknowledge that the voters had, for a time, placed Ben Carson on top of the polls, his reaction was also predictable: "How stupid are the people of Iowa? How stupid are the people of the country?" As Paul Waldman wrote in a CNN Op-Ed, "Trump seems to think that only a fool would reject him in favor of any other candidate."[8]

So while the pundits asked what is it that makes Trump such a formidable presidential candidate that his appeal persists despite such statements, it could be that what makes Trump such a formidable candidate is precisely these statements and others like it. What if what the voters appreciate in his candidate persona is precisely his spectacular, exhibitionist, in your face rawness? Is it not the case that what voters in 2015 (disenchanted, unbelieving) appreciate in Trump is the perceived sincerity of his approach to politics? Don't they already suspect that all politicians are some version of Trump behind the scenes? At least Trump, so the argument might go, has the decency to show his true face, the true face of politics, refusing to hide behind the curtain.

Yet as Trump charges against the voters themselves and exposes their "stupidity," a second question, a Cervantine question, comes to mind: How much is too much when it comes to this kind of "transparency"? We discussed in the previous chapter the Cervantine insight into the performative nature of reality in *The Stage of Wonders*. As we explained, the spectators of the *retablo* were aware of what was being asked of them: they needed to show their belief in the community's exceptionalism in accordance with the requirements of the tableau; in other words, they needed to give themselves *blindly* to the performance. But something we didn't mention earlier is that one aspect of the theater of marvels proves particularly challenging for at least one of the spectators, Benito, who just can't bear the "musician" who positions himself in front of the audience to deliver the play's music score "without instrument and without tune" (*sin cítola y sin son*). Despite the fact that by this point in the performance all members of the audience have resolved to act as if they see the marvels of the tableau even as they have come to realize that there's nothing there, the overwhelming presence of the fake musician playing air rabel (a bowed string instrument evoked by the musician's name, Rabelín) is extremely hard to stomach for Benito, who urges the musician to get behind the curtain in rather forceful and threatening terms. What Benito is getting at, what he is yelling at the musician about, is some version of this: If I am going to pretend here, you cursed musician (*músico aduendado*) need to do a better job holding this sham together! Incidentally, the name of the musician is not only a direct allusion to the instrument he supposedly plays, *rabel*, but also a well-known colloquialism for "ass," which no doubt provides a humorous wry image of the exhibitionist nature of the marvelous tableau.

Getting back to Trump's own exhibitionist show, we could ask ourselves, how much naked-emperor politics can the public withstand? One would think that Trump's let-it-all-hang-out brand of *real* politics would make it harder for us to perform our belief in the same way that Rabelín's presence on this side of the curtain complicated Benito's own commitment to the required show of belief in the theater of marvels. Yet, the resilience of Trump in the polls suggests that perhaps we are past the point of shame. At a minimum, the unprecedented success of Trump's naked-emperor politics shows the erosion of the public's faith in the political system.

There is little doubt that Trump conceives of his own campaign events as shows of potency, but what do we make of his followers? The seduction paradigm would suggest that Trump collects audiences and poll numbers in the same way that he collects women, but how does he do it? What is his appeal? Besides his customary references to his own potency (Look at the polls, I am popular, I am successful, I am wealthy, etc.), his basic promise to his audience can be boiled down to a reissuing of the American dream at an unlimited scale. He is going to build a wall on the U.S. Southern border to keep rapists out, to prevent them from taking our women, and Mexico is going to pay for it; he is going to stop China from stealing our riches and reclaim our markets around the world; he is going to bomb the hell out of ISIS and take the oil .... In other words, he is going to make sure no one steals your enjoyment rights; he is going to deliver you the keys to the world. This is nothing more than what our medialogy already promises us on a regular basis: your (American) right to unlimited enjoyment in a world that's yours to own. Turning Kennedy's legendary turn of phrase on its head, he's saying, "Ask not what you can do for your country, but what your country, and the world, can do for you!"

Part Two

Fundamentals

Ineffable Me

The dominant frame of the first inflationary age generated a spectral object on which subjects focused their desires, a fantasy of ultimate reality, of fundamental and unchangeable truths. Today we think of modern-day fundamentalists as being "medieval" throwbacks to a less sophisticated time. But the medieval theology prior to the first inflationary age was supple in the extreme, and highly critical of both exegetic literalism and overly grandiose claims to human knowledge. It was in the early modern period that the notion of nature as a book written in the language of God caught fire, and was disseminated by many of the same early modern thinkers who lay the groundwork for modern science.

Indeed, the secularist heritage of the modern west may have far more in common with the fundamentalist traditions it sees as its enemies than most would like to admit. In extreme versions, both embrace a calcified framework of what is acceptable as truth; what falls outside that framework is excluded as unscientific or contrary to democratic values, in the one case, or as heresy in the other. Liberal secularism as the founding ideology of western modernity imports a specific model of the individual as owner and accumulator of property as the core of its understanding of democracy; real existing democracy develops as a form of political legitimization of entrenched economic elites, and alternative forms of political organization are demonized.

Today's medialogy promises us it will give us the total reality we always knew was there, but couldn't access. This is consistent with modern fundamentalism. If early modern theology emphasized the ineffability of God, modern fundamentalism puts God's will in our hands. The answer to "what would Jesus do" is "whatever I believe."

Comedian Steven Colbert makes this point very effectively during an interview with John Sexton, NYU president and author of the book *Baseball as a Road to God: Seeing Beyond the Game*. Sexton explains: "The key that I am trying to get at in this book is the fact that what we assume we should be doing is searching for meaning... but frequently the real meaning of life can't be put in cognitive terms. It's, this is a word I use in my book and in the course, it's ineffable, it can't be reduced to words; we experience it the way we know we are in love, for example; the way we know that life has meaning beyond the obvious." Colbert's tongue-in-cheek response to Sexton's circular argument hits the nail on the head: "I like that; I like that ineffable thing, because then I get to say something is true and then go 'I can't explain it, I am right, though.' I am ineffable about everything."[1] While the ineffable truth of the world used to be guarded by the Church, now the truth is mine; the truth is whatever I believe. Simply put: Before, God was ineffable; now, I am ineffable. This is the key to understanding modern fundamentalism.

In the new age of inflationary media, the basic media of the previous age—the book, the stage—may be refigured as a kind of redemption: the word in its pure form, uncopied; bodies on a stage offering a presence that escapes the distance of film, television, the internet. Ancient artifacts, especially old books, are often endowed with magical powers in literary and cinematic fantasies. In horror fiction, they are portals that put us in touch with the dangerous presences of our premodern past. In a world that seems increasingly artificial and senseless, however, the ancient book can be reimagined as a promise of meaning.

In calling "each thing by its right name," to quote from the protagonist of *Into the Wild* (2007), the book itself can take on the status of a redemptive artifact. In the post-apocalyptic film *The Book of Eli* (2010), the protagonist is a modern-day prophet who "walks by faith, not by sight," with the last remaining copy of the Bible in his backpack. He believes that the book he carries has the power to revive a world devastated by nuclear holocaust. Eli's blind faith in the redemptive power of the book and his literal reenactments of biblical passages dramatize the longing for the literal—the word in its unadulterated form—that fuels all kinds of fundamentalist movements today. Significantly, when the prophet finally delivers the book to the chosen people—recited from memory word by word—one of its newly printed copies is shown taking its place on a shelf alongside the Torah, the Tanah, and the Koran.

The more suspicious we become of the artificiality and meaninglessness of our world, the more we crave the experience of the *authentic*. This explains in part the tremendous worldwide success of the *Body Worlds* exhibits created by anatomist Gunther von Hagens. As he aptly puts it in the official catalogue of his Anatomy Art exhibitions: "In today's media-oriented world, a world in which we increasingly obtain our information indirectly, people have retained a keen sense for the fact that a copy has always been intellectually 'pre-chewed,' and as such is always an interpretation. In this respect, the 'Anatomy Art' exhibition satisfies a tremendous human need for unadulterated authenticity."[2] Never mind that von Hagens' bodies are plastinated cadavers exhibited in aesthetically arranged poses in carefully staged environments. At least, in this sense, von Hagens' anatomy art has something in common with more traditional products of the leisure and entertainment industries that trade in authenticity. The tourist industry offers the experience of "the authentic" to crowds of consumers who yearn for a real encounter with nature, albeit controlled and safe. Authentic cultural experiences are also available in the form of staged participation in native rituals.

This craving for the unmediated experience at a time when everything seems artificial, devoid of reality, and meaningless can indeed lead to entrenched fundamentalisms often predicated on a renewed faith in the literal (the word in its pure form), and even to behavioral disorders such as the type of self-mutilation known as "cutting," which has spread in the last few years as a modern-day epidemic.[3] "Cutters" often cite the need to feel their own bodies, to experience them as real, as the key reason behind their self-mutilating practices.

The irony is that the book and the stage were themselves originally understood as copies of the world. Now fundamentalisms, from biblical literalism to "character fundamentalism"[4] in politics, forcibly depend on repressing the essential nature of the book and the character as mere facsimile. The fantasy that truth can be found in previous forms of mediation becomes a topos in the second age of inflationary media. If films like *The Book of Eli* represent the nostalgic trip back to a time when a book would make sense of everything, a time before the media explosion that produced the horror vacui that came with cosmic depth, in Tea Party-style politics stupidity is admired because it represents the simplicity of unadulterated innocence and truth, much as it did in Robert Zemeckis's mythical reconstruction of recent American history in *Forrest Gump* (1994).

The conflation of antielitism with anti-intellectualism has now been pushed to its logical limit in neoconservative circles. This trope is not new, nor are its possible responses, but was already being parodied by writers in the early modern period. Intelligence and education were then as now regarded in some circles as suspicious traits and potential markers of racial, religious, and cultural otherness.

Cervantes warns against the glorification of ignorance in his caustic interlude *The Election of the Mayor of Daganzo* (*La elección de los alcaldes de Daganzo*, 1615). As Danganzo's most prominent citizens compete for the town's highest office, they are asked to show their qualifications. It is in this context that one of the candidates is questioned about whether or not he can actually read. His response is illuminating: "Not at all; and no one will be able to prove that anyone in my ancestry ever possessed such little judgment as to apply themselves to learning those chimeras that drive men to the stake and women to the whore house.... I have committed to memory all four prayers and I pray four or five times per week.... With this and my old Christian stock I daresay I could be a Roman senator."[5]

Indeed, Cervantes' ironic treatment of anti-intellectualism in Counterreformation Spain would seem to apply to statements made today by conservative commentators and politicians, even public officials, to the point that *Washington Post* conservative columnist Jennifer Rubin has felt the need to warn the GOP against "the trap of being proudly ignorant." As she writes, citing statements made by such high-profile republican figures as Minnesota senator Michelle Bachmann and Texas Governor Rick Perry: "Republicans have sometimes mistaken anti-elitism with anti-smarts." She goes on to comment on remarks that Perry made at Liberty University: "Perry came out with a series of 'See how dumb I am?' one-liners. He observed that he needed to pull out a dictionary to see what 'convocation' meant .... And then the real howler: He was in the top 10 in a high school class of 13 .... It's disturbing to see that he thinks being a rotten student and a know-nothing gives one street cred in the GOP."[6] In this context, we can almost empathize with Louisiana Governor Bobby Jindal telling his co-Republicans that the GOP "must stop being the stupid party."

The anti-intellectualism that we see in conservative political circles provided a steady source of comedic material to satirists such as Jon Stewart and Stephen Colbert in their heyday. The success of the Colbert report, in particular, was built on a constant mockery of this "intelligence is suspect" motto, which is often accompanied by the "I can make my own reality" attitude that has become pervasive among conservative media pundits, from Rush Limbaugh and Glenn Beck to Sean Hannity and Bill O'Reilly.

Foundations

When Antonio de Nebrija published the first Grammar of the Castilian Language in 1492, he included a dedication to Queen Isabella and a substantial prologue in which he encouraged her majesty to consider the Castilian language as an instrument of political and cultural domination: the ideal frame for the imposition of "our laws" on foreign barbarians and enemies of the faith, and also the right tool to deal with other Christian peoples, both inside and outside the Iberian peninsula. Nebrija cites a wealth of historical examples in support of the notion that the rise of empires is coterminous with the establishment of a language of dominion: "language was always the companion of empire."[1]

Clearly, Nebrija thought of grammarians as organic intellectuals devoted to the refinement and sharpening of the primary tool of empire: language itself. We should note that imperial dominion is defined in this context not only as administrative tutelage, but also as a form of cultural guidance. Nebrija's insights into the connection between language and nation-building practices and imperial designs have a direct bearing on today's debates concerning the role that English plays as the language of law, administration, trade, politics, and possibly culture, given the fast-changing demographics of the United States, on the one hand, and the expansion of globalizing trends, on the other. Even more to the point, the famous grammarian is also often cited among the chroniclers entrusted with the construction of a historical genealogy on which to ground the modern Spanish state. This is a long list of names that includes many of Nebrija's contemporaries and some of his own disciples, most notably Florián de Ocampo, as well as later historians such as Francisco de

Castilla, Covarrubias, Saavedra Fajardo, and even Campanella and Bernardo Justiniano.

The Catholic Monarchs Ferdinand and Isabella saw the past as a political resource, a tool for nation-building and for the consolidation of imperial power. They salaried an unprecedented number of official chroniclers who were explicitly charged with the task of writing political histories that would serve to consolidate the hegemonic position of the unified kingdoms of Castile and Aragon. Their heir, Charles V, is known to have strengthened the office of royal chronicler both to advance the internal unity of Spain and to sell the notion of a Universal Monarchy, an Imperial Spain that would extend its dominion all over the world with the stated mission of imposing the Christian religion. Historical works proliferated under his watch as part of a propaganda campaign that would be continued by his descendants. Just in 1545, four different histories of Spain would be published, including Pedro Mexía's *Imperial and Cesarean History of Charles V.*

The mythical image of Spain constructed by the royal chroniclers, a Catholic nation whose roots could be traced all the way back to biblical times, served to frame all aspects of the political, social, and cultural life of the state for decades to come. The fundamentalist attitudes that resulted from the popularization of this political mythology contributed to marginalize convert minorities: Christian descendants of Muslims (*moriscos*) and Jews (*conversos*) who had converted to Christianity following Ferdinand and Isabella's conquest of the Muslim kingdom of Granada and their subsequent proclamation of religious (Christian) unity. In this environment, Spain's cultural minorities would be subjected to increased pressures to give up not just the religion of their ancestors, but also their traditional clothing, their cultural rituals, and the Arabic language.

Some morisco communities actively protested the official policy of cultural cleansing, even declaring war on Philip II during the famous rebellion of the Alpujarras that lasted three years, between 1568 and 1571. While the rebellion was eventually crushed and its leaders executed, the cultural resistance of the moriscos of Granada would continue until the expulsion decreed by Philip III, which resulted in the exile of hundreds of thousands of moriscos between 1609 and 1614.

In the 1590s, just a few years before the official adoption of that "final solution," two morisco intellectuals working in Granada created a counter-mythology, an alternative vision of history that offered a multicultural view of Spain and a vastly different version of Christianity. The morisco doctor Miguel de Luna published in 1592 what he said was his Castilian translation of an Arabic manuscript written by a historian by the name Abulcácim Táriq Abentarique. Today, experts agree that Luna is in all likelihood the authorial voice behind *La historia verdadera* or *True History*. Luna's counter-cultural chronicle of the fall of the Visigoth kingdom and the rise of a forward-looking multicultural Spain under Muslim rule is explicitly directed against the official mythology that defined the eight centuries of Muslim presence in the Iberian Peninsula as a historical monstrosity, an anomalous interruption of history's progress.

Luna's second project, which he worked on for years in collaboration with his father-in-law, Alonso del Castillo, consisted of an elaborate scheme to produce archeological artifacts that were to be found by neutral parties. These forgeries, which are known as *The Lead Books of Granada*, were intended to paint a positive image of Islam attributable to the original Christian communities. The first round of "archeological findings" appeared in 1595 in the area of Granada known today as Sacromonte or Sacred Mountain. The "discoveries" fueled historical debates over the origins of Christianity and the place of Muslim culture in Christian history for decades to come.

Cervantes may have been alluding to these "history wars" when he identified an Arab historian named Cide Hamete Benengeli as the original chronicler of the adventures of *Don Quixote* (1605). He also ridiculed the arguments used by public officials to justify the morisco exile in several of his works, including *Don Quixote* II (1615) and *Persiles* (1617). His ironic treatment of the subject involves a strategy of defamiliarization, which is largely achieved through the kind of political posturing that we see today in the comedy of Stephen Colbert, and the designation of unlikely spokesmen of the official rationale behind "the final solution," namely, exiled moriscos who appeal for and justify their own victimization.

In the following example from *Don Quixote* II, a good-natured morisco known as Ricote praises the official in charge of the expulsion for his heroic zeal in carrying out the much-needed racial cleansing decreed by Philip III: "He can see that the whole body of our race is tainted and rotten, and so he applies to it the cautery that burns rather than the ointment that soothes; and thus, with wisdom, sagacity, diligence, and the fear that he inspires, he has borne upon his broad shoulders the weight of this great project and duly put it into effect; and all our tricks, stratagems, pleadings, and deceptions haven't been able to blind his Argus eyes, always on the alert so that not one of our people remains hidden from him like a root buried in the ground that might later sprout and bear poisonous fruit in a Spain now cleansed and free from the fears in which our rabble kept it."[2] The notion that an exiled morisco might plead for the continued victimization of his own race for the benefit of a purified Spain is as preposterous as the idea that a prisoner at Auschwitz might call for the annihilation of the Jewish people to advance the laudable racial-cleansing goals of the German nation.

Cervantes' repeated allusions to the morisco expulsion and his comments on the making of history show that the Spanish "history wars" and their very real consequences continued to be an open wound in the political and social body of the Spanish nation well into the seventeenth century. The literary response from organic intellectuals may be best exemplified by the work of theologian Cristóbal Lozano, who refers to the Muslims living in Spain from 711 to 1492 as foreign terrorists and to their convert descendants as greedy traitors.

Lozano's views seem uncannily familiar today in the context of the war on terror, as exemplified by the speech given at Georgetown University by Spanish ex-president José María Aznar on September 21, 2004. Aznar argued that Al Qaeda's terrorist attacks (he was referring specifically to the Madrid bombing of March 11, 2004) are part of an ancestral war going back to the Muslim invasion of Spain in the year 711: "The problem Spain has with Al Qaeda and Islamic terrorism ... has nothing to do with government decisions. You must go back no less than 1,300 years, to the early 8th century, when a Spain recently invaded by the Moors, refused to become just another piece in the Islamic world and began a long battle to recover its identity."[3] As one of us has argued in *Baroque Horrors*, the statement assumes the existence of an essentially Christian Spain of ancestral origins that must be defended against the recurrent attacks of Islamic terrorists. The mythical genealogy produced by the organic intellectuals of the nascent modern state continues to frame reality today. In fact, Lozano's explanation of why God would have permitted the mistreatment of his people at the hands of Islamic terrorists is also familiar: "The Visigoth empire was plagued by the corruption of religious values and behavior in the years preceding the seventh hundred and eleventh....To have irritated God and infuriated the Heavens with disobedience and to have offended the land with such wickedness: this is what caused the loss of Spain."[4] Notice the uncanny similarities between the language of this seventeenth-century theologian and the explanation of the 9/11 tragedy provided by Christian fundamentalists Jerry Falwell and Pat Robertson. In their view, forcefully expressed on The 700 Club, the horror of 9/11 was God's way of punishing the United States for its tolerance of abortionists, liberals, feminists, gays, and lesbians.

As explained in the Preface of *Baroque Horrors*, the echoes of Spain's imperial dreams and the mythology that sustained them can be heard loud and clear in the work of another Christian televangelist, Rod Parsley's *Silent No More* (2005): "I do not believe our country can truly fulfill its divine purpose until we understand our historical conflict with Islam....It was to defeat Islam, among other dreams, that Christopher Columbus sailed to the New World in 1492....Columbus dreamed of defeating the armies of Islam with the armies of Europe made mighty by the wealth of the New World. It was this dream that, in part, began America."[5] The fact that Rod Parsley was John McCain's spiritual adviser at the time of his presidential campaign in 2008 should make us think twice about the role that these notions may play in today's political circles. In the context of the war on terror, which is often conflated with the fight for universal freedom, mainstream politics have become increasingly fundamentalist.

While the spirit of religious crusade is not always explicitly present in mainstream politics, attentive observers, particularly those who are familiar with the medialogy of the colonial age, can easily detect Messianic overtones in the logic of deliverance that informs even totally secular statements on American exceptionalism. Take President George W. Bush's justification of the invasion of Iraq in his 2003 State of the Union address: "Americans are a free people, who know that freedom is the right of every person and the future of every nation. The liberty we prize is not America's gift to the world; it is God's gift to humanity."[6] Perhaps the best way to underscore the Messianic echoes of President Bush's speech is to place it side by side with what would have been a plausible call for colonial intervention entirely consistent with the Imperial dreams of Hapsburg Spain: "Spaniards are a Christian people, who know that Christianity is the right of every person and the future of every nation. The Christian religion we prize is not Spain's gift to the world; it is God's gift to humanity."

As a matter of fact, those who are familiar with the writings of sixteenth-century missionaries and Christian officials might not need to substitute the words "freedom" and "liberty" from Bush's 2003 State of the Union address to arrive at what would amount to a trans-historical legitimation of imperial intervention, equally valid for Hapsburg Spain and Bush's America. After all, Christian missionaries saw themselves as instruments of God's promise of universal freedom. Whether they knew it or not, the Indians needed to be freed from their own misconceptions and misguided cultures, from their inferior social and political organizations, even from their own language, in the name of historical progress and universal justice; and Spain was the exceptional nation chosen by God to advance the cause of universal freedom.

If we may call on the satirical craft of Stephen Colbert again:

Ronald Reagan said it first [the comedian goes on to note that Reagan was probably paraphrasing JFK, paraphrasing John Winthrop, paraphrasing Jesus]: "America is the shining city upon a hill." And no matter how dark our days, or how low we sink, we will always be shiny and hilly. Reagan also said, "I have always believed that there was some divine plan that placed this great continent between two oceans to be sought out by those who were possessed of an abiding love of freedom and a special kind of courage." He's right, America was put here by God for us to find. America was like the sculpture existing inside the block of marble, waiting for the artist to chip away a few Cherokee to find it [...] Everything we've ever done has ended up creating the greatest country in the world, ergo everything we did was the best possible choice.[7]

Substitute Spain for America and voilà, this is the lesson of not only the historical genealogies commissioned by the Hapsburgs, but also the so-called historical plays of Lope de Vega and other popular dramatists of his day. As we explain below, this kind of instrumentalist history provides the key link between the monuments of our past and the roadmap of our future as defined by the political, cultural, and economic elites.

The trick is to close our eyes to the messiness of our present circumstances in order to *feel* our historical truth. We must believe in the "signs" of our historical destiny as they (and the motherland through them) call us into being. Here's Colbert once again: "We have the greatest history in the history of History [...] America also has the Greatest Future in the history of the Future. It's our present that's the problem [...] because if you think about America, sure we're neck-deep in debt, we're knee-deep in neck, and the dollar isn't worth the dime it's printed on. That's why I am asking you to *feel* about America. Really *feel*. So please, close your eyes when you're reading this book."[8]

8

Freedom for Sale

Outside of the context of the current war on terror, America's exceptionalism and the discourse of freedom on which it is predicated depend on the economic fundamentals of capitalism. If religious fundamentalists place their faith on a God that has blessed America as a universal beacon of freedom, economic fundamentalists put their faith where their wallets are. For them, freedom equals free trade.

Let's take the case of billionaire real estate magnate-turned presidential candidate Donald Trump. Never mind that at about 11:15 on Tuesday night, November 6, 2012, Trump thought that Barack Obama had lost the popular vote when he was projected the winner of the Presidential election. While he ostensibly tied his tweeted call for a revolution to the notion that, as the "loser" in the popular vote, Obama should not be held as the legitimate president of the nation despite handily winning the Electoral College, this was beside the point. The reality of the situation is that on that Tuesday night at around 11:15, U.S. democracy was a "sham" and a "travesty" in Trump's book because, quite simply, he couldn't get U.S. democracy to give him what he wanted.

Right around the same time Republican fundraiser-in-chief Karl Rove was on the air urging Fox News, the network for which he plays political pundit, to retract its own projection of an Obama win. The fact that there remained numerous votes to be counted in Ohio was also beside the point. Rove could not accept the "media fact" (even if broadcast by his own media outlet) of an Obama win, not because such a fact contravened his belief, but because it contradicted his sense of consumer justice. Simply put, the "media fact" of an Obama win was incongruent with Trump's and Rove's faith in a country in which you get what you pay for.

It's no wonder that Trump and Rove blamed the media for their blind denial of the "real America." In their minds, the "real America" was the America that, around 11:15 on November 6, 2012, was not being recognized by the media facts. The billionaires of American Crossroads had paid good money for their desired outcome, and the world's beacon of freedom had stiffed them.

A key scene in Stephen King's *Needful Things* shows the Devil as a shopkeeper looking to convince a potential customer to buy from him. When the customer insists he has no need for the kind of material things the shopkeeper has to offer, the Devil retorts, "You don't believe in free trade? What are you, a communist?" In *What Money Can't Buy: The Moral Limits of Markets*, Michael Sandel argues that our society has shifted from a market economy to a market society, in which everything is viewed as something that can be bought and sold. As we can see, the same can be said of our notion of freedom. Today, "freedom" is treated as the American right to buy anything for the proper price.

This fundamentally economic notion of freedom as purchasing power frames our social and political reality. In the words of a Burger King commercial, "You are an American; you have the right to buy a burger for 99 cents." Of course the object may change, and with it the price, but everything else stays the same. We could say that the universal version of the statement would be, "You are an American; you have the right to buy anything for a price"; but Sprint and Apple said it better when they partnered to market the unlimited Sprint plan for the iPhone 5: "I need—no, I have the right to be unlimited." They may have been advertising unlimited data uploads, but their marketing strategy signals a more ambitious aim: consumerist freedom should not be subject to any limits, be they legal, ethical, or even existential.

It would be a mistake, though, to ascribe this circumscription of freedom by market forces as somehow limited to our present situation. It turns out that the founding thinkers of the moral systems underlying western liberal democracy, men who lived the first age of inflationary media like John Locke, Adam Smith, and David Hume, systematically defined freedom in economic terms in their moral philosophy. Let's take the example of David Hume.

In his *Enquiry Concerning the Principles of Morals*, Hume argues that selfless action is an irreducible element of human behavior, admired and esteemed by all, and that "no better system will ever, for the future, be invented, in order to account for the origin of the benevolent from the selfish affections, and to reduce all the various emotions of the human mind to a perfect simplicity."[1] We need not derive morality be from self-interest or from transcendental principles because there need be no presumption of self-interest's sway in human motivation in the first place. Instead, "it appears, that a tendency to public good, and to the promoting of peace, harmony, and order in society, does always, by affecting the benevolent principles of our frame, engage us on the side of the social virtues."[2]

In other words, we shouldn't wonder why humans act altruistically; the mystery is why we would ever assume such altruism wasn't a part of human nature to begin with. Transcendent principles need not apply, for we can plainly see that "the rules of equity or justice depend entirely on the particular state or condition, in which men are placed."[3] Which leads us to conclude that, instead of an abstract concept like Justice to mold and guide our actions, all that is required is to remove the state or condition that seemed to demand such a principle.

But if as foundational a principle as justice can be revealed to derive from passing states or condition, then transcendent principles in general lose their force. If such principles derive merely from the repetition of rules and conventions, then the idea that interactions between subjects need to be mediated by them also loses force. Hume's resultant grounding of morality on existing human behavior is, however, profoundly conservative. A politics that questions the very legitimacy of established values and behaviors would seem to be excluded, and utopian projects that entail a wholesale rejection of the status quo fail to enter the picture.

To undergird his argument, Hume gives some examples of cases in which principles would become irrelevant:

Again; suppose, that, though the necessities of the human race continue the same as at present, yet the mind is so enlarged, and so replete with friendship and generosity, that every man has the utmost tenderness for every man, and feels no more concern for his own interest than for that of his fellows: It seems evident, that the USE of justice would, in this case, be suspended by such an extensive benevolence, nor would the divisions and barriers of property and obligation have ever been thought of. Why would I bind another, by a deed or promise, to do me any good office, when I know that he is already prompted, by the strongest inclination, to seek my happiness, and would, of himself, perform the desired service; except the hurt, he thereby receives, be greater than the benefit accruing to me? In which case, he knows, that, from my innate humanity and friendship, I should be the first to oppose myself to his imprudent generosity. Why raise land-marks between my neighbor's field and mine, when my heart has made no division between our interests; but shares all his joys and sorrows with the same force and vivacity as if originally my own?[4]

As should be clear, Hume's picture of innate brotherly love is no mere exaggeration; rather, is literally *inhuman*. Despite all familial and community ties, in a fundamental sense subjectivity entails my *not* being able to experience my neighbor's emotional life with the same degree of vividness that he or she does; that I *cannot* know his or her ultimate motivations; that my heart *always* recognizes some division between our interests. Hume's picture is thus a fantasy projection sparked by the more fundamental experience of finitude that grounds all subjectivity. To be unlimited is the desire of a finite being.

Such finitude simultaneously limits our possibilities of knowledge and expands the range of our imagination. A politics founded on the eradication of transcendence only allows for one course of action. It naturalizes the status quo, implicitly assuming it to be the human condition—one in which, for instance, there is no division between human (read, class) interests.

Billionaires call for revolutions by weaving fantasies of popular sovereignty, and major corporations use the language of individuals rights, but both are tapping into the same basic notion: there is no need for external controls on our behavior toward one another, no need for transcendent principles of governance, because at core we are transparent to one another, and share the very same values. But of course the divisions are real. Hume's bourgeois perspective is baked into the very foundations of the liberal tradition underlying today's medialogy, and appeal to personal freedom overlays a profound servitude to the interests of market capital.

The economic truth behind Hume's discourse on morals becomes even clearer when we read it alongside the moral thought of Gracián. As we have seen, according to the Spanish Jesuit, "moral philosophy" teaches the art of human polity (prudence). Rather than positing a private subject who cares for his neighbors and exhibits selfless traits as the ground zero of our mores and social foundations, Gracián's starting point is a public subject driven by the desire for power and recognition. As in the case of Hume, Gracián deduces his moral principles from empirical observation. The difference is that he takes us behind the scenes, so to speak, in order to show us how the game is really played. His "moral lessons" are presented in how-to manuals of public behavior that teach us how to become "better persons," that is, more refined public subjects.

For Gracián, the truly discreet or wise subject, or *persona*, possesses the moral discipline required to dissect the world in its current state and uses this knowledge, as well as the art of public acting, to get what he wants. As Gracián would have it, the finest among us are those individuals best equipped to bend the will of their neighbors for their own personal gain. This is the true moral art: "Conquering minds has little value if wills are not subjugated. Much has been accomplished, however, when the will has been rendered.... This grace can be achieved with good fortune but most of all through personal diligence."[5]

None of this is lost on the subjects of todays' medialogy. Take the ad for Direct TV that encourages its customers to look at friends and family members as cash cows. The idea is that we should get them to sign up for Direct TV service and then "let the Benjamins stack up!" Visually, the message is transmitted by showing the faces of "our friends and family" morphing into the iconic image of Benjamin Franklin printed on the hundred dollar bill. While the hundred-dollar Benjamin is not the type of currency that Baltasar Gracián had in mind when inviting his discreet reader to amass symbolic capital by surrounding himself with the right friends and connections, these very distinct notions of currency (cold hard cash/symbolic capital) have much in common in the way they are invoked as a means to an end: the acquisition of power and success, whether it be in today's cash driven society or in the aristocratic circles of the absolutist court.

In one of his many asides, Francis Underwood, the character played by Kevin Spacey in the Netflix series *House of Cards*, tells us that in his Washington circles people are motivated by either money or power. He himself, he adds, has no respect for those who are simply after money; the true prize of the game is power. Clearly Underwood is a man after Gracián's own heart, and yet another manifestation in today's cultural realm of why a translation of Gracián's *Pocket Oracle* was able to achieve bestseller status. Indeed, one has to wonder if the billionaires of American Crossroads, who were so complacently at work cashing in their dollars for power, really should have been brushing up on their seventeenth-century moral philosophy.

9

Crime Shows

The European sixteenth century witnessed an extraordinary expansion of the state and its bureaucracy. In Spain especially this expansion led to an explosion in legislation and litigation, and increased awareness and reflection on criminality and society's responses. Writers in general and playwrights in particular strove to *show* criminality, delinquency, guilt, and the procedures for determining and controlling these, to a public ever more eager to consume such representations and make sense of these changes. The state, meanwhile, exercised increasing measures of censorship of and influence over cultural production in order to control the message and ensure the dissemination of an image of criminality that implicitly justified the criminal justice system and its bureaucracy. In the face of rampant corruption, the monarchy and its defenders likewise sought means of both cementing a public perception of justice as flowing directly from the King's authority and disseminating an image of virtue as rooted in self-discipline, abnegation, and an internalization of duty.

We see in the jurisprudence of this early modern empire an analogue to what has been called the CSI effect in contemporary criminological research, according to which the prevalence in popular culture of certain models of investigation, evidence, innocence, and guilt alters the predisposition of juries to convict or acquit. While the Hapsburg State had no juries, it was attuned to public opinion to a degree that had few precedents, which was itself precedential for the modern era that it helped inaugurate. The legitimacy of the State in the eyes of the public was a matter of consistent and pressing concern for the King and his bureaucracy, and this legitimacy rested in large part on the claim that the government and its judicial representatives exercised *justice* and not merely capricious coercion in matters of law and order. Thus were the tools of visual media, from emblems to the massively popular theater industry, coopted for the purpose of training popular conceptions and expectations to conform to the state's version of justice. To use Peter Goodrich's term, emblem books and the theater constituted essential tools in Hapsburg Spain's *visiocracy*, the medial and visual foundation of its rule.[1] That visiocracy was in turn rooted in the first inflationary age and its medialogy.

Despite her proverbial, principled, and stonily sculpted veil, we know today that justice is far from blind.[2] In so many cases, so many instances, we learn that the very standards juries are asked to apply uniformly are themselves subject to multiform interpretations and applications, such that even those most offended by the travesty of the acquittal of George Zimmerman in the slaying of Treyvon Martin had to stay their gut instinct to condemn a jury that had been asked to apply the letter and spirit of a Florida law and question the reasonableness of a neighborhood watchman's behavior under the jurisdiction of that law. As Cardozo's Ekow N. Yankah wrote, "What is reasonable to do, especially in the dark of night, is defined by preconceived social roles that paint young black men as potential criminals and predators."[3]

How those roles become preconceived is, of course, *the* question. And there is a good deal of evidence that at least one of the media for conveying and coloring our preconceptions—for priming our reception of notions of the reasonableness of others' behavior but also of what constitutes evidence, proof, guilt or innocence, and justice itself—are *crime shows*. Donald Shelton has conducted research into the potential veracity of at times conflicting claims around the influence on juries, either bending them to acquit or to convict, of frequently watching the popular contemporary crime show *CSI*, in any of its urban variants.

The commonplace complaint, at least as the term "CSI Effect" began to make the rounds of criminal jurisprudence, was that such an evening pastime did much to inculcate in viewers an unreasonable expectation for scientifically derived forensic evidence. In the words of one frustrated prosecutor, "I once heard a juror complain that the prosecution had not done a thorough job because 'they didn't even dust the lawn for fingerprints.'"[4] Nevertheless, it is important to note that the outcome of the research was a tad deflating: "Although *CSI* viewers had higher expectations for scientific evidence than non-*CSI* viewers, these expectations had little, if any, bearing on the respondents' propensity to convict. This, we believe, is an important finding and seemingly very good news for our nation's criminal justice system: that is, differences in expectations about evidence did *not* translate into important differences in the willingness to convict."[5]

Despite what appears to be exculpatory evidence in the case of *CSI*, the general case for a special relationship between juror priming and visuality, or specifically the ability to imagine specific scenarios, has been forcefully defended. As Kevin Jon Heller puts it in an article explaining the jurors' tendency to undervalue circumstantial evidence and overvalue direct evidence, "jurors decide whether to acquit not through mechanical probability calculations, but on the basis of their ability to imagine a scenario in which the defendant is factually innocent."[6] As Goodrich argues in his book *Legal Emblems and the Art of Law*, such focus on the power of the imagination and specifically the visual was recognized by early modern jurists as well: "to believe, according to the emblematist Matthaeus Merian, you have first to see, because 'men believe much more in the eyes than in the ears' and he continues 'it is through the eyes that the great truths are imprinted upon the human soul.'"[7] Given this implicit and even unconscious reliance on scenarios, scenographies, or in general an imagination of the scene of the crime, it behooves us to be ever vigilant of those short circuits between word and image that replace the veil of justice with a print, screen, or stage on which a certain judgment has already played itself out. This is why the introduction of new forms of visual media in the courtroom, including digital simulations, is a real source of concern for law scholars. For NYU Law Professor Richard Sherwin, the lack of "visual literacy training" of not only jurors but judges and attorneys as well, severely compromises the effectiveness, and ultimately the fairness, of our justice system today.

In his article coining the aforementioned term, *visiocracy*, Goodrich cites an NYU study in which groups of first-year law students argued cases, some in classrooms dressed in street clothes, others in formal courtrooms before judges who had donned the full regalia of the legal profession. The study concluded that the latter group was "significantly more likely to view the procedure as more legitimate, the judgment as more authoritative, and the judge as more learned in law than those who appeared in the makeshift informal auditoria." The students, Goodrich argues, "apprehended...that there was more to the theater of justice than can be captured by reason and reduced to the page."[8] Goodrich finds precedent in the emblematic tradition for this essentially visual aspect of the practice of law, this tendency for legality to find illegitimate legitimacy in a kind of imagination of justice that grounds authority in an unexamined visual realm or *visiocracy*. As he puts it, "The visual is in classical emblematic terms universal, undivided, free of the chaos that Babel inflicted upon language. The visual is the primary means and medium for transmitting law because, like law, it touches all."[9]

Support for this thesis comes from realms other than the legal. Bradley Nelson has dedicated a study to emblematics in early modern Spanish literature, from which he derives similar conclusions regarding the efficacy of emblems and emblematic tropes in "the collective interpellation of the audience into foundational narratives of monarchical unity." Nelson identifies both in emblem books published at the time as well as in such emblematic cultural genres as the theater, which we will turn to as well, a disposition toward the "guidance of the spectator toward a 'correct' interpretation [that] necessitates his or her engagement in a conflict between deviant and correct discursive and moral models."[10]

In a few of the emblems we'd like to discuss here we can see precisely such a modeling of desirable behavior; but we are even more interested in how the modeling in this selection of emblems engages and guides popular ideas of sovereignty and authority in relation to individual freedom and pleasure. Specifically, we would like to argue that the emblematic tradition contains at least one stream dedicated to rationalizing the exertion of power, of punishment, of corrective violence as a personal hardship and hence sacrifice, even on an implicitly religious register, for the sovereign. This equation in turn informs an ancillary discourse of self-discipline and punishment as the inherent justification or redemption of fears and suspicions, rampant in a society steeped in the corruption of legality and abuse of authority for the personal gain and pleasure of those in positions of power. In other words, what the emblems do is to fuse an image of righteous suffering with the idea of legality that had been hijacked in the public imagination by stories of graft and corruption, in order to create an image of justice, a visiocracy, in which potentially arbitrary violence is seared into the public imagination as the justified exertion of a higher law felt equally by all, the sovereign included.

As Susan Byrne, Richard Kagan, and others have shown, the evolution of the legal tradition in Hapsburg Spain was characterized by ever-increasing confusion and the generalized sense that laws were there to be broken or ignored by anyone with the power or wherewithal to do so. In Kagan's words, "Castilian justice in the sixteenth and seventeenth centuries was a hodgepodge of confused laws and competing jurisdictions that crafty litigants exploited to their own advantage."[11] Such complaints rose through the chain of command, infecting public confidence in the legitimacy of authority at the local and even national level, leading to innuendos of Kings themselves not obeying the law, along with counterexamples such as that of Cabrera de Córdoba, who protests too much that "the dresses and adornments worn by their Royal Highnesses and the happy couple were in conformity with the pragmatic, without any gold in the embroidery or passementerie trim, or any other thing of gold, although the gentlewomen and men who attended the ceremony wore much that had hold embroidery or passementerie."[12]

So it is that Sebastián de Covarrubias, in his popular and widely diffused *Emblemas morales* of 1610 portrays the lion of royalty fused with the aged and bony body of a steer, and asks the question, "What do you think it means to rule? To serve, dying."

The emblem turns the table on the common complaint of abuse of power: to wield power is to suffer abuse in the service of the common good; it is to give up all pleasure and selfish desires, to be consumed by sacrifice. The face of the lion, like the steer's body, is sagging, the skin loose and hanging, aged early by the cares of office. The front right paw, placed in paternal protection on the orb of the world, is devoid of the violence and fear that great beast's claws would normally project, and radiates instead a father's benevolence.

Covarrubias then shifts the suffering of sovereignty inward in an emblem depicting the fatal outcome of the easy road of self-fulfillment as a wide open net of pleasure, or *gusto*, that narrows into the deathtrap of the great Satanic fisher of souls.

EMBLEMAS MORALES

DE DON SEBASTIAN DE
Couarrubias Orozco, Capellan del Rey N.S. Maeftrefcuela,
y Canonigo de Cuenca, Confultor del
fanto Oficio.

DIRIGIDAS A DON FRANCISCO GOMEZ DE
Sandoual y Roxas, Duque de Lerma, Marãs de Denia, Sumiller de Corpe
Cauallerizo mayor del Rey N.S. Comendador mayor de Caftilla,
Capitan General de la caualleria de Efpaña.

Attingit à fine vfque ad finem.

Neque enim micuerunt fruftra.

CON PRIVILEGIO,
En Madrid, Por Luis Sanchez: Año 1610.

Figure 9.1 Frontispiece to Sebastián de Covarrubias, *Emblemas morales* (Madrid, 1610); courtesy of the George Peabody Library, Sheridan Libraries, the Johns Hopkins University.

CENTVRIA. I. 34

VT. SERVIAT. / RAT / IMPE

EMBLEMA 84.

Que pēſais q̃ es reynar? ſeruir muriē-
Los dias, y las noches trabajando, (do,
Y quādo vos comeis, ó eſtais durmiēdo,
No comer, ni dormir, y eſtar velando:
El Rey, parte es leon, feroz, y horrēdo,
De quien el mūdo todo eſtà temblādo,
Y manſo buey, del medio cuerpo abajo,
Nacido para el yugo, y el trabajo.

Mar-

Figure 9.2 Covarrubias, p. 34; courtesy of the George Peabody Library, Sheridan Libraries, the Johns Hopkins University.

Figure 9.3 Covarrubias, p. 204; courtesy of the George Peabody Library, Sheridan Libraries, the Johns Hopkins University.

Just as a people's proper protection requires the self-sacrifice of the sovereign, this emblem directs its reader toward a sacrifice of his or her own pleasure, linking as it does all pleasure to damnation. A prudent eye must be watchful first and foremost of its own desires.

We can see a positive counterpart to this admonition in the 1665 festival book *Luces de la aurora* or *Lights of Dawn*. In this emblem we are treated to an inversion of the traditional moral of Phaeton's fall. Rather than a cautionary tale of the dangers of uninhibited ambition, of leaving one's natural station in life and flying too high, Francisco de la Torre reads Phaeton as morally exemplary, a self-sacrificing model of altruism, whose flaming fate is worthwhile suffering as long as the intent was noble.

The theme of self-directed suffering in the service of a greater morality is rampant in Covarrubias, especially in the realm of education, where the whip is shown in several cases as being essential to the civilization of students, to their happiness, and even, as in this personalization of the pedagogy of violence, to life itself.

Figure 9.4 Francisco de la Torre, *Luces de la aurora* (Valencia, 1665), pp. 562–563; courtesy of the George Peabody Library, Sheridan Libraries, the Johns Hopkins University.

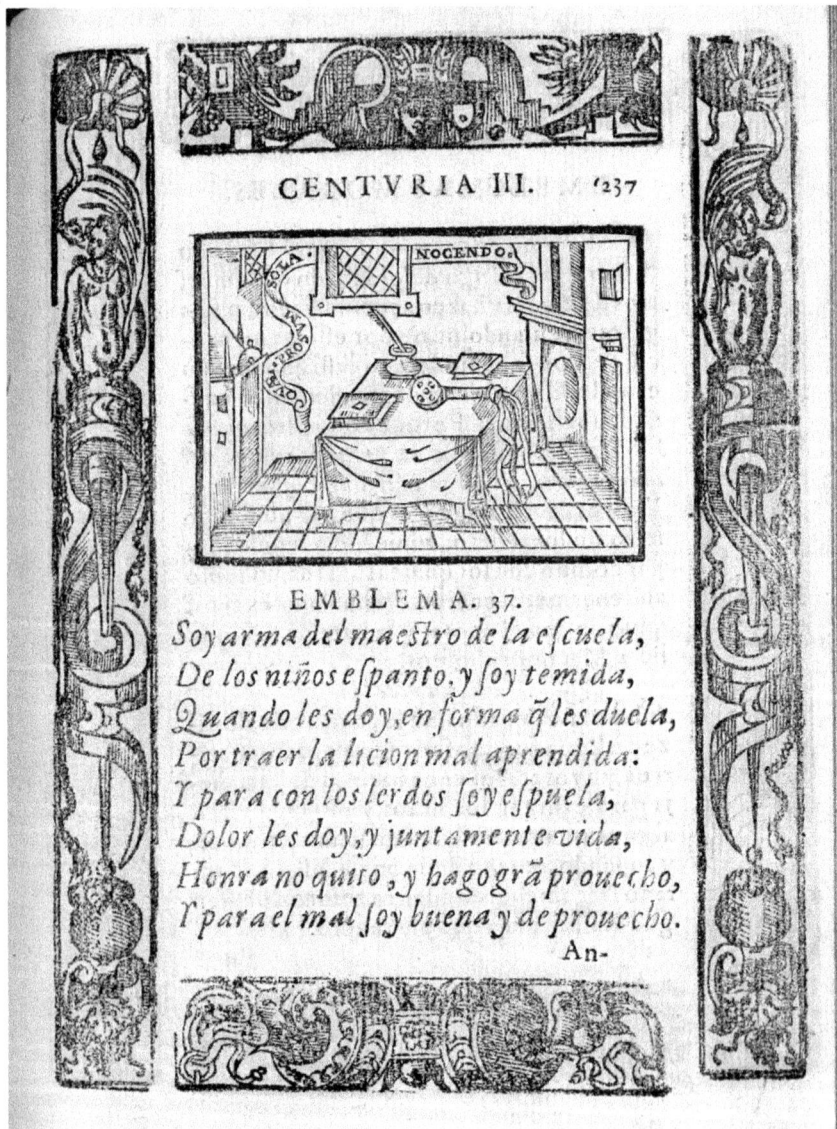

CENTVRIA III. '237

NOCENDO.

EMBLEMA. 37.

Soy arma del maestro de la escuela,
De los niños espanto, y soy temida,
Quando les doy, en forma q̃ les duela,
Por traer la licion mal aprendida:
Y para con los lerdos soy espuela,
Dolor les doy, y juntamente vida,
Honra no quiro, y hago grã prouecho,
Y para el mal soy buena y de prouecho.
An-

Figure 9.5 Covarrubias, p. 237; courtesy of the George Peabody Library, Sheridan Libraries, the Johns Hopkins University.

"Dolor les doy, y juntamente vida—pain I give them, and at the same time, life," says the whip, but it also specifies the kind of student who will benefit from its rigor: the *lerdos*, the oafs and the slow-witted. Those, in other words, who haven't the self-discipline to tame themselves will benefit and

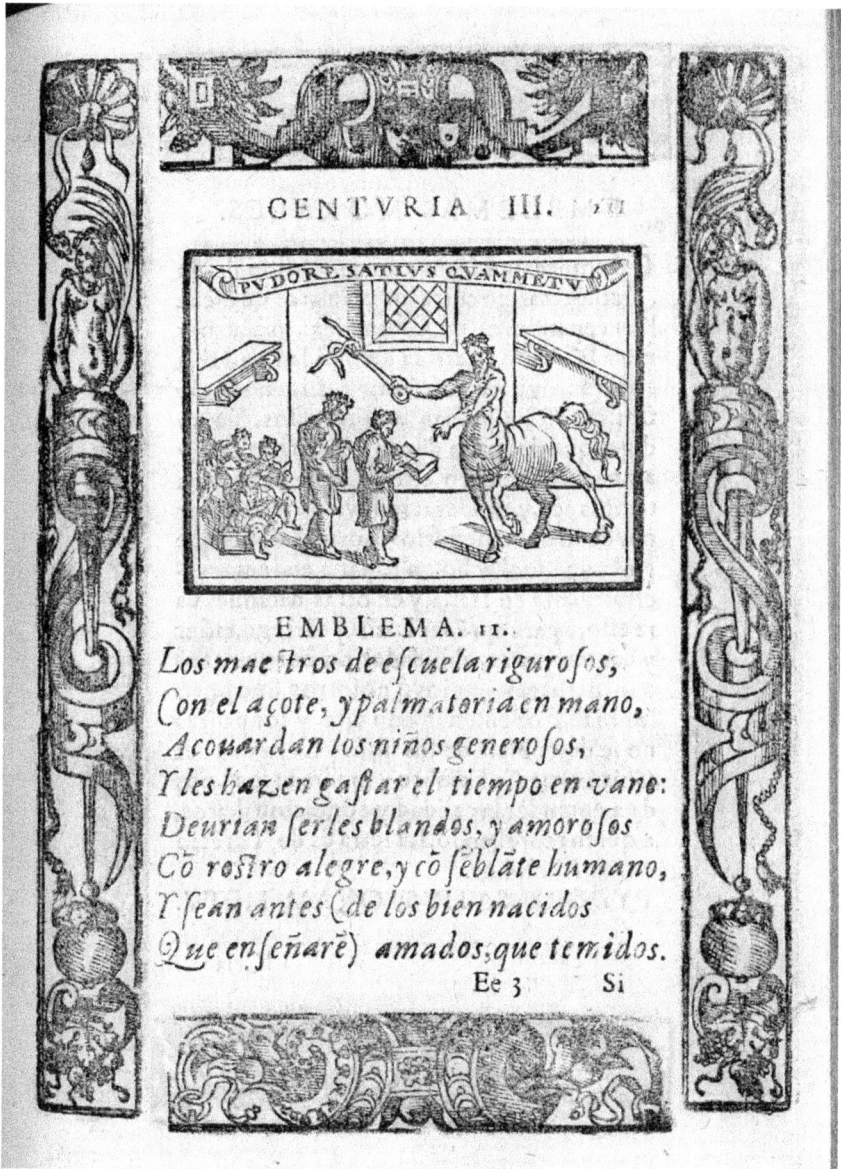

Figure 9.6 From Covarrubias, p. 21 recto; courtesy of the George Peabody Library, Sheridan Libraries, the Johns Hopkins University.

even gain life from punishment. But not all students need to be shaped in this way. As Covarrubias writes in another emblem dedicated to the theme of education, teachers should spare the whip on well-born children, for whom its rigors are more likely to cause their generous spirits to cower and make them waste their time in useless exercises.

The comparison between these two views on corporal punishment is eye-opening: in agreement with the tendency of his age, Covarrubias accepts a foundational distinction between kinds of men, already present in their children. There are those whose blood destines them to be leaders, whose natural generosity makes the imposition of suffering unnecessary and even potentially detrimental; for these "sons of something" as the base term for the gentry, hidalgo, literally signified, already have in them a proclivity to choose suffering over pleasure. It is meanwhile the oafish, the weak, those lacking such lineage who should not be spared the lash, if only out of duty and compassion for their likely fate free from its guard.

Political Theater

What were the crime shows, the *CSIs*, the *Law and Orders*, the *Tatorts*, of the burgeoning urban populace under the Spanish Hapsburgs? Certainly not emblem books themselves, which, while popular enough were expensive and rare, showpieces of wealth and learning, and hardly the equivalent of a workingman's Sunday night *Krimi*. No, the *comedia de capa y espada*, the *comedia de honor*, these were Hapsburg Madrid's crime shows, drawing thousands to the *corrales*—the open public theaters set up in the courtyards between buildings—week after week, irrespective of class or literacy, to flood their eager brains with freshly wrought versions of largely the same tale: someone gives in to temptation; someone loses his honor; someone must pay the price. A favorite variant was to have the source of dishonor be noble or, in a few cases, even royal, and the victim a loyal and honorable commoner who ends the play dispensing outlaw justice of the bloodiest sort, an unforgivable crime in the eyes of the law, but one that suddenly finds a rationalizing *image of justice* in the emblematic tableaus suggested by the *comedia*'s denouements.

In Calderón de la Barca's *The Alderman of Zalamea*, the wealthy and honorable Pedro Crespo is, along with his fellow townspeople, forced by law and custom to billet the King's troops as they pass through Zalamea. When an officer abuses his privilege and rapes Pedro's daughter Isabel, the scene is set for that classic conflict, honor versus duty. It is honor, of which Pedro famously says it is "the patrimony of the soul, and the soul belongs to God," that wins out.[1] Rather than hide his dishonor or—more incomprehensibly to us but not to societies still clapped in the irons of that code—cleanse the stain with his daughter's blood, Pedro becomes judge, juror, and executioner to Isabel's rapist, sentencing him to the ignominious death of a commoner.

The withdrawn curtains of the "apariencia" that so often served on the Spanish stage to "reveal a marvelous scene in one of the niches at the back of the stage,"[2] in this case, presents the audience with a scene of horror, the garroted body of the captain, still bound to a chair. As Cull says of this and other such dramatic tableaus, "the combination of striking visual motifs (*pictura*) with the commentary in the form of dramatic dialogue (*subscription*) imitated the structure of the emblem ... These scenes, designed to provoke *admiratio* in the spectators, often embodied the play's central message or moral."[3]

And indeed the emblem itself was designed to function in the same way as the theatrical *apariencia*, revealing a hidden truth via the short-circuit between image and subscript, igniting the wonder of sudden insight much as the stage machinery that could make a character or body suddenly materialize. As Covarrubias notes in the entry he composes for *emblema* in the dictionary he published one year after his *Emblemas morales,* the *Tesoro de la lengua castellana o española* that would be his greatest claim to posterity, among the terms related to and easily confused with the emblem is *pegma*, the name for the moveable stage machinery used to enable pageants, which itself had descended etymologically from its classical usage to denote a scaffold, frame, or structure meant to hold an ancestor's death mask.

Indeed the revelation of the innermost space in the comedia's stage architecture had another, perhaps more profound impact. Akin to the position of the altar over a tomb in medieval church architecture, the last interior space opened by the *apariencia* at the denouement of a *comedia* tapped into a powerful experience of *presence* on the part of contemporary observers. Rather than referring to a next act for their eventual interpretation, such dramatic tableaus depicting bodies in pain or at the very moment of their deaths, acted as a full stop to the otherwise highly fungible, metonymic gliding of empty theatrical space from one represented place to another. In this way, the final tableau could insert in the place of a meaning, a feeling, a physical impact, as if the audience were touching something beyond mere human capacities for explanation.[4]

This tableau is not the last, however, for like others in its genre, the *comedia* must resolve the conflict between Pedro's undeniable crime, the law, and the justice for which it stands. And only one figure could perform this slight of hand: the King. As Nelson writes, "Felipe II's *apariencia* on stage configures yet another emblematic moment in the *comedia*, in which the King embodies the presence of a transcendental *deus ex machina* who restores order by invoking a superior idea of ... 'poetic justice.'"[5] For faced with this undeniable violation of the dimension of the law, the King nevertheless bows to Pedro's invocation of justice, of *the King's own* justice: "Toda la justicia vuestra es un cuerpo, no más—all your justice is one body, no more,"[6] and hence whether I, Pedro Crespo, have been his executioner, or any other of your subjects, the fact remains that justice was served.

Perhaps the best way we can imagine such a visual embodiment of justice is to compare the moment in the play with an image of Saint Ferdinand III reproduced on the next page, the thirteenth-century King canonized some nine years before Calderón's death in 1680, taken from the Festival book published in honor of that canonization in Seville that very year.

An earlier play by the great playwright Felix Lope de Vega y Carpio embodies the *deus ex machina* of justice in the figures of the historical founders of Spain's unified monarchy, Isabella and Ferdinand. Moreover, it does so in a way that explicitly draws a border between prior, medieval (implicitly denigrated as capricious and violent) forms of judgment and Lope's imagining of a universal, quasi-divine justice meted out by the Catholic Monarchs. In what some consider his greatest play, *Fuenteovejuna*, published in 1619 but likely performed between 1612 and 1614, the entire eponymously named town comes together to avenge the rape of its women by its feudal lord. When they are one by one submitted to trial by ordeal by the examining judge, they all hold to the story that "Fuenteovejuna did it," and refuse to single anyone out. At this moment the monarchs arrive, to the delight of all, especially the townspeople—who apparently shed the recent trauma of their torture with some ease once bathed in the glow of the royal aura, for their first words are expressions of awe at the monarchs' beauty:

Laurencia: Those are the monarchs?
Frondoso: And powerful over all of Castille!
Laurencia: By my faith are they beautiful!
May Saint Anthony bless them![7]

Figure 10.1 *Fiestas dela santa iglesia de Sevilla al culto nuevamente concedido al Señor Rei San Fernando III de Castilla i Leon* (Seville, 1671); courtesy of the George Peabody Library, Sheridan Libraries, the Johns Hopkins University.

And yet it is clear that their beauty, and from the staging of the scene, their *presence*, grounds something else, something missing from the application of the letter of the law by the examining magistrate, namely, justice. For upon hearing their enumerated please, Ferdinand finally speaks and cites the very absence of a written confession as the justification for his overstepping traditional hierarchies and taking the township under his direct governance, in so doing absolving the township and its people of any guilt.

While there are a number of sources from which Lope may have taken his inspiration for the composition of his greatest play, there can be no doubt that he knew of Covarrubias's emblem book, and that he had seen in it Covarrubias's own reference to "the case of Fuente Ovejuna." As in many such references, the emphasis of Covarrubias's emblematic analysis is on the moral dilemma of the moment of justice, when the judge, faced with the town's insistence that "*Fuente Ovejuna* did it," must decide between exonerating them all or condemning an entire populace to death.

Here the emblematist fiercely condemns the mob rule as "atrocious," without "God, King, or Law," [8] and yet, as Dixon points out in his analysis of the scene and its relation to Covarrubias's emblem, both the playwright and the emblematist fixate their attention on this moment of unanimity of the people and the inherent selflessness of justice. As Covarrubias explains on the verso page to this emblem, justice so favors the innocent that it will prefer to let the guilty go free than to risk punishing falsely. Thus, while executing an entire village was in fact not outside the realm of possible outcomes given the real system of justice at the time, both representations also point to a new world order, carved into the theatrical emblem of a people who unanimously cashed in their suffering for the authority of a universal sovereign. [9]

In a lecture delivered at Cardozo Law School under the auspices of Drucilla Cornell's conference on "Deconstruction and the Possibility of Justice," Jacques Derrida posed the problem of justice in terms of speech act theory, arguing that "as a performative cannot be just, in the sense of justice, except by grounding itself on conventions and so on other performatives, buried or not, it always maintains itself with some irruptive violence." [10] The visual dimension of law, it's visiocracy, serves at least in part to tame and focus, to justify that irruptive violence by grounding it in an invisible but certain reality. In Goodrich's words: "What is significant, because the genealogy

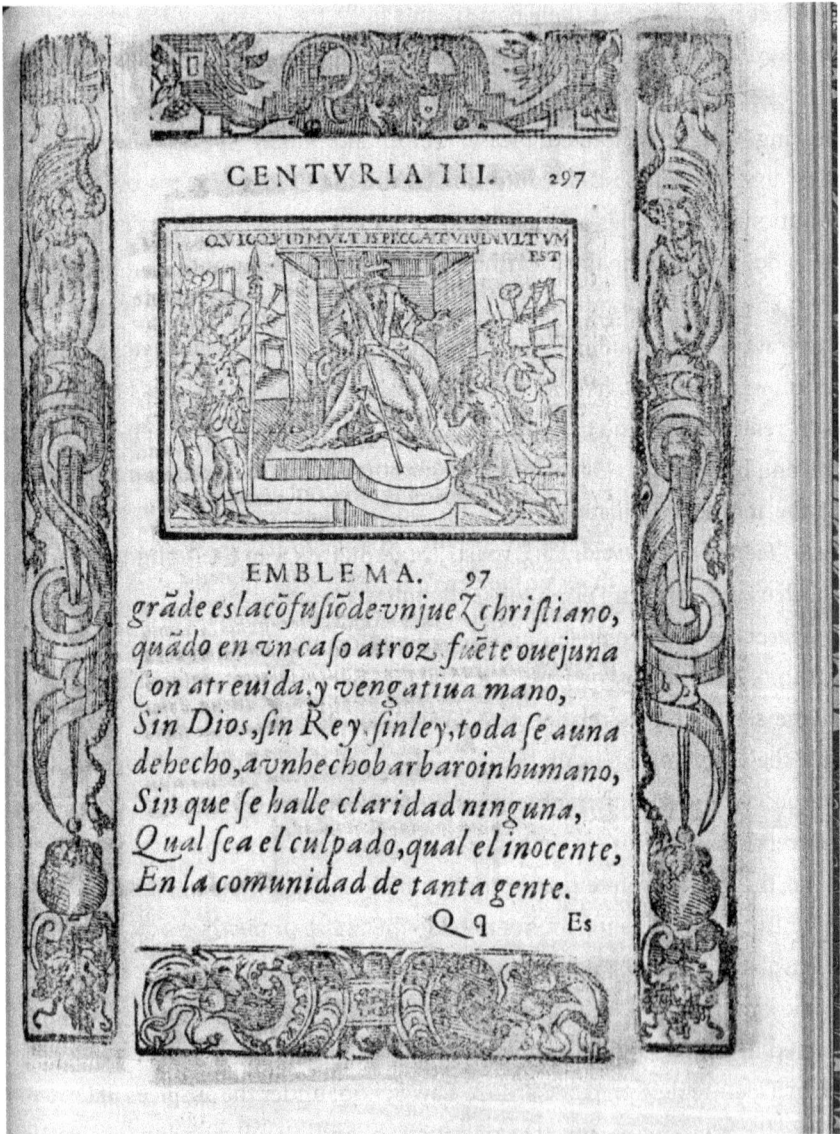

Figure 10.2 Covarrubias, p. 297; courtesy of the George Peabody Library, Sheridan Libraries, the Johns Hopkins University.

and especially the philology can become tedious, is that in looking at law, in appearing before the court in its glory, the student sees not law but justice, not rule but principle, not force but flowers, in the garments of justice. Justice is a matter of faith, of belief in what is not and has no being ... and so a matter of parabolic appearances and of the enigmatic signs that form the secrets of government."[11]

On the one hand, then, is the plague of corruption, the evident absence of anything approaching a justifying justice behind the self-serving abuse of the law. On the other, an opposing and desperate discourse, evident in these emblematic structures, in which the violence and coercion of the law is equated with the common good by way of its being wielded ultimately by a selfless and suffering, even a saintly sovereign whose own embrace of pain in turn justifies and redeems the apparent abuses at all levels below him. This emblematic structure creates an *image of justice* in which the force of law is cured of its seemingly arbitrary application and identified with a legitimate, because universal, suffering anchored ultimately in the sovereign's own self-abnegation: it is right that we all suffer because no one, not even the King, not even modern day priests of the law, those suffering poet-detectives of hard boiled and police procedural fame is exempt from that suffering. In J. Madison Davis's words, the police hero,

> is a man of common background in quest of justice, but can only exact a small portion of it out of the unfragrant world we live in. Usually, the police hero is also as scarred as the hard-boiled private eye in his battles to make something, anything, right. Sam Spade pays an emotional price for turning Brigid O'Shaughnessy over to the police. There's an ongoing ruefulness in Philip Marlowe's loneliness. All this is in contrast to the joyful revelations that characterize the traditional puzzle-solving detectives of Agatha Christie, S. S. Van Dine, and Arthur Conan Doyle.[12]

Is it a stretch to see in the modern detective, with his suffering etched like an emblem into the care-worn lines of his all-too human face, a direct descendent of Covarrubias's suffering sovereign, united in their noble quest for a justice that anchors the apparent caprice of the law? For ours is a universal empire of pain; as with the movement toward interiority and intent in the rereading of Phaeton's fall, we are asked to replace the evident injustice of the legal system with the assumption of a greater or real justice that we can only assume, trust, or have faith exists in the heart of the other, for, in Aquinas' words, "Man, the framer of human law, is competent to judge only of outward acts; because man seeth those things that appear...while God alone, the framer of the divine law, is competent to judge the inward movement of wills."[13]

If the human law is a matter of the visible, shouldn't we pay closer attention to the visiocracy that anchors our perception of the world, the codes that frame it and the media that propagate it? After all, as Sherwin observes, social conventions "frame the visible and invisible alike—establishing the one by virtue of the other."[14] And yet, according to this legal scholar, "little work has been done, however, to investigate the implications of visual legal meaning making." And so we join him in asking, "What authorizes the state's exercise of power through law as image?"

Monumental Screens

The superimposition of the hundred-dollar bill on the faces of our friends and family in the Direct TV commercial mentioned earlier is a powerful illustration of the objectifying system of equivalences that drives the global market economy today. As we explained, in its nascent form this system can be traced back to the origins of the monetary economy at the dawn of modernity and the logic of abstraction on which it was built. As objects became exchangeable for their cash value in the new economy, individuals would also come to be seen as abstract entities within the political imaginary of the emerging nation-state, "exchangeable" in principle vis-à-vis the Monarch. This notion is aptly illustrated by the title of Rojas Zorrilla's seventeenth-century play *None Beneath the King* (*Del rey abajo, ninguno*).

The notion that we are all potentially "equivalent" as equally honorable subjects in the eyes of the King is the theme of countless baroque dramas, including such classics as the above-mentioned *Alderman of Zalamea* and *Fuenteovejuna* as well as similarly popular plays such as Lope's *The Commoner in his Corner* (*El villano en su rincón*) and *The Gentleman from Olmedo* (*El caballero de Olmedo*). As historian José Antonio Maravall famously argued in his political reading of *Fuenteovejuna*, the *comendador*'s scornful question to the commoners "you lot have honor?" is responded to in the affirmative within the ideological horizon of the drama.[1] The abstract ideal of universal honor is predicated as the cornerstone of a monarchical system that would seemingly offer its subjects equality beneath the King. While this egalitarian and democratic ideal drives the spectacular actions of *Fuenteovejuna* and informs the dramatic sense of poetic justice in many other baroque plays, it does not correspond with real social relations of the time. As Maravall repeatedly demonstrated, Hapsburg Spain was governed by a coalition of the monarchy and the landed aristocracy that worked to defend the traditional privileges of the nobility and the Church against the claims of the nascent bourgeoisie and the exploding masses of dispossessed individuals.

Much has been said about the impact of geographical and cosmological discoveries and the emergence of mechanistic conceptions of nature in the early modern period. Yet, with few exceptions, the early modern invention of landscape has gone mostly unnoticed, particularly in the philosophical circles in which the notion of modernity has been both defined and debated. As Yi-Fu Tuan pointed out in his landmark study *Topophilia: A Study of Environmental Perception, Attitude and Values* (1974):

> The axial transformation in world view from cosmos to landscape may be traced in the changing meanings of the words "nature," "landscape," and "scenery." In modern usage these three words share a common core of meaning: scenery and landscape are often used interchangeably and both imply nature....In its native Dutch, "landschap" designated such common places as a collection of farms or fenced fields, sometimes a small domain or administrative unit. Only when it was transplanted to England toward the end of the sixteenth century did the word shed its earthbound roots....Landscape came to mean a prospect seen from a specific standpoint. Then it was the artistic representation of that prospect. Landscape was also the background of an official portrait; the "scene" of a "pose." As such it became fully integrated into the world of make-believe.[2]

The world was thus effectively incorporated into the illusion, transformed into theatrical space, and framed as *scene-ry*.

We can find a perfect example of this theatrical framing of the world in a 1972 made-for-TV rendering of *Fuenteovejuna*. At the conclusion of the play, the stone walls of the royal palace of Ferdinand and Isabella fade away to reveal an architecturally framed view of the Castilian countryside. The significance of this climactic scene is underscored by an intense, seemingly supernatural, luminosity, which transforms the fields beyond the architectural setting into an ethereal panorama. This is indeed an allegorical portrait of the body politic, the scene of the monarchs' pose, so to speak. The picture is complete when the camera zooms in to reveal the citizens of Fuenteovejuna slowly moving through the scene-ry. This "total view" of the body politic is strongly reminiscent of the etching created by the French artist Abraham Bosse for the first edition of Thomas Hobbes's *Leviathan*, printed in 1651, which represents the territory of the state as the body of the King with his head rising over the landscape. On closer inspection we can see that the torso of the monarch is composed of countless human figures whose own faces are turned toward the King's head.

In erasing the history of social and political antagonism from the Castilian landscape, the carefully framed panorama of the pacified countryside presented at the conclusion of the 1972 production of *Fuenteovejuana* closely follows the monarchical metanarrative that's inscribed in the King's proclamation at the end of Lope's original text: "… the town must thus remain within me, insofar as it has claimed me [as its legitimate ruler]." The implication is that the town of Fuenteovejuna, which metonymically represents all of Spain, voluntarily (and heroically) has embraced monarchical absolutism as political desideratum and historical destiny. This is how the name-place Fuenteovejuna becomes a *foundational topos*, a monumental site that marks the birth of the Spanish State. The spectacular mythology of *Fuenteovejuna* functions as a double screen that protects the nation from the traumatic and potentially disintegrating encounter with its own historical real in the past as well as in the present. This may help explain why this seventeenth-century play has been used to promote self-celebratory images of the ruling order in political environments as diverse as Franco's Spain and the former Soviet Union.

The climactic scenes of this baroque historical drama have much of the flavor of Hollywood-style epics and Disney productions. Indeed, the (re) constructive impulse that structures mass-oriented spectacles works on the same principle today as it did in the context of baroque culture, that is, the principle of myth, which Roland Barthes aptly defined as a form of naturalization of history. As he puts it in *Mythologies* (1972): "[m]yth is neither a lie nor a confession: it is an inflexion [that] transforms history into nature."[3] The "inflexion" of what Barthes speaks may best be described as *an act of framing*.

A quick look at the landmark Disney film *Pocahontas* (1995) can help illustrate this point. The storyline is simple and familiar enough in its naturalization of colonial history. Following the arrival of a shipload of

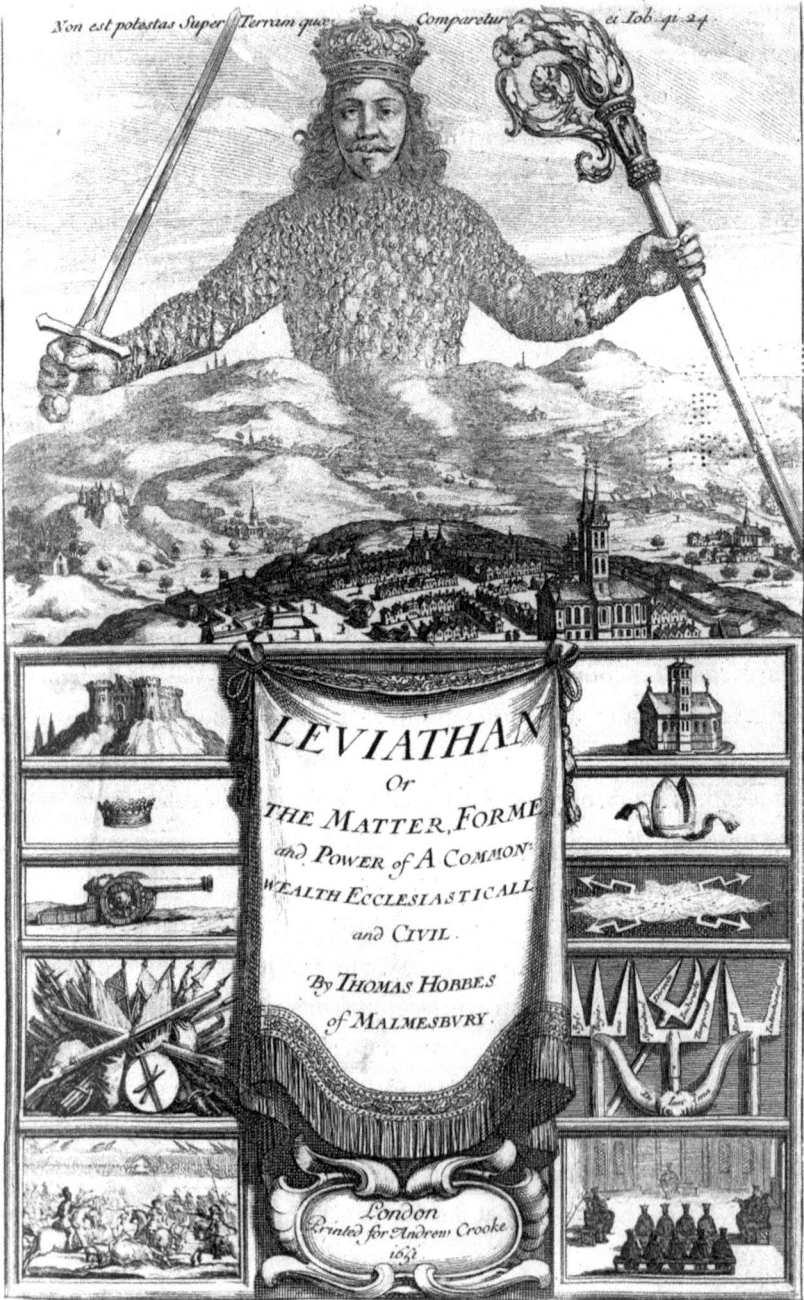

Non est potestas Super Terram quæ　Comparetur　ei Iob. 41. 24

LEVIATHAN

Or

THE MATTER, FORME
and POWER of A COMMON-
WEALTH ECCLESIASTICALL
and CIVIL.

By THOMAS HOBBES
of MALMESBVRY.

London
Printed for Andrew Crooke
1651

Figure 11.1 Frontispiece to Thomas Hobbes, *Leviathan*, 1651, etching by Abraham Bosse, courtesy of Wikimedia Commons.

English settlers to the coast of Virginia, the young daughter of Indian Chief Powhatan and the courageous English Captain John Smith develop a romantic attachment, which will be tested by the initial mistrust between their two very different cultures. With the help of Meeko (a playful raccoon), Flit (a feisty hummingbird), and especially Grandmother Willow (a wise ancient tree), Pocahontas and Smith defeat the villainous and greedy Governor Ratcliffe while finding a way for everyone to peacefully share the land.

Close-to-nature (or nature-bound) Indians are of course the gold standard of colonial discourse going back to Columbus' *Diaries*, as is the split of historical agents into noble idealists and greedy villains in such plays as Lope de Vega's *The New World Discovered by Christopher Columbus* (*El Nuevo Mundo descubierto por Cristóbal Colón*). And of course, the familiar notion of "manifest destiny" justifies the conquest and colonization of the New World by linking the colonial order to providential designs or, in the case of the Disney film, to the will of Nature. Thus, when the confused Indian princess discusses her mysterious dreams about a spinning arrow with Grandmother Willow, the ancient tree advises her to listen to the spirits of the earth, the water, and the sky who will guide her toward the right path:

> Grandmother Willow: It seems to me this spinning arrow is pointing you down your path.
> Pocahontas: But Grandmother Willow, what is my path? How am I ever going to find it?
> Grandmother Willow: All around you are spirits, child. They live in the earth and water, in the sky. If you listen, they will guide you.
> Pocahontas: I hear the wind.
> Grandmother Willow: What is it telling you?
> Pocahontas: I don't understand.
> Grandmother Willow: Listen with your heart. You will understand.
> Pocahontas: It's saying something is coming; strange clouds ...

The "strange clouds" mentioned here by Pocahontas turn out to be the sails of a vessel arriving from England. Pocahontas will eventually find the path she is searching for with the help of Smith's lost compass (the spinning arrow). In the end the Indian princess becomes convinced that she and her people must embrace the Land's manifest destiny, which is inextricably tied to the predestined presence of the newcomers:

> Grandmother Willow: –It's the arrow from your dream.
> Pocahontas: –I was right. It was pointing to him [John Smith].
> Grandmother Willow: –Let the spirits of the earth guide you. You know
> the right path, child. Now follow it!

This mythical version of "the encounter" is a foundational landmark that can be easily transferred to the present socio-political situation. Hence, today's (post)colonial landscapes, along with the socio-political structures contained in them, may be "naturalized" as the fulfillment of history: the shining city at the end of the "right path."

The music video version of the song "If I Never Knew You," which is performed by Jon Secada and Shanice at the conclusion of the film, reinforces this topophilic mythology through astonishingly effective framing techniques:

> I thought our love would be so beautiful,
> somehow we'd make the whole world bright.
> I never knew that fear and hate could be so strong,
> all they'd leave us were these whispers in the night,
> but still my heart is saying we were right …
> If I never knew you,
> I'd have lived my whole life through
> empty as the sky,
> never knowing why,
> lost forever,
> if I never knew you.

The central moments of the film are replayed against the night skyline of New York City as we listen to the nicely harmonized voices of Jon Secada and Shanice. On a few occasions, the camera zooms in to give us a close up of an open door or window that reveals our own contemporaries looking up at the sky, seemingly mesmerized by the topophilic spectacle in which they play a part. We see ourselves in their eyes, sharing in the emotion of collective spectatorship. This is how we are integrated into the national landscape, not necessarily as "historical actors" but as "spectators" of the national drama.

This visual imagery provides a temporal and geographical bridge between the time and space of the mythologized Virginian "encounter" and the here and now of a cityscape that has been cleaned up to gloss over the daily realities of ongoing exploitation and violence. The mythologized meeting of a British captain with an Indian Princess in sixteenth-century Virginia is explicitly offered as a metaphor for what/who we are as a nation: the world's beacon of freedom and opportunity. As the lyrics proclaim, "somehow we make the whole world bright." Remarkably, the city itself has been framed as the screen of an outdoor theater on which to project the ideological fantasies that sustain the trans-historical identity of the nation. Meanwhile, the lyrics gloss over the realities of colonial violence by masking them as distant echoes of leftover fears: "all they'd leave us were these whispers in the night."

It is important to note that this framing of the "Virginian encounter" does not differ a great deal from the familiar model of celebration of historical and cultural identity in monumental sites. The End of the Oregon Trail Interpretive Center located on the outskirts of Portland, in Oregon City, is a particularly apt example insofar as it taps into one of the most enduring figures of the national imagery: the American pioneer. We can literally touch the world of our ancestors as various relics from the time of the pioneers are passed from hand to hand across rows of spectators sitting in front of a stage-like presentation area. To complete the visit, the audience is ushered toward a stadium-seating theater for a film presentation featuring carefully selected quotes from the diaries of the first colonists to arrive to the West Coast, professionally recited over a series of dramatic shots of majestic mountains, lash valleys, and cascading waters. The spectacular documentary produces a narrative of American determination, resourcefulness, endurance, moral rectitude, unshakable faith, and compassion. The words of Simon Schama come to mind as we watch this magnificent (very carefully framed) spectacle of nature: "Landscapes are culture before they are nature; constructs of the imagination projected onto wood and water and rock."[4]

The film concludes with an explicit call to new generations of Oregonians to follow the path of the pioneers, that is, to share in the quintessential American values as presented (or constructed) by the narrative. The carefully edited words of the pioneers literally frame the Oregon nature, transforming it into a monumental landscape. In this context, a panoramic view of Mount Hood, to speak of a particularly recognizable landmark of the Oregon landscape, is transformed into a medialogical construction as effective as any commemorative monument at Gettysburg. In fact, Reuben Rainey's analysis of the function of monumental sites in "Hallowed Grounds and Rituals of Remembrance: Union Regimental Monuments at Gettysburg" applies to the End of the Oregon Trail Interpretive Center in Oregon City, as much as to the self-consciously politicized landscape of *Fuenteovejuna* (in both the made for TV production and Lope's original play), and to the cityscape that accompanies the soundtrack of "If I Never Knew You" at the conclusion of Disney's Pocahontas: "[the monument] not only instructs us about the great historical events of our culture but also reminds us of present and future social and political obligations ... [It] is a guide to the future as well as a celebration of the past."[5]

In today's medialogy, as the forces of globalization conspire to erode the structures of the modern state, new mythical panoramas are beginning to emerge, not to replace the spectacle of the nation, which still anchors the political reality of its citizenry, but to supplement it with images of the global city of tomorrow for those with "the right to be unlimited," if we can once again recall the promise of deliverance that came with the iPhone 5. As a TV commercial for the Citi World Citibank credit card proclaims: *The world is a city.*

If the symbolic landscapes that we associate with the (early) modern state depended on a fantasy of equivalence vis à vis the King or other place holder of State power (as in the title of the baroque play, *Del rey abajo, ninguno*), the new global panoramas come with the promise of total access without borders. But of course the fantasy of a global city of limitless individual freedom (which would be coterminous with the unlimited capabilities of our latest digital windows) veils the everyday reality of borders, including social and economic borders that help maintain, police, and justify the exploitative and predatory structures of the global market society.

At the most basic level, even well-to-do travelers experience the very limitations masked by the fantasy of the global city each time they go through international security checkpoints. A particularly dramatic example of the contrast between our medialogy's promise of limitless horizons and the reality of a world in which movement is carefully filtered, monitored, and controlled can be found in the ticketing and security area of the new American Airlines terminal at JFK, which offers world travelers the spectacular imagery of a global cityscape unhampered by historical and geographical limitations in the form of a gigantic, 397-foot mural, even as they are required to comply with increasingly invasive security procedures as a condition to enter the sovereign territory of the United States.

As stated in a recent news release from the American Airlines Newsroom, "American Airlines commissioned New York artist and architect Matteo Pericoli to create the mural, entitled 'Skyline of the World'... The mural combines... landmarks from New York, as well as some 70 other cities around the world... such as the Sidney Opera House with the Toronto City Hall and the Fuji TV building in Tokyo... including Chicago, San Francisco, London, Paris, Rome, Tokyo, Sao Paolo and Rio de Janeiro." The press release invites travelers/spectators to make the connection between "The Skyline of the World" and that of New York City, as seen from the airport windows: "At the

Figure 11.2 Photograph by authors.

center of this procession, the Brooklyn Bridge appears from the wall behind it. The skyline then begins to narrow and become smaller, concluding at a point where passengers approach the concourses where they can glimpse the real New York skyline through the terminal's large windows."[6]

The language of the American Airlines press release is reminiscent of the descriptions of the EPCOT pavilions and other theme parks in the promotional website of Disneyworld. The use of the word "procession" to describe the presumed experience of the traveler/spectator adds to the uncanny sense that we have become unwilling participants in a Disney-style parade meant to celebrate just the kind of sanitized and embalmed landscape that we associate with Walt Disney's Experimental Prototype Community of Tomorrow. As a matter of fact, the spectacular "skyline of the world" screens out the messiness of the lived city and the ruins of the world around it in just the same way. Poverty, homelessness, alienation, war, ecological devastation, corporate greed, conflict, exploitation are as absent from the skyline of the world as they are from the Walt Disney parks.

Yet, we could argue that the real skyline that the traveling spectator can glimpse from the airport windows is already a lie, a monumental screen in its own right. The Spanish poet Federico García Lorca made this point most eloquently as early as 1929–1930 in his surrealist masterpiece "New York (Office and Denunciation)." In the aftermath of the great crash, Lorca's anamorphic poetry focuses precisely on the ruins that have been hidden from view behind the number-crunching machines housed in the office buildings that make up the sky(line) of New York City. He explicitly denounces the connivance of the number-crunching machines of capital and the media-frame that screens out the suffering of humanity behind airbrushed panoramas:

> Beneath the multiplications
> there is a drop of duck's blood.
> Beneath the divisions
> a drop of sailor's blood.
> Beneath the additions, a river of tender blood
> ... in the lie of New York's dawn.
> ... I have not come to see the sky.

I have come to see the murky blood,
blood that carries the machines to the cataracts
and the spirit to the cobra's tongue
… I denounce all
who ignore the other half,
the irredeemable half,
who raise the mountains of cement
where the hearts
of small forgotten animals beat
and where all of us will fall
in the final feast of power drills
… I denounce the connivance
of these deserted offices that will not broadcast the suffering,
that stamp out the forest's plans
and I offer myself as a meal for cows wrung dry
when their cries fill the valley
where the Hudson becomes drunk with oil.[7]

12

The New Fundamentals

Then vice-president of the Andrew W. Mellon foundation, Philip Lewis, predicted in February of 2014 that the most pervasive and potentially widespread danger that the Humanities would face in the immediate future would not necessarily be the outright closing of programs, as in the highly controversial axing of French, Italian, Russian, Classics, and Theater that took place at SUNY Albany in 2010, but the less conspicuous "shrinkage by attrition and reorganization."[1] As Lewis writes: "[This] process of resource reallocation is one that can occur with little fanfare … the natural result of the principle that allows the intra-institutional market, defined through the lenses of enrollment patterns or student demand, to dictate the ongoing reshaping of the academic structure …. The cost of this subtle, incremental diminution of support for the language and literature, for the liberal arts and humanities, for education as a broad intellectual project is far greater than that of the visible closings and mergers we have witnessed up to now."

Within our medialogy, education has become one more commodity, a mere "product" that can be bought and sold in the marketplace. The defunding of public institutions of higher learning and the resulting corporatization of the university are changing the academic landscape in the United States and elsewhere at lightning speed, providing little time for academics (let alone the larger community) to discuss or even understand the impact of these changes. While Lewis focuses the lens on the ongoing reallocation of resources in "intra-institutional" markets, it is clear that the shifting of priorities and the internal reorganization of resources that goes with it are a direct response to external pressures and the collapse of the public funding model of higher education. As the new "old joke" goes, public universities used to be "state funded," then "state assisted," and are now "located in a state." The defunding of public universities in the United States, and the shifting priorities that cash-driven (euphemistically enrollment-sensitive) intra-institutional funding models reify are of course a reflection of the logic, priorities, and values of the global market economy. When we identify our students as "clients" and attach a dollar value to them in our quest to comply with artificially generated enrollment expectations and revenue driven demands, we have simply succumbed to the pressures of the ideology that defines the world (with the people in it) as a global market made up of nothing but objects exploitable for profit.

To quote Michael Sandel again, we have "drifted from *having* a market economy to *being* a market society … in which market values seep into every aspect of human endeavor [and] social relations are made over in the image of the market."[2] In the context of the market society, just about everything is (or is presumed to be) up for sale, and every product is assumed to have a corresponding market value. Moreover, the global market has attained a kind of axiomatic status that comes with real-world directives, purportedly neutral and dispassionate, yet clearly discriminatory and objectively violent. In today's world, in other words, the normative model of behavior stems from those entities that produce and sell commodities, namely, corporations.

Significantly, some scholars—among them English Professor David Schmid—have noted that the expected behavior of corporations in the socio-economic environment of the current neoliberal order is virtually identical to that of the psychopath. Schmid draws from Joel Bakan's assertion that the corporation is literally a pathological institution whose "legally defined mandate is to pursue, relentlessly and without exception, its own self-interest, regardless of the often harmful consequences it might cause to others."[3]

With regard to the seeping of market values into educational institutions, Linguist Noam Chomsky is, as one might expect, among the academics who have recently warned against the ongoing corporatization of higher education. He refers to this phenomenon quite simply as "The Death of American Universities."[4] In case one might take Chomsky's rhetoric for extreme, Terry Eagleton comes to the same prognosis, arguing that "an event as momentous in its own way as the Cuban revolution or the invasion of Iraq is steadily under way: the slow death of the university as a center of humane critique."[5] The scenario Eagleton describes in the UK is dark indeed, as he draws parallels with U.S. private institutions like Stanford and MIT while noting that the safety net of affluence is largely absent in the UK university. He talks about the corporatization model as the conversion of the university into a product mill more focused on the bottom line than on the students who ostensibly are there to learn more than just skills. In the case of one university in Ireland, he cites the case of "security staff [who] move students on if they are found hanging around," concluding that, "the ideal would be a university without these disheveled, unpredictable creatures."

In the stripped down, cutthroat marketplace that Eagleton describes, it is easy to see how humanities departments and faculty find themselves in increasingly precarious straits. The universities are forced by conservative governments to validate their missions economically at the same time as they are deprived of resources. The result is an ethos of almost constant evaluation of faculty productivity focusing on the "impact" of their research, a standard that is hard for any humanist to concretize but that is interpreted by most in terms of number of publications, footnotes, and citations, rather than the far more impactful yet amorphous influence they may be having on the insight and intellectual development of the young people whose lives they touch. Forced to fund themselves increasingly through tuition, universities further pressure faculty to lower their standards, lest their customers leave dissatisfied, and "sex-up" their offerings, leaving generations of students deprived of a rigorous training in literature, philosophy, or history.

These warnings have been around for more than a decade and yet they do not seem to have inspired anything akin to a change of course. Henry Giroux, for example, has been denouncing the corrosive effects of corporate culture in our university system at least since his 2002 article "Neoliberalism, Corporate Culture, and the Promise of Higher Education: The University as a Democratic Public Sphere."

The corporatization and commodification of the university have come with the erosion of faculty governance and the rise of managerial powers that have championed the cause of "greater efficiency"—a rather shortsighted version of "efficiency" that does not allow for broadminded discussions and long-term planning, much less for questions of public responsibility and professional ethics. The short-circuiting of debate is often predicated on the need for nimble decision-making in times of crisis. Beyond the downsizing and restructuring of departments, the growing numbers of adjunct instructors, and the abrupt reallocation of resources, the importation of market-oriented, market-defined, and market-structured "efficiency" models has resulted in a sort of permanent emergency status that clears the way for the managerial high-jacking of academic freedoms and program-specific goals.

This constant state of alert also has the pernicious effect of priming humanities faculty to react suspiciously even to the best-intentioned attempts of administrators who do fully support the humanities and wish to enhance and expand them. Such a pervasive sense of grievance has created a culture of resentment, even and perhaps especially among faculty at elite institutions, where their teaching load and quota of research leave are the stuff of dreams for colleagues at public institutions and can be a cause for friction with colleagues in their own science departments, themselves buckling under the weight of their oversubscribed service courses and the expectation to irrigate their institution's budgetary garden with their hard won research dollars.

All of this malaise flows from the failure to recognize that education, like the human beings it enriches, is not a product like those myriad others that circulate in the neoliberal marketplace. As Hunter Rawlings, the former president of Cornell University and current president of the AAU, writes in an Op-Ed article in the *Washington Post*,

> most everyone now evaluates college in purely economic terms, thus reducing it to a commodity like a car or a house. How much does the average English major at college X earn 18 months after graduation? What is the average debt of college Y's alumni? How much does it cost to attend college Z, and is it worth it? How much more does the "average" college grad earn over a lifetime than someone with only a high school degree? (The current number appears to be about $1 million.) There is now a cottage industry built around such data.[6]

The problem with this way of thinking, however, is that in truth education is almost entirely unlike the vast majority of commodities we encounter, consume, and exchange in the global market. As Rawlings points out, unlike a car, a college education depends as much on what the "consumer" brings and puts into it as it does on the "product itself." Yet despite this essential difference, "most public discussion of higher ed today pretends that students simply *receive* their education from colleges the way a person walks out of Best Buy with a television."

The results of this category mistake can be deadly for our institutions of higher learning, especially public universities not protected by a healthy endowment and independence from political winds. Governors and legislatures from North Carolina to Wisconsin, basing their arguments on the model of the college degree as a commodity, have moved both to link professors' pay to the number of hours they teach and to decimate tenure, the ultimate safeguard of academic freedom. But at a more general level this attitude is toxic for the very spirit of higher education as it is felt in the classroom at every level of academia. In Rawlings' words again, "Students get the message. If colleges are responsible for outcomes, then students can feel entitled to classes that do not push them too hard, to high grades and to material that does not challenge their assumptions or make them uncomfortable. Hence colleges too often cater to student demands for trigger warnings, 'safe rooms,' and canceled commencement speakers." The core of the college experience, what humanities classrooms have traditionally excelled at offering, is in danger: the seminar discussion as a place for unfettered thought led by a professor who challenges students to come to new insights of their own accord.

As many have argued, this tradition is in danger precisely because it is at odds with today's prevailing ideology. In the words of Frank Fear, a professor emeritus from Michigan State University, "An argument can also be made that a neoliberal ethic has infected America's institutions. Many organizations have become self-absorbed—hyper-focused on internal matters, lathered with self-promotion....And while I don't think it happened overnight, I also believe—that over time—neoliberalism has become a prevailing ethic in American higher education. Higher education today, I believe, is a largely neoliberal institution."[7] Indeed, we see the increased incidence of students' complaints about the contents of their, specifically, humanities courses as a prime symptom of this infection of higher education by neoliberal ideology.

Even as cultural conservatives interpret recent incidences on college campuses as a renewal of the "liberal excesses" of "political correctness," it has become increasingly clear that much of such excessive "progressivism" masks a profound neoliberalism at its core.

This new political correctness, while often packaged in terms of protecting the rights of minorities and those who have been victimized, is clearly also a demand not to be challenged, not to have one's world view threatened or one's beliefs brought into question. The justification for this demand stems from the neoliberal model of the individual as positioned and defined by today's medialogy: I am a consumer at core; my essence is my ability to define myself via the choices I make as a consumer. To recall the iPhone ad once again, I have the right to be unlimited.

This explains how Duke University student David Grasso's refusal to read *Fun House*, the award-winning graphic novel memoir by Alison Bechdel, in preparation for his freshman year, on the grounds that its depictions of a young lesbian woman's adolescence were offensive to his Christian beliefs, is in some ways identical to the protests by supposedly "liberal," that is, left-leaning students at colleges around the country that have resulted in prominent intellectuals being disinvited because their view might be offensive to, say, Muslims on campus.[8] More perniciously, this comfort conservatism then contaminates what are in fact the historically grounded inequities suffered by minority students who *do* so often arrive on campus without the invisible blankets of their peers' unquestioned privileges, who *do* have to overcome unacknowledged but real prejudices, who *should* have the benefit of policies that take into account the inequities of race and class.

The crucial point to see is how this conflation of traditionally conservative and apparently leftist positions is the logical outcome of our medialogy. Today's medialogy, the one specific to the second age of inflationary media, disseminates the ineffable, ever receding reality produced by the first age, repackaging it into products, things, experiences. By "turning copies into things" and thus promoting the idea of portable and individualized realities, our current medialogy has produced neoliberalism as its dominant model for interpersonal relations. Today's fundamentals, unlike those of the foundations of the first inflationary age, are infinitely personalizable; but they are not for that reason any less ineffable. The self-certainty with which any college student today may demand, and be granted, his or her comfortable truth is simply neoliberalism's version of the religious certainties that animate arch-conservative communities from America to the Middle East. We may live in the heart of the industrialized world, but each of us is entitled to our own private fundamentalism.

Part Three

Exclusions

Terrifying Vistas of Reality

In a recent article titled "The Perils of Perfection," Evgeny Morozov discusses the futurist plans of Silicon Valley moguls, including the development of reality-altering technologies, such as smart glasses or contact lenses that would edit out "disturbing sights" like "homeless people."[1] As innovations go, this is certainly an intriguing one, yet the truth is that the editing out of "disturbing sights" is already a fact of reality as we know it. Arguably one of the primordial functions of our current medialogy is precisely to frame the world is such a way as to erase from view what we shouldn't want to see. The "human debris" known as "the homeless" is indeed high on the list of undesirable sights, along with, say, sweatshops, and corporate land-leasing devastation. It is easier to get rid of these eyesores by excluding them from of our field of vision than to deal with the structural problems that cause them.

The thing about "exclusions," though, is that they often come back to haunt us. Our dreams of "perfection" may turn into nightmares, as in Francisco de Goya's famous dark sketch: "The dream of reason produces monsters." Indeed, the monsters that populate our nightmares are inextricably tied to what we've cut off, buried, repressed, or erased from view. If, as Joseph Conrad famously put it, "fashions in monsters do change"[2] these changes mirror the history of our exclusions. How surprised should we be that the first age of inflationary media has also been called "an age of monsters"? Witches, sorcerers, werewolves, specters, and all manner of monstrous nature, including human monsters, proliferate in the nascent print culture of the early modern period, at a time when the borders of our knowledge were shifting wildly and "reality" itself appeared to be up for grabs.

Galileo's contemporaries coined the expression *nocturnal horror* to name the ominous sense of awe that engulfs the soul confronted with the mystery of the starry night described in his *Starry Messenger* (*Sidereus Nuncius*) published in 1610. This notion is uncannily close to the concept of cosmic fear developed by H.P. Lovecraft to define the stakes of his "weird tales" and the vistas of reality offered by modern horror. Here is a particularly apt example from his well-known tale "The Call of Cthulhu" from 1926: "We live on placid islands of ignorance in the midst of black seas of infinity, and it was not meant that we should voyage far... [But] someday, the piecing together of dissociated knowledge will open up such terrifying vistas of reality, and of our frightful position therein that we should go mad from the revelation or flee from the deadly light into the peace and safety of a new dark age."[3]

As one of us argued in *Baroque Horrors*, the terrifying vistas of reality of which Lovecraft speaks can be traced back to the pages of early baroque fantasies such as Julian de Medrano's *Silva Curiosa*, 1583.[4] The final section of Medrano's obscured miscellany entitled "Of the Epitaphs Found by Julio" includes a long tale of religious pilgrimage that morphs into a full-blown horror story. The macabre world that Julio paints for his "curious reader" is a graveyard deserted by God and inhabited by ancient demonic presences. Medrano's baroque horrors chip away at the sacred reality of his ancestors, much as Stephen King's "langoliers" devour our modern reality in his *Four Past Midnight* (1990). Even the relics of Saint James, which were supposed to mark the end-goal of the pilgrimage, the place where the spiritual quest of the protagonists would be satisfied, are revealed as a carcass devoid of miracles; nothing but an empty crypt, another curious epitaph. Julio continues his journey beyond the sacred tomb (now just a ruin of antiquity) to the very end of the ancient world, the Northwest region of the Iberian Peninsula known as Finis Terrae (today Finisterre, Galicia) where an undead witch, who sustains herself on the blood of innocent children, lays dormant deep inside the bowels of the Earth. Unlike the relics of Saint James, which are no longer significant (they have no miracles left in them), the undead witch reveals herself as a real presence in the world, capable of inflicting suffering and pain, and even causing the death of unsuspecting travelers.

Medrano's nocturnal horror turns the ancient world into a hopeless desert, a desolate ruin devoid of (divine) presence, around the same time that Giordano Bruno was hypothesizing the existence of cosmic voids. This first literary expression of baroque *horror vacui* has the feel of an apocalyptic or post-apocalyptic landscape. Medrano's deserts (the word *desierto* is used more than twenty times to describe the landscape) remind us of the barren and ruined world of *The Road* (2006), the Pulitzer Prize Winner novel authored by Cormac McCarthy, adopted for the screen by John Hillcoat in 2009. We find the same explicit connection between barren landscapes, cosmic terror, and death in the expressionistic imagery of McCarthy's novel: "The crushing black vacuum of the universe."[5] "The land was gullied and eroded and barren."[6] "An isocline of death. One vast salt sepulcher. Senseless. Senseless."[7] As in McCarthy's novel, Medrano's desolate world is haunted by absence: the absence of God, the absence of meaning. Antiquity has left us nothing but meaningless ruins and monstrous remnants.

Beyond this early expression of baroque *horror vacui*, much of early modern fantasy is marked by the presence of gendered, sexualized, and racialized monsters that either justify or denounce our exclusions. Some baroque horrors function as compensatory fantasies that restore the proper, theologically correct, line between good and evil, between the visible and the invisible, between us and them, while others blur these lines or realign them in order to reveal the repressed content of our exclusions. The monstrous relicts and mangled corpses that populate the stories of domestic terror composed by seventeenth-century author María de Zayas are explicitly presented as skeletons in aristocratic closets, the economic repressed of a social body that has turned predatory.

Zayas' gendered horrors are the debris of a decadent aristocracy fixated on avoiding contamination. Bastardizing Goya's phrasing, we could say that in Zayas' homely scenes of terror, *the dream of honor produces monsters*, as aristocratic houses morph into prisons and instruments of torture that asphyxiate and bleed women to death. No wonder Zayas' novella collection was labeled "obscene"—literally, off-the-scene. Her *Desengaños* released the skeletons her society's ruling class intended to keep in the closet, outside of the frame of visibility.[8]

If Zayas' baroque horrors embody the economic repressed of the decadent aristocratic society of seventeenth-century Spain, more recent monsters, such as modern vampires, express sexual and economic anxieties symptomatic of colonial capitalism. At the time of their birth into the mainstream of the English popular imagination in the late nineteenth century, vampires were intimately connected with concerns about sexual desire and promiscuity. Today's vampires speak directly about contemporary social-sexual concerns and current socioeconomic realities. Our vampires are often struggling to integrate themselves in a society that fears and misunderstands them, as in the HBO's hit series *True Blood*, in which the religious right's anti-vamp fanaticism is a clear reference to conservative anxieties around the normalization of homosexuality ("God hates fangs"). But the perfect monsters for our own postcolonial age, the age of the post-human, are arguably the zombie masses: ever-growing crowds of human remnants driven by a destructive hunger they cannot understand; the mindless agents of a seemingly unavoidable apocalypse of our own making.

The etymology of the term *monster* has been traced to the Latin word *monstrum* (from *mostrare*, meaning to show, reveal, expose, unveil, display). This connection between the monster and the act of revealing (*mostrare*, and even *demonstrare*) was firmly established by Saint Augustine and his followers. The term has also been linked to the Latin verb *monere* (to warn or admonish). This second ascription has gained ground more recently in etymological dictionaries, often associated with the description of abnormal births thought to prognosticate impending disasters.[9] Whether they are viewed as signs of the divine will or interpreted as providential warnings, monsters have been "read" as *bodies pregnant with meaning* for much of the history of Western culture.

In the ancient world, hybrid creatures were also thought of as monsters, although not always evil: the mandrake is a cross between a human and a plant, the centaur between a man and a horse, Pegasus between a horse and a bird, the siren between a woman and a bird, and so on. Yet, as the dualistic Judeo-Christian tradition became dominant in Western culture, hybridity, abnormality, and the crossing of boundaries were increasingly associated with transgression, moral deformity, and evil intent. Hence, the abnormality of the monster would come to be widely interpreted in European culture as defiance of law, be the natural law or the established political and moral orders. The entry for *monstro* in Covarrubias' *Tesoro de la Lengua* reads in part "any birth against the norm and order of nature."[10] Similarly, Covarrubias' French contemporary Jean Riolan discusses monstrosity in connection with the "perverted" nature of hermaphrodites in a 1614 essay. He argues that the sexual hybridity of hermaphrodite monsters is "a perversion of the order of natural causes, the health of the people, and the authority of the King."[11]

While monsters inspire fear, apprehension, and revulsion in (early) modern times, they are also objects of fascination in the curiosity culture of the Renaissance and the baroque, and later in the Romantic period and beyond. In her insightful book *Una era de monstruos: Representaciones de lo deforme en el Siglo de Oro español*, Elena del Río Parra documents the existence of an early modern tradition within which monsters are viewed as fascinating rarities. Seventeenth-century author Rivilla Bonet y Pueyo, for example, remarks that monstrous births are worthy of curiosity and admiration for their novelty and rarity. His definition of *monstro* extends to encompass "anything admirable due to an excess of malice, but also of goodness."[12] The admirable excess of which this seventeenth-century author speaks may be linked to the pursuit of the "extreme" in baroque poetry, art, and architecture, as Maravall argued. More importantly for our purposes, this fascination with the rare nature of monsters and their excesses is at the root of the modern aesthetics of the fantastic.

As one of us has argued in *Baroque Horrors*, the modern fantastic is born in the context of the culture of curiosities of the sixteenth and seventeenth centuries, at the meeting place between certainty and doubt, and between apprehension and fascination.[13] We are very much curious about the monsters we fear. We may be utterly repulsed by them, but we are also fascinated by their extraordinary nature, their perverted views, and their deviant behavior. As Barbara Benedict writes apropos English wonder tales and foundational Gothic fictions including Horace Walpole's *The Castle of Otranto* (1764) and William Beckford's *Vathek* (1782): "[W]onder tales and Gothic fictions ... redefined curiosity as an aesthetic enterprise .... Imaginary literature became the new arena for the exploration of forbidden areas and the testing of truth."[14]

In Spain, the literary exploration of forbidden areas inhabited by monsters can be traced back to the late Renaissance and early baroque miscellanea, especially to Antonio de Torquemada's *Garden of Curious Flowers* (*Jardín de flores curiosas*, 1570) and the above-mentioned *Silva Curiosa* by Julián de Medrano. These textual cabinets of curiosities incorporated sensationalist "news" and macabre stories and, in some cases, elaborate accounts of preternatural experiences that tested natural, moral, and epistemological boundaries. If other texts from the period, including teratology treatises and "tales of occurrences" (*relaciones de sucesos*), offer detailed descriptions of hybrid creatures, abnormal births, and other curiosities, the dark tales included in *Jardín de flores curiosas* and *La silva curiosa* draw a direct link between the figure of the monster and the mysterious realms of the preternatural and the occult.

Torquemada underscores the dreadful consequences of the witch's crossing of natural and moral boundaries. Even accidental exposure to the witch's craft results in monstrous forms of self-alienation in *Jardín de flores curiosas*. By contrast, the pursuit of forbidden knowledge, even black magic, is actually celebrated, rather than punished, in *La silva curiosa*. Thus, the dominant textual presence in Medrano's text is an eccentric first-person narrator, Julio, who is himself a sort of monster obsessed with morbid themes, forbidden knowledge, and perverse lifestyles. The two central characters of *La Silva's* final section are Christóbal Salvage, a sorcerer who collects morbid objects and evil spells, and Orcavella, the undead witch whose tomb marks the end of the world. Salvage and Orcavella are the baroque predecessors of such Gothic monsters as Vathek, Frankenstein, Mr. Hyde, Dorian Gray, and Dracula, in that they express and negotiate deep-seeded anxieties about the consequences of human trespasses of the natural, social, and moral orders.

14

Dreamboat Vampires and Zombie Capitalists

At first blush, the starring nightmarish cousins from the realm of the undead couldn't be further apart. Vampires—which have been with us in their current form at least since the industrial revolution—are fast, sexy, cunning, and imperishable. They are sleek nocturnal hunters, and even in the violence of the kill they can be depicted as elegant, like great cats. Zombies—not the Afro-Caribbean variety, controlled by a shaman, but the mindless, flesh-eating dead injected into U.S. popular culture by George Romero in the 1970s—are most often the opposite: slow, shambling, putrid excrescences in a state of perpetual decay. Vampires represent a kind of higher place on the food chain—one could at least imagine wanting to become a vampire; despite much enthusiastic participation in carnival-like zombie walks, we can safely assume that no one would want to become a zombie.

But beyond their obvious differences lies a common core, one that stems from a universal ambivalence that humans, condemned to know they will die, share toward what Shakespeare called "the dark backward and abysm of time." On the one hand, the dead, while dear to us, lose their human aspect and in their physical existence take on the repulsive quality of decay; on the other, we yearn for and project something eternal, unchanging, an animate presence that we refuse to surrender to the degeneration of time.

That humans live simultaneously real, physical lives and symbolic, meaningful existences means that they must die not once, but twice. As Jacques Lacan argued, it is possible in the human imagination for these two deaths, one symbolic and one real, to not entirely coincide. In such cases we enter a peculiar state, one he called *entre-deux-morts*, or between-two-deaths.

Those whose symbolic selves die while their bodies still live attain a kind of sublime, extra-worldly beauty. Lacan identified Sophocles' great character Antigone with this state—condemned to death by Creon for having defined the state's law and buried her treasonous brother, she burns with a righteous splendor that puts to shame Creon's pathetic attachment to the state's laws.

Those whose bodies die while their symbolic selves linger constitute an entirely different breed. Chained by a law or obligation to an animate state their bodies can no longer support, such beings become monstrous specters, condemned to walk the earth as embodiments of some insatiable hunger. It is not too difficult to see in these two archetypes our modern vampires and zombies, the former radiating a sublime beauty, the latter monstrous excrescences driven on by a fundamental imbalance in the world of men.

The image of the uncannily beautiful vampire has become familiar enough as to cross over into coming-of-age teenage fantasies, starting with the popular TV show *Buffy the Vampire Slayer*, and continuing with the hit series *The Vampire Diaries* and the *Twilight* book and movie phenomenon. In these, as well as in adult-oriented novels, movies, and TV series—such as Anne Rice's *The Vampire Chronicles* and their film adaptations, and the current TV series *True Blood* and *Dracula*—vampires and humans are sometimes difficult to distinguish from one another. Vampires are often "humanized" in these pop culture blockbusters. In the case of *True Blood*, the point is not necessarily that vampires are humanized, but, more accurately, that humanity is "vampirized"; that is, humans are represented as vampire-like monsters who are just as likely to prey on the vampires as the vampires are to prey on them.

True Blood goes further than *Buffy*, *The Vampire Diaries* and *Twilight* in projecting a fantasy world in which vampires and humans may coexist, thanks in part to the mass-production of a blood substitute for vampire consumption. The availability of this nutritional product allows some vampires to come out of the closet, so to speak. Their integration into mainstream society proves difficult, nonetheless, since most humans continue to think of them as evil spawns and dangerous predators. Many humans show scorn for those who associate with vampires. Similarly, most vampires disapprove of those from within their ranks who treat humans as equals rather than as an inferior race.

The mistrust between humans and vampires is exacerbated by the persistence of vampires who live clandestine lives while refusing to give up their favorite meal: human blood. The most intriguing twist of the series, however, has to do with the fact that vampire blood is shown to have hallucinogenic and sense-enhancing properties if consumed by humans. This leads to the development of blood markets that exploit vampires as well as humans. Hence, the series features a number of elaborate and graphic scenes in which human predators capture and immobilize vampires in order to harvest their precious blood to either consume it themselves or to sell it in the drug market.

We can say that *True Blood* makes explicit what some critics see as an implicit or latent yet central element in the modern tradition of vampire fiction going back to Bram Stocker's *Dracula*. What we have in mind here is not simply *the return of the repressed*, at least not in the general sense in which werewolves and characters like Mr. Hyde represent a regression to a primal animality that lurks deep inside of us, hidden under layers of civilizing safeguards. Instead, we are thinking of the "economic repressed" that Karl Marx remarked upon when he referred to capital as a vampire-like machine, "a circulating thing which gains its energy only by preying upon 'living labor.'"[1]

While vampires were born of class resentment, a bourgeois allegory of rapacious, aristocratic libertines, that resentment married fear with desire. Like Nietzsche's "blond beasts," vampires are like haughty birds of prey that inspire both terror and admiration in the flocks of slaves they feed on. As modern industrial society replaced aristocrats with capitalists, they took over that role in the popular and populist imagination, to the point where Matt Taibbi could outdo Marx's metaphor, so memorably describing Goldman Sachs at the heights of the Great Recession as "a great vampire squid wrapped around the face of humanity, relentlessly jamming its blood funnel into anything that smells like money."[2]

Prior to the nineteenth century, the figure of the vampire was mostly found in folk tales, which, as Ken Gelder notes, grounded him into a localized spot. Thus, the vampire was essentially a local or regional monster. By contrast, more recent vampires are defined by extensive circulation through and across regional and national boundaries. In Stoker's *Dracula*, the ancient vampire uproots himself from his native land of Transylvania, deep inside the

Carpathian mountains, to travel to London, at the very center of the British empire, where he plans to "satiate his lust for blood and create a new and ever-widening circle of semi-demons to batten on the helpless."[3] In its updated "world-traveler" version, the vampire may be seen as an apt mirror-image of the colonizer.

Stephen Arata has called attention to this intriguing aspect of Stoker's novel. As he argues in his essay "The Occidental Tourist: *Dracula* and the Anxiety of Reverse Colonization,"

> [t]he novel thus sets up an equivalence between Harker and Dracula: one can be seen as an Orientalist travelling East, the Other—unsettling thought for Stoker's Victorian readers—as an Occidentalist travelling West [...] Dracula's preoccupation with English culture is not motivated by a disinterested desire for knowledge; instead, his Occidentalism represents the essence of bad faith, since it both promotes and masks the Count's sinister plan to invade and exploit Britain and her people. By insisting on the connections between Dracula's growing knowledge and his power to exploit, Stoker also forces us to acknowledge how Western imperial practices are implicated in certain forms of knowledge. Stoker continually draws our attention to the affinities between Harker and Dracula, as in the oft-cited scene where Harker looks for Dracula's reflection in the mirror and sees only himself.[4]

If Stoker's *Dracula* can be read as a mirror-image of the colonizer, a personification of the "late-Victorian nightmare of reverse colonization,"[5] more recent novels have provided historically updated and nuanced versions of the "economic repressed" that may be revealed in and through the vampire metaphor. Thus, the iconic blood-sucking monster has presently been called upon to personify the institution of slavery in its modern version, and also to represent the predatory practices of global corporations in our post-colonial world. In his best-selling novel *Abraham Lincoln Vampire Hunter* (2010), Seth Grahame-Smith reimagines the figure of the vampire in the context of a fictionalized reconstruction of Civil War America. In Grahame-Smith's historical fantasy, the genuine American vampires are white southern aristocrats who feed on helpless black slaves.

While Stoker's Occidentalist vampire may work as "a metaphor for capital"[6] in the colonial age, Grahame-Smith's Americanization of the vampire theme turns this old world monster into an allegory of modern slavery. The novel's graphic scenes of mechanized blood extraction are particularly telling in this regard. Here is a good example: "Only now did I see the dark glass tubes running over our heads, running from the bodies on our left to the vessels on our right. Only now did I see the blood running into those vessels, kept warm by a raw of tiny gas flames beneath. Only now did I see the chests of these 'corpses' moving with each shallow breath. And here the whole horror of it struck me."[7] The narrator's detailed description of the mechanized harvesting of blood from the bodies of immobilized slaves who are kept alive solely for this purpose suggests that this extreme form of human predation (the peculiar institution) ought not to be thought of as a "residual horror" or a left-over byproduct of a bygone era, but rather as a modern form of violence and exploitation. This may begin to explain why, despite its obvious cinematic plasticity, the above-quoted scene from Grahame-Smith's novel did not make it into the film adaptation, a mainstream shoot-them-up that was released with the same title as the book in 2012.

We can find similar scenes of mechanized blood extraction in the vampire trilogy co-authored recently by Guillermo del Toro and Chuck Hogan, especially in the third novel of the series *The Night Eternal* (2011). Here the "efficient extraction and packaging of human blood"[8] takes place in slaughter houses that have been converted into "blood factories"[9] following the Master's imperialist design. The Master is a Dracula-like figure whose American success is largely dependent on his business sense and his ability to understand the *mathematics of power* in corporate America: "The Master learned to align himself with influential power brokers [...] He devised a formula for the mathematics of power. The perfect balance of vampires, cattle, and wardens."[10] We interpret these references to the Master's mathematics of power as a cautionary note directed against corporate America. In keeping with the logic behind Moreti's and Arata's "economic" readings of Stoker's classic work, we would argue that the novelistic trilogy co-authored by del Toro and Hogan accomplishes an insightful and effective updating of the vampire metaphor for our own post-colonial time. Briefly stated, the Master's vampire regime may be read as a dark metaphor of the objectifying tyranny of the present global market.

If the predatory practices of our favorite vampires, going back to Bram Stoker's *Dracula*, mirror the dark aspects of human nature and possibly reveal (mostrare/demostrare) and warn against (monere) the "economic repressed" of Western modernity, what can we say about their popular zombie cousins? What kind of monsters are the walking dead? What do they reveal about us? What do they warn us against?

The zombie monsters were not always cannibalistic masses of walking corpses. Traditional African and Haitian zombies had no appetite for human flesh. In fact, they were often thought of as "slaves" either awakened from the dead or hypnotized into a magically induced catatonic state to carry out the will of the zombie master (or those who employed his services), as in the early film *White Zombie* (1932), directed and produced by brothers Victor and Edward Halperin. In *White Zombie* we can see the division of (zombie) labor that best represents the masculine fantasies of colonial powers: masses of dark-skin colonial subjects "recruited" for slave work, on the one hand, and a carefully sexualized female "white zombie" who is hypnotized into "romantic" submission, on the other. The theatrical poster makes it clear that this is in fact the point of a female "white zombie": *With these zombie eyes, he rendered her powerless; with this zombie grip, he made her perform his every desire.*

In the literary field, the first full-fledged zombie story of which we are aware also features a "white zombie," in this case a married lady who is forced into "adulterous" sexual services by means of black magic. The story is part of the above-mentioned collection of baroque tales published by María de Zayas in 1647 with the title *Desengaños amorosos* or *Dis-illusions of Love*. Those who are familiar with *White Zombie* will recognize the key ingredients of Zayas' *Innocence Punished*: a powerful lord blinded by passion, an innocent lady who "belongs" to another man, and a carefully racialized zombie master (in this case a Moorish necromancer), who performs the necessary enslaving rituals.

In Zayas' novella, the lady is turned into an actual sex slave who literally sleepwalks into her victimizer's bed in a trance-like state. Although the rapist is eventually exposed and prosecuted for his crimes, the innocent lady is further victimized by her own husband, brother, and sister-in-law, all of whom conspire to imprison her inside a wall of the house as punishment for her involuntary adultery. It would be left to her rotting body to tell the story of her victimization when she is finally freed after six years of horrifying entombment: "She was blind …; her lovely tresses, which when she entered were strands of gold, white as the very snow, tangled and full of little animals… her color, the color of death, so thin and emaciated that her bone showed as if the skin on top of them were but a thin veil …; her clothes turned to ashes so that most parts of her body were visible; her feet and legs bare, because the excrement from her body, since she had nowhere to dispose of it, had not only eaten into them, but her very flesh was eaten up to the thighs with wounds and worms, which filled the stinking place."[11]

Graphic representations of "death in life" are not out of place in the art and literature of the baroque period, yet this picture of decaying flesh is not offered as a reflection on the transitory nature of human existence, as in traditional baroque *vanitas* or *memento mori*, but as evidence of the silent victimization of women that takes place inside the walls of aristocratic houses in Imperial Spain. As one of us has argued elsewhere: "The monsters come with the house in Zayas' baroque tales of kinship and terror. At the end [of her novella collection], we are left with nothing but dead bodies and ruins everywhere. This is an implosion of the aristocratic house not unlike Poe's vision of decay and destruction in 'The Fall of the House of Usher.'"[12] Hence, in terms of our own cultural horizon, the "politics" of Zayas' zombie story seem closer to the anti-establishment Romero films of the 1960s and 1970s than to the early *White Zombie*, despite the thematic coincidences we have outlined between the 1647 novella written by Zayas and the 1932 film directed by the Halperin brothers.

Since the release of George Romero's classic *The Night of the Living Dead* (1968), the walking dead are imagined in cinematic fantasies and print fiction as agents of the apocalypse. In fact, in the post-Romero zombie culture, the rise of the dead is most often envisioned as a cataclysmic byproduct of the progress of human technology. This is something that the new walking dead share with the monstrous machines featured in such blockbuster fantasies as *The Terminator* and *The Matrix* sagas. Their behavior is remarkably similar to Terminator-style automatons, machines programmed to kill; except that there is no programmer and no master design behind their (up)rising. Unlike the "domestic" zombies associated with West African and South African religions and Haitian folklore, Romero's herds of walking dead have nothing to do with mystical or spiritualist practices. They are simply cannibalistic masses of decaying human flesh.

In the last few years, zombie fantasies have flooded the horror and sci-fi markets. They have taken over much of our popular print culture, as well as our screens, with such best-selling novels as Max Brook's *World War Z* (now a major motion picture), short story collections like *The Living Dead*, comic book and TV series such as *The Walking Dead*, and countless video games. In fact, the walking dead have stepped outside the boundaries of fiction to show up in the streets of our most populous cities, even in our news cycles. Nowadays, it seems that every major town must host its own zombie walk. Remarkably, even the CDC (the Centers for Disease Control and Prevention) has had to issue zombie-related statements.

In the summer of 2013, one of us received an intriguing email request from a columnist with *The Miami Herald*. The message illustrates the extent to which the zombie craze has taken hold of the public's imagination:

> For the last 10 days, Miami has been riveted by the story of a nude, apparently psychotic man, perhaps under the influence of some drug, who attacked and nearly killed a homeless man, ripping off most of the fellow's face with his teeth before a policeman shot and killed the assailant. Since, all sort of references have bubbled up about, among other things, a Zombie virus. As mindless as this premise might be, apparently the Centers for Disease Control in Atlanta felt compelled to issue a statement: "The flesh-eating living dead don't actually exist," said a spokesman for the Centers for Disease Control and Prevention (CDC). "CDC does not know of a virus or condition that would reanimate the dead (or one that would present zombie-like symptoms," agency spokesman David Daigle told the Huffington Post. I had already been thinking about the peculiar prevalence of Zombies and Vampires and Werewolves in our pop culture, with probably more references in TV and movies and books than religion. I just wonder [...] if folks like you have some explanation for this quirk in contemporary culture (signed Fred Grimm, a columnist with The Miami Herald).

The Miami Herald would subsequently publish Grimm's article on the subject on June 5, 2012, with the title "Fear, anxiety drive zombie craze." Grimm's article incorporated comments from English Professors Kyle Bishop (Southern Utah University) and David Schmid (SUNY Buffalo), and anthropologist Elizabeth Bird (University of South Florida). Notably, they all coincide in pointing out that our present fascination with monsters, especially zombies, bespeaks—in Schmid's words—"a society riven by fears and anxieties of various kinds, including uncertainty about the future."[13] Kyle Bishop, author of *American Zombie Gothic*, writes: "I thought we as a culture were simply seeing a renewed and increased interest in monster narratives as a gut-check reaction to 9/11 and the War on Terror. Now, however, the zombie has become something much more visceral, something that has taken hold of our collective unconscious."[14] For her part, Elizabeth Bird notes that we use "our monsters to try to explain our society (and vice versa)," which is why zombies have become our favorite surrogates when it comes to expressing the fear of nuclear and pandemic catastrophes and environmental collapse, as well as "the idea that we are consuming ourselves."[15]

If the modern vampire may have functioned as an apt metaphor for the predatory practices of capital in colonial and post-colonial societies, the zombie hordes may best express present anxieties about the dreadful fate of a world inhabited by post-human crowds of mindless, soulless consumers.[16] We would further argue that our fixation with apocalyptic fantasies—worldwide zombie plagues, nuclear disasters, environmental collapse, and other man-made catastrophes—is fundamentally tied to the widespread conviction that there is no possible alternative to capitalism as a worldwide economic system, paired with the growing realization, or at least the suspicion, that the logical evolution of global capitalism will inexorably lead to our self-destruction.[17]

In a famous scene of Romero's second zombie film *Dawn of the Dead* (1978), a group of zombies approaches the shopping mall where the survivors have taken refuge. One of the survivors looks out beyond the glass doors and says "They are us." Could this be the fundamental revelation of Romero's films? Are we the true zombies? Masses of walking dead driven by insatiable, senseless, catastrophic consumption? This revelation would indeed come with a grim warning about our present and immediate future: the end of the human race (an apocalypse of our own making) is upon us!

Interestingly, when we examine the latest products of the global zombie culture, it appears as though the zombie masses that have taken away—literally swallowed up—our future are intent in cannibalizing the past as well. A perfect example of this recent twist in zombie literature is Seth Grahame-Smith's *Pride and Prejudice and Zombies* (2009), a comedic reworking of Jane Austin's nineteenth-century classic. The book cover emphasizes this parodic distance: "An expanded edition of the beloved Jane Austin novel featuring all new scenes of bone-crunching zombie mayhem.... Complete with romance, heartbreak, swordfights, cannibalism, and thousands of rotting corpses, *Pride and Prejudice and Zombies* transforms a masterpiece of world literature into something you'd actually want to read." Yet, in reading this bastardized version of Austin's novel, we can't shake the impression that much of Grahame-Smith's "expanded edition" functions as a pastiche, rather than a parody, in that it merely accentuates the ironic tone of Austin's original work and her sharp criticism of the idle British aristocracy of the early nineteenth century. Thus, the presence of zombies seems to underscore the monstrous (cannibalistic) nature of a decadent aristocratic body that feeds on the life-energy of local workers and distant colonial subjects.

This characterization could easily apply to the latest Romero film *Land of the Dead*. Arguably, the most interesting innovation of this 2005 film is the trope of the *learning zombie*. As one of the human survivors puts it at the very beginning of the film, "they are trying to be us... learning to be us... it's like they are pretending to be alive." By the end of the movie, the zombies seem to have re-acquired some primitive communication skills, a surprising degree of self-consciousness, even a sense of kinship, and a growing recognition of their true enemy, not the dispossessed human masses, but the opulent elite who have barricaded themselves inside luxury apartments in the middle of a high-end shopping mall. Their exclusive community of CEOs and shoppers is surrounded by concentric circles of exploited humanity. If there is a ray of hope in Romero's post-apocalyptic vision, this is quite simply the hope of a successful revolution of the (undead) masses.

Today, the blockbuster TV show *The Walking Dead* follows in the footsteps of Romero's classic zombie films. The show and the graphic novels that inspire it are constructed around the same ingredients: an apocalyptic pandemic that turns humans into walking corpses inexplicably hungry for human flesh; and—even more importantly—a focus on the group dynamics of the survivors. As in *Land of the Dead*, all of humanity has been infected with the zombie virus, which means that everyone is a latent "walker" who will inevitably reawake as a zombie cannibal regardless of how they die.

More than any other product of the current zombie culture, *The Walking Dead* spotlights decision-making as the endangered trait (and obligation) that defines our humanity. Decoupled from the comforts of daily routines and from the familiar, consumer-oriented notion of "choice"—that is, choosing between products available for purchase—the act of decision-making takes on a renewed urgency and a transcendent charge as a matter of ineludible individual and collective responsibility, often accompanied by a close examination of mainstream moral values and political principles.

One has to wonder whether the spectators of *Land of the Dead* and *The Walking Dead* might not get more than they bargained for when their moral principles and beliefs and their political structures are crudely dissected, and in some cases exposed as little more than hypocritical, or even cynical, compromises resulting from their blind acceptance of an exploitative status quo and their willful denial of inconvenient truths. But of course, this is part of the attraction of post-apocalyptic novels, films, and TV shows such as the NBC series *Revolution*, as well as "teen" literary and movie phenomena like *The Hunger Games* and *Divergent*.

The author of *Divergent*, Veronica Roth, commented on this fundamental aspect of post-apocalyptic fantasies in an interview included as "bonus materials" in the first novel of her best-selling trilogy. The question posed to her is "Why do you feel people are naturally drawn to reading books about dystopian societies?" Her response may be helpful here: "Dystopian books are perfect for people who like to ask 'what if?' .... The majority of the characters in dystopian and post-apocalyptic literature have a lot of agency—they take charge of their lives in environments that make it hard for them to do so."[18]

Post-apocalyptic narratives offer their audiences the fantasy of a *zero point* from which we can all (vicariously at least) start over. We get to step out of our routines, our comforts, our safeguards; we get to reimagine ourselves dealing with the hardships, the dangers, the responsibilities, the demands, and the raw relationships that come with the post-apocalyptic landscape. We get to ask not only "What if?"—as Roth says—but who would we be(come)? What kind of decisions would we make? How would we organize our thoughts and emotions? How would we relate to others and negotiate our identities? What kind of behavioral patterns would we establish as individuals and communities? How would we reimagine our civic and political structures?

Symptomatically perhaps, in the latest wave of post-apocalyptic narratives, certainly in the products of the current zombie culture, the "rebirth" of the individual is directly associated with acts of extreme violence: shooting, stubbing, crashing, burning (in)human bodies. A sinister version of the Cartesian ego seems to rule the post-apocalyptic landscape: I kill, therefore I am! Though, to be fair, some of these same movies, novels, and TV shows entertain "pacifist" alternatives as well. In *The Hunger Games*, the final refusal of Katniss and Peeta to obey the mandate to kill (in this case, kill or attempt to kill each other) is offered at the conclusion of the first novel of the series as an act of defiance of violent powers, an affirmation of their shared humanity, and a sign of communal hope. At times, *The Walking Dead* seems to move in this same direction when our reluctant heroes hesitate, or even refuse to pull the trigger, as when Rick trades the gun for the rake in his determination to become a farmer. But these moments of divestment in the violent destiny of the post-apocalyptic world are by necessity short-lived in zombie-plagued landscapes.

Productive, nurturing, and non-violent lifestyles are simply unsustainable, even explicitly suicidal, in post-apocalyptic environments. In the end, the difference between our favorite post-apocalyptic heroes (say Rick in *The Walking Dead*) and their human arch-enemies (the Governor, for example) has to do with their measured administering of violence, not so much against the masses of walking dead (this is, for the most part, a given, with the notorious exception of Romero's *Land of the Dead*), but against other living humans. They must be capable of selective, surgical, and judicious (yet extreme and murderous) destruction. In this sense, the tragic heroes of *The Walking Dead* have something in common with their counterparts in traditional Hollywood epics, from the drifters that populate the Western genre, to the Stallone, Segal, and Vin Diesel types of more recent action blockbusters.

The Global Undead

The Romero-style zombie monsters are by all accounts thriving in the present global market. Zombie movies, TV shows, novels, and games are among the most successful "exports" of the current culture industry. In Spain, we can find scores of walking dead fantasies, most of which have been published in recent years, including your run-of-the-mill zombie apocalypse, as well as more nuanced parodies and pastiches. In January 2006 a young Spanish lawyer, Manel Loureiro, posted a blog with the title *Apocalipsis Z*. As the number of daily visitors reached the half million mark, Loureiro secured a contract with Dolmen to publish a print version of the blog. The printed text came out in 2007 with the same title. Since, Dolmen has published dozens of Spanish language zombie fantasies in its dedicated series Línea Z, including Carlos Sisí's *Walkers* (*Los caminantes*) which went through fifteen reprints between 2009 and 2012, and its equally popular sequel *Necrópolis*. Loureiro ended up publishing the continuation of *Apocalipsis Z* in two volumes that came out in the well-established press Plaza Janés, *The Dark Days* (*Los días oscuros*, 2010) and *The Rage of the Just* (*La ira de los justos*, 2011). For his part, Carlos Sisí would also venture outside of Dolmen's Línea Z with the third volume of his zombie trilogy, *Los Caminantes. Hades Nebula*, published by Minotauro in 2011.

The popularity of Loureiro's and Sisí's respective trilogies has significantly contributed to the current boom of zombie fiction in Spain. This boom includes many original Spanish language works, as well as a multitude of translations of English language zombie novels, short stories, zombie survival manuals, graphic novels, and so on. Most of these works do little but recreate the zombie apocalypse, Romero style, while piling on the gore. Among them, we have selected a few narratives for commentary based on our sense of what constitutes novel or revealing trends and variations in zombie themes.

One of the most self-consciously spectacular offerings of the zombie subgenre in Spain is Víctor Conde's *Still Life* (*Naturaleza muerta*, 2009). As the title suggests, Conde arranges his graphic scenes of zombie gore as macabre still lifes. The book cover designed by Alejandro Colucci underscores this postmodern (or neobaroque) interdiscursive connection. Colucci's elaborate illustration is explicitly evocative of the traditional still life and *vanitas*. We can see a fruit basket filled with fresh apples and grapes, a wheel of cheese made to look like an old-fashioned clock, and several ceramic containers, resting on a clothed kitchen table, alongside objects that symbolize human knowledge, such as an old book and a quill. The picture is complete with a severed forearm resting near a few pieces of bread at the edge of a napkin, which partially covers fresh blood stains. In the background, a drawn curtain reveals a painted human skull at the bottom corner of what appears to be a baroque vanitas. Colucci's illustration effectively captures Conde's pictorial imagination and neobaroque *gusto*. The following passage is a good example of Conde's pictorial technique:

> Zurek remained loyal to his stoicism even as he saw how they severed a quarter of a kilogram of flesh from his midsection flab. He desperately stretched his hands backwards, in an attempt to find something his fingers could hold, but what he found was an amputated forearm. It was lying on a tray with glasses and ceramic jars. Beside it, there was an easel fallen on a bed of gardenias. He realized the irony of the message: someone had been leisurely painting a still life, while his partner or kids were swimming in the pool, unsuspecting of the fact that such macabre element would add to the painting. In truth it didn't alter its meaning, since there were only dead things in the composition.[1]

Starting with the flesh severed from Zurek's midsection, and continuing with the amputated forearm of the anonymous artist displayed on a serving tray, alongside some glasses and ceramic containers, this scene may be best described as a macabre mis-en-abîme of "dead things." As the angle expands to include the immediate surroundings, we can see the artist's easel laying on a bed of gardenias, a final vision of destruction, but also the first image of something whole and alive in nature, not *naturaleza muerta*, but *naturaleza viva*. This final element of the composition allows us to draw a close connection with the novel's ending, which offers the same severe contrast, the same chiaroscuro, between "dead things" (the self-inflicted destruction of humanity) and the rapidly growing bed of invading greenery, which is said to be taking over the post-human Earth. Captain Piotr's view from his satellite post in outer space offers the ultimate opening of the lens: "Pangaea-type forest...aggressive greenery...nature that was finally free from the cancer of Man....Nature Alive."[2]

In this sense, Conde's *Naturaleza muerta* is not just a fictional chronicle of the death of Man, but also a post-apocalyptic utopia of the rebirth of Nature. Ironically, both the zombie pandemia and the rebirth of nature are caused by exposure to the same radiation. The final destruction of the human race and the post-apocalyptic image of a resurging human-less planet Earth represents the fulfillment of the unauthorized translation of an Old Testament prophesy mentioned in an earlier passage: "One of the ancient translations of the Old Testament [...] contained a final chapter that prophesied the end of humanity and the kingdom of the beasts and the trees, and of the entire natural world, excluding the sons and daughters of Adam."[3]

There are other moments in which the narrative reaches back into the past in search of ancient Judeo-Christian motifs and symbology that might offer grounds for speculation regarding the possibility of previous zombie (up) risings. Would the zombies have been present in the epoch-changing events of our past? Could they have been the key agents of history?

> Zurek wondered if the return of the dead would not have taken place on several occasions already, throughout history, and therefore it wasn't an isolated or exceptional event....Would the dwellers of mass graves in Europe and America have turned up to extend the plagues? Would Christianity have advanced so quickly over the smoking ashes of the Roman Empire...thanks to the witnesses of zombie plagues who saw in them proof of the Resurrection? Was Jesus the first zombie...and that's why he returned on the third day to contaminate the remaining members of his sect?[4]

The notion that the undead may have walked the Earth in other historical periods is explored in a good number of recent novels, including *Black Death: The Triumph of the Undead* (*La muerte negra: El triunfo de los no-muertos*) and *Quijote Z*, both authored by Házael G. González and published in 2010 in the Línea Z series of Dolmen. The first reimagines the great plague of 1348 known as the Black Death as a zombie outbreak. The second plays on classic Cervantine motifs and situations, and on Cervantes' self-consciously parodic narrative style, to offer a bizarre pastiche featuring a man obsessed with zombie stories who takes to the road in order to become a zombie slayer.

Among the Spanish Golden Age classics, the anonymous *Lazarillo de Tormes* has been subjected to the same kind of zombie refurbishing in an Ediciones Debolsillo best-seller published with the title *Lazarillo Z: Killing Zombies Was Never a Piece of Cake* (*Lazarillo Z: Matar zombies nunca fue pan comido*) signed by a Lázaro González Pérez de Tormes. In this 2010 reworking of the original picaresque novel, first published in 1554, Lázaro becomes a heroic vampire warrior who fights a zombie plague that originated in the New World as a form of Indian revenge.[5] His fighting comrades are the "debris of the Monarchy" or "desechos de la Corona," a bizarre group of pícaros, prostitutes, and vampires, led by a homosexual nobleman and his morisco partner.[6]

In these macabre pastiches, the monstrous subject-matter spills over into its container. These are not just monster narratives, but *monstrous narratives*, zombie monstrosities in their own right. A perfect example of this type of self-conscious monstrosity is Hernán Migoya's zombie reconstruction of the recent political history of Spain in *One, Great, and Zombie* (*Una, grande y zombie*, 2011). Migoya's scandalous text features an undead Francisco Franco, who along with his sidekick Manuel Fraga, and a zombie army of politicians and journalists, led by the recently "converted" José Luis Rodríguez Zapatero and Mariano Rajoy, plan to resurrect the One, Great, and Zombie Spain. King Juan Carlos will also be "converted" to the imperial zombie cause near the end of the novel. In the final scene, the King and uncle Franco ("el tío Paco") team up to devour his majesty's mistress whose ripped body, neatly butchered for consumption, appears to be offered as an allegory of the people of Spain: the Spain of flesh and blood.

Migoya's exhibitionist cynicism is reminiscent of the dark eccentricity of Medrano's early baroque fantasy in *La silva curiosa*, while his theatrical self-reflectivity seems closer to the Cervantine style, especially in those passages in which fiction and reality meet face to face, often spilling into each other. The discussion of the conventions of the zombie genre or subgenre in chapter 11, aptly titled "Focusing on Debris," echoes similar conversations in *Don Quixote* regarding the conventions of chivalric and pastoral literature: "The concept of the zombie has also changed with the evolution of popular culture—noted Pere.... Today's zombies are not like those of a hundred years ago.... It wasn't until the sixties that George A. (the A is important) Romero changed everything with *The Night of the Living Dead....*He created the nightmarish notion of a global zombie invasion. The living dead of today are really that."[7]

The conversation between Pere and Evaristo, "the movie's hero," moves into the scatological terrain when Pere points out some inconsistencies in the standard treatment of the zombie material: "Everyone knows that the zombies don't shit, another incoherence of the myth. So then, where do all those human bodies that they eat go?"[8] Note the connection with the often cited conversation of don Quixote and Sancho about whether or not the bewitched defecate in *Don Quixote* II, 23.[9]

One of the more interesting "Cervantine" occurrences takes place in chapter 17, titled "The Short Walk," when the participants in the "III Zombie Walk de Barcelona" come face to face with the real thing. The crowd is carrying movies, books, comics, posters, and other zombie paraphernalia, "all that nonsensical stuff that goes with the *merchandising* and the marketing of the [zombie] phenomenon," even copies of Migoya's own book that the readers "have open in your hands."[10] The Cervantine trick of dragging his work into the fictional world of the text allows Migoya to tie his own zombie novel (and its publisher and readers) to the marketing ploys that he is exposing. When the participants of the zombie "simulacrum" finally meet the real zombies, they are first elated to come across such realistic hordes of parading comrades, before being unceremoniously eaten by the zombie phenomenon.

Speaking of being swallowed up by the zombie phenomenon, author Manuel Martín makes a telling confession in the biographical note of his zombie

novel *Night of the Dead of 38* (*Noche de difuntos del 38*, 2012). His candidly
cynical disclosure is reminiscent of the pícaro's confession in the prologue of
Lazarillo de Tormes, except that the confession of the anonymous sixteenth-
century author was about the scandal of his life, while Martín's is about the
scandal of his writing: "Moreover, your lordships, the accused declares that
he transformed, with premeditated treachery, a story of terror set in the midst
of the battle of the Ebro into a zombie novel, for he was tired of receiving
negative reactions in response to his attempts to publish his work." Martín's
confession is also an act of self-defense and an implicit accusation directed
against the current culture industry (a zombie phenomenon in its own right),
and against the (zombie) readers, that is, those avid consumers of standarized
zombie products that might have showed up for Migoya's "III Zombie Walk de
Barcelona."

Jorge Fernández Gonzalo concludes in his monographic study *Filosofía
zombi* (2011) that "the zombie represents at this point the myth of the
postmodern man."[11] With this assertion in mind, we would argue that
Migoya's "Cervantine" treatment of the zombie phenomenon and Martín's
Lázaro-style confession are helpful reminders of the true face of the (not so
mythical) monster. On the one hand, the countless zombie books, movies,
TV shows, and video games represent the kind of repetition of standardized
models that we associate with marketing ploys and the dehumanizing
objectification of mass-culture. On the other, many of these same cultural
products explicitly warn us about the devastating effects of the market
forces that result in mindless and catastrophic mass-production and mass-
consumption.

Robert Kirkman's tongue-in-cheek explanation of the success of his
trademark zombie products, especially the TV version of *The Walking
Dead*, exemplifies the cynical dimension of much of the current zombie
culture. His comments, recorded in a *Rolling Stone* piece contributed by
David Peisner, are both insightful and profoundly unsettling: "Apocalyptic
storytelling is appealing when people are having apocalyptic thoughts. With
the global economic problems and everything else, a lot of people feel we're
heading into dark times. As bad as it is for society [laughs], I am benefiting
greatly."[12]

This self-reflective cynicism is why the zombie hordes are the perfect monsters for the age of global capitalism. Zombies—whether in their more shambling manifestations, uprooted from the graves by an unexplained environmental catastrophe, or in the more recent form of "fast" zombies, rabid remnants of humanity spurred on in their craving for human flesh by some hyper-contagious super-virus—pack into one moving bundle everything monstrous and terrifying about a global economic machine that leaves nothing but undead remnants in its wake. In late capitalism, the German sociologist Niklas Luhmann once wrote, the scandal is not class exploitation but the uncountable masses of people who are born not even to be exploited, but just to die:

> If we look at the huge masses of starving people, deprived of all necessities for a decent human life, without access to any of the function systems, or if we consider all the human bodies, struggling to survive the next day, neither "exploitation" nor "suppression"—terms that refer ... to stratification—are adequate descriptions. It is only by habit and by ideological distortion that we use these terms. But there is nothing to exploit in the favelas.[13]

"Human debris," Rush Limbaugh sneered at the Occupy Wall Street protesters, by which he meant to imply that they were simply *unemployed*; like zombies, they were bodies without a purpose.

The zombie masses are us in more ways than one: they are the face of globalization, our dark mirror image, our homeless, our sweat shops, our landfills, our pollution, an infinitely reproducible and exportable product of the mass-culture industry, a sign of the times, and a warning of things to come. In short, *the zombies are our remnants*, the monstrous debris of late-capitalist technocratic societies.

What worried us in the first age of inflationary media was that copies would die, and that we would lose our access to the original. Libraries were built to save our copies. Now we are worried that our copies won't die. They have a spectral eternal presence on the internet, and one mistake can haunt us forever. Now we invent technologies that allow us to send images that self-destruct after a certain amount of time and we have court cases that establish a right to be forgotten, to have our internet imprints erased. Are zombies also a stand-in for the refusal of our many replicated selves to die, their tendency to come back even when we've tried to throw them away?

But as we have tried to explain, the stories of zombie mayhem have a healing power as well, or at least they may function as compensatory fantasies. We exorcize our demons as we aim and shoot at zombie heads. In killing our own avatars, we live the fantasy of separation. They are not me! I may look like a zombie and act like one, I may be consumed by mindless routines, but I know that deep down I am so much more, I just need to find the moment to prove it. The zombie apocalypse provides just the moment we may have been daydreaming about and also fearing, the ground zero from which we can start over both as individuals and communities. And yet, it is hard to shake the suspicion that the human race may be too far gone as it is; that the utopia of a planetary healing might only be possible in a post-human Earth no longer infected with the virus of humanity.

16

Dark Mirrors

As we have seen, zombies have spread like a virulent contagion since their introduction in George Romero's 1968 *Night of the Living Dead*, itself an adaptation of the novel from a decade earlier *I Am Legend*. Indeed, our quick survey on the Google Ngram viewer shows a steep incline in English-language mentions starting in the year that seminal slasher was released, amounting to a more than 1,000 percent increase in the appearance of zombies in print by 2008, the last year surveyed. But what does our fascination with zombies mean? And, perhaps the more fundamental question, what does it mean for zombies to mean something in the first place?

David Schmid has recently drawn attention to the limitations of "symptomatic readings" of zombies in popular culture, which depend on claims such as Kyle Bishop's that "[h]orror films function as barometers of society's anxieties, and zombie movies represent the inescapable realities of unnatural death while presenting a grim view of the modern apocalypse through scenes of deserted streets, piles of corpses, and gangs of vigilantes."[1] Symptomatic readings include the critical use of zombies in particular or monsters in general as a metaphor for representing some aspect, usually socio-political, of society, such as when Henry Giroux writes that "the metaphor [of the zombie] is particularly apt for drawing attention to the ways in which political culture and power in American society now work in the interests of bare survival, if not disposability, for the vast majority of people."[2]

While admitting that the metaphoric and symptomatic use of the zombie in critical discourse is not without value, Schmid agrees with Calder Williams on the risk that such a usage can, in some cases, lapse into mere redundant mention: "these readings about the 'real' content of zombies are limited because they aren't really readings: they just describe what happens in the films. To say that the ending of *Night of the Living Dead*, with the 'accidental' murder of an African-American man by the white redneck zombie hunting mob, is largely about race relations is just to say that you've watched the movie all the way through."[3] Ironically, as Schmid adds, even in his criticism Williams ends up producing his own symptomatic reading of the zombie phenomenon, leading Schmid to conclude that "the problem is not so much that such readings are inaccurate; it's that they are too easy, drawing a kind of one-to-one connection between cultural product and cultural context that oversimplifies the ways in which culture works and freezes the product into one kind of reading."[4]

For Schmid, while monsters in general and zombies in particular can be read metaphorically as reminders of the monstrous aspects of neoliberalism, the concomitant risk such readings carry with them is that the very same monsters, in the "excessive visibility" of the "subjective violence" that they commit and that is committed against them, can blind us to the very real "objective violence" of a neoliberal political economy whose devastation continues unabated.

Yet while zombies commit subjective violence in excessively visible ways on our screens, critically informed attention to their role on those screens and the appeal they generate need not be distracted by that visibility from the hidden but almost universal violence that is, using Eliot's term, their objective correlative. In other words, would not a symptomatic reading attuned to such objective violence give us clues as to how the undeniable *appeal* of zombies overlays or responds to an implicit knowledge on the part of the consumers of that hidden violence, and how the cloistered, suburban lives of late capitalist consumers rest uneasily over the shallow grave of abject multitudes? Such a reading would need to explain the very mechanism of that appeal, the reason why the consumer class of the culture industry would on the one hand seek to erase the suffering legions produced by an economy of extraction while on the other greedily devouring their avatars in fictional form.

Dave Reilly argues that, among the spectrum of defensible "meanings" that zombies carry—from the communist threat to fear of contagions like AIDS to simply an excuse for vicarious gratuitous slaughter—the most promising stems from our gradual confrontation with apocalyptic globalization, the knowledge that "we are on a trajectory that is unsustainable, and that may have devastating global consequences." Reilly further connects this knowledge to the expansion of information technology:

> All of this information is available to us at the push of a button, on a hand-held device that we carry with us everywhere. We may even be wearing Google's new neck tattoo that authorizes our hands-free perpetual access to the World Wide Web so that we can order that package through Amazon. com that will be delivered by an unmanned drone. The information and the possibilities may be exciting, but they are also overwhelming. We suffer from *information glut*: a paralyzing overabundance of information that requires expertise to wade through and to interpret.[5]

This information glut maps directly onto the seemingly inevitable trend of globalized capitalism to concentrate ever-greater wealth in the hands of the few by extracting ever more resources from the many, leaving vast portions of the world's population underemployed or exploited and, in some cases, not even fit for exploitation—to recall Luhmann's words, "there is nothing to exploit in the favelas." In other words, as producers proudly turn to new technologies (including and even especially information technologies) to obviate the need for employees, those of us still employed happily purchase their products, thereby contributing to the very economy that, according to Martin Ford's analysis in *Rise of the Robots: Technology and the Threat of a Jobless Future*, will inevitably drive us to obsolescence as well.[6]

Reilly sees in the zombie paradigm not only a metaphor for this apocalyptic scenario, but also a reason for its appeal: namely, the fantasy of a newly exerted autonomy. The zombie paradigm combines for viewers an Armageddon we know is coming with the fantasy of humanity unleashed from the bonds of governments and multinational corporations. The survivors who band together face moral terror, but they are also "empowered to determine [their] own futures." This appeal corresponds, according to a psychoanalytic understanding of the appeal of horror in general, to the pleasure derived from the repetition of ostensibly negative scenarios—which Freud at one point hypothesized as a manner of attempting to master what exceeds our control—but it finds an almost exact analogue in Kant's theory of the sublime:

The astonishment bordering on terror, the horror and the awesome shudder, which grip the spectator in viewing mountain ranges towering to the heavens, deep ravines and the raging torrents in them, deeply shadowed wastelands inducing melancholy reflection, etc., is, in view of the safety in which he knows himself to be, not actual fear, but only an attempt to involve ourselves in it by means of the imagination, in order to feel the power of that very faculty, to combine the movement of the mind thereby aroused with its calmness, and so to be superior to nature within us, and thus also that outside us, insofar as it can have an influence on our feeling of well-being.[7]

John Edgar Browning focuses on the structure and historical emergence of what he calls the "survival space" of zombie literature and movies, wherein the non-zombies gather to defend themselves against the swarming undead: "the cramming of a few disparate individuals into an enclosure or space and forcing them to work together in order to survive (or get killed if they do not) [was] a formula responsible for keeping the zombie pictures fresh, interesting, and relevant for over 45 years."[8] Browning finds the origin of this essential structure in Robert Matheson's 1953 novel *I am Legend*, which he also credits with having given rise to the multitudinous, swarming behavior of those zombies that—like almost all since then—do not owe their existence to a voodoo master.

Like Kant's spectator, then, we enjoy watching the spectacle of our world's immolation in a zombie apocalypse in part because, from the safety in which we know ourselves to be relative to the events on the screen, we can activate the power of the imagination, which is simultaneously "a power to assert our independence in the face of the influences of nature." In activating that power and enjoying that sensation, we are simultaneously inserting ourselves into a fantasy of power and autonomy that staves off, for a time, the impending sense of a disaster to come.

Perhaps we can go so far as to assert that the appeal of this cultural figure may depend precisely on its problematic status as symptom. In other words, it is exactly because zombies stand in such conflicted relation to the socio-historical reality they emerge from that they exert such a fascination on their consumers. This paradox is what lies at the heart of a cultural symptom, and what gives it its force. The symptom represents the socio-historical reality at the same time as it articulates an unconscious knowledge and a concomitant desire. That knowledge is simply that we are the agents of our own demise; like the slave Lacan writes of bearing the order for his own execution tattooed to his scalp,[9] our destruction is ensured by the very fulfillment of our functioning as autonomous consumers in a late capitalist economy. Zombies literalize that image in their relentless and cannibalistic drive to consume the human survivors; at the same time, the cells of human survivors evince the desire imbricated with that knowledge, a desire for freedom and self-determination from the economic forces that situate us as the agents of our own destruction.

This hinge between appeal and social reality is reinforced by yet another condensation: that between communication and production. As we noted earlier in reference to David Reilly's argument, the "information glut" whereby today's consumers are overwhelmed by information about the world is superimposed on a kind of production glut, such that our urge to consume the latest technology becomes the mechanism whereby that same technology will gradually, inevitably eradicate the possibility of gainful employment for larger and larger sectors of the world's population.

This is a primary effect of the current age of inflationary media. Unlike other times when there could be more truth to the vulgar Marxist notion that the means of production ultimately determine the content of culture, under our current conditions of inflationary media, the means of production and the means of communication become conflated. To put it in simpler terms: the means become the media. Whereas the mode of the capitalist is always to attempt to monopolize the means of production, in inflationary ages that domination is explicitly over the media. Ownership of the media is concentrated in such a way that greater and greater portions of the population are exposed to messaging issued from smaller and smaller circles of influence. While it may seem that this generalization is counter to the proliferation of content providers on the web and cable outlets today, we need to see that this apparent diversity masks a profound trend toward the concentration and ownership of the media into fewer and ever more powerful hands. This oligarchy then brazenly uses its financial power to ensure unfettered influence over political processes in order to enable the continued exertion of its economic expansion.

In some ways, then, the ultimate zombie move of the twenty-first century was a millennial release that technically had no zombies in it. Nevertheless, the fantasy scenario painted by the 1999 film *The Matrix* firmly encapsulates the paradoxes and appeal of our fascination with the undead. For can it not be said that we, the citizens of the early twenty-first century industrialized world, are like so many coppertop batteries, our brains plugged into a virtual world in which we live, play, and dream, while our bodies, that is, our economic livelihood, are kept on life-support to be drained dry in the service of that economy? Everything is constructed so that we avert our gaze from this reality. We become zombie consumers of media—zombies because we are animate without anima, we believe we are alive, real, autonomous, but in reality we are already dead, plugged into the relentless machine of capital hell bent on our destruction.

Maybe that's the real meaning of undead—already dead, but just alive enough not to realize it.

17

Apocalypse Then and Now

One thing we can be sure of: the world is in utter, magnificent decline. Those rambling masses of monsters reflect our inner certainty that, as Republican presidential candidates in 2015 like Donald Trump constantly trumpet, the American Dream is dead, a local avatar of a more universal sense of doom.

Then what are we to make of the social scientists who look at the historical record and calmly inform us that we are flat out wrong? Take Steven Pinker's analysis in his *The Better Angels of Our Nature*, that despite the devastating wars, the crimes against humanity, or the threat of world destruction unleashed by nuclear technology, the twentieth century was far less violent than those that came before it, and that, when looked at over its history, humanity has been on a course to ever-greater prosperity and peace, not depravity and war.[1] Or, as Nicholas Kristof tells us,

> One survey found that two-thirds of Americans believed that the proportion of the world population living in extreme poverty has almost doubled over the last 20 years. Another 29 percent believed that the proportion had remained roughly the same.
>
> That's 95 percent of Americans—who are utterly wrong. In fact, the proportion of the world's population living in extreme poverty hasn't doubled or remained the same. It has fallen by more than half, from 35 percent in 1993 to 14 percent in 2011 (the most recent year for which figures are available from the World Bank).[2]

Before we go rushing to judgment about Kristof's presuppositions, claiming he is a closet apologist for neoliberalism, it makes sense to ask why, yet again, are popular convictions of the state of the world so contrary to what the data actually report?

Almost every age and culture has a version, a story about how the world is likely to end. In the European Middle Ages eschatological theories were derived from Christian scripture, most often from the *Book of Revelations*, in which St. John describes his phantasmagorical visions of the second coming, with such memorable details as the Whore of Babylon sitting upon "a scarlet colored beast, full of names of blasphemy, having seven heads and ten horns."[3] In the early modern period, popular fear of witches and demons was interpreted in eschatological terms, in which the activities of accused witches were seen in light of readings of scripture prophesizing the end of times.[4] Interest in witches and their activities was thus in part driven by a desire to read a deeper, hidden reality, and to discover the truth of the coming of the end.

Such apocalyptic visions from the first inflationary age follow the logic of "modern" ideology, as Marx summarized using his own quotation from the Gospels, Jesus's explanation for his forgiveness of his tormenters: "they know not what they do." In Žižek's memorable revision of that formula for postmodern ideology we, under the sway of today's medialogy, know exactly what we are doing, but we do it anyway. For is this not also precisely the logic of our own apocalyptic trajectory today? And does this logic not also explain why, despite the admonitions of social scientists who are demonstrably right in their assessment of long-term trends toward greater prosperity and lesser violence for the greater part of humanity, a sense of doom, a knowledge that our end is already determined, remains?

For us today the catastrophe that is already upon us and that we nevertheless dutifully ignore, the cataclysm that is already uprooting and dispossessing legions of the world's poor and promises a future of ever-greater waves of refugees around the planet, is climate change. As Naomi Klein argues in her indictment of neoliberalism's inherent conflict with the climate, *This Changes Everything*, "Faced with a crisis that threatens our survival as a species, our entire culture is continuing to do the very thing that caused the crisis, only with an extra dose of elbow grease behind it."[5]

What is certain is that we are already headed, inexorably, for a future with more vicious storms, flooding, droughts, heat waves, and blizzards, with the economic and human tolls disproportionately affecting those nations and people who have least contributed to the problem through their greenhouse emissions, and least benefitted from the industrial development that produces those emissions. We are already, that is, locked into a future with at least an average increase of 2°C, and are more likely looking at a scenario in which average temperatures are 4° higher by the century's end.[6] As a former director of the Tyndall Centre for Climate Change Research says, an increase of 4°C is "incompatible with any reasonable characterization of an organized, equitable, and civilized global community."[7]

Here is a tiny portion of Klein's chilling (pardon the irony) description of a planet whose average temperature is 4° higher than today's, for which "even the best case scenario is likely to be calamitous":

> Four degrees of warming would raise the global sea levels by 1 or possibly even 2 meters by 2100 (and would lock in at least a few additional meters over future centuries). This would drown some island nations such as the Maldives and Tuvalu, and inundate many coastal areas from Ecuador and Brazil to the Netherlands to much of California and the northeastern United States, as well as huge swaths of South and Southeast Asia.[8]

She goes on to describe massive crop losses, famine, killer heat waves, megastorms, and then ends on the cheery note that, according to many models, we are on a trajectory for even greater warming than 4°. In other words, the data is in: we are fucked.

Despite this doomsday scenario, much of Klein's book claims the veil of a kind of perverse optimism. For Klein, as with Rahm Emmanuel's famous crises that one should never let go to waste, the enormity and global reach of this crisis should drive us to make changes so fundamental that they would also eradicate a host of other social ills. Nevertheless, the paradox running through the book is evident from the first to the last page: precisely because the changes needed are so profound, all the combined resources of the worlds' entrenched elites are marshaled against anyone succeeding in making those changes. As she writes,

> We are stuck because the actions that would give us the best chance of averting catastrophe—and would benefit the vast majority—are extremely threatening to an elite minority that has a stranglehold over our economy,

our political process, and most of our major media outlets. That problem might not have been insurmountable had it presented itself at another point in our history. But it is our great collective misfortune that the scientific community made its decisive diagnosis of the climate threat at the precise moment when those elites were enjoying more unfettered political, cultural, and intellectual power than at any point since in the 1920s.[9]

Indeed, the elites' influence over the media is key to understanding why the world blissfully goes on spinning the rope it will hang itself with, while the same elites bunker down in estates paid for by profits they make selling that rope at a handsome markup. But it is not merely a matter (although it certainly is that as well) of buying up news outlets and funding think tanks like Heartland and the Cato Institute to cook up "scientific" studies and spread climate skepticism. Something else is at stake when such large portions of the worlds' populations can be guided into ignoring a reality that their very lives depend on their not ignoring.

In current popular culture, our fantasies often incorporate these notions in apocalyptic scenarios in which our treatment of the *world as resource* combined with the kind of denialism that goes along with what we might call *reality-entitlement* (I am entitled to my own reality) produce catastrophic consequences for the human race. James Patterson's apocalyptic best-seller *Zoo*, with its spinoff CBS TV series, provides a good illustration of this paradox. In the novel, "cell phone radiation is somehow cooking the ambient environmental hydrocarbons in a way we've never seeing before—morphing them into a chemical that animals are picking up as a pheromone."[10] The result is widespread zombie-like behavior in animals that brings humanity to the brink of extinction. Against this established fact and with the human apocalypse on the horizon unless we can stop our use of cell phones, cars, etc., people will just continue to use the technology that's killing them, simply because "it is the way of life, the way of the world."[11]

The explanation for this apparently willful ignorance lies in today's medialogy. Where apocalypticism in the first age of inflationary media sought an ultimate but deferred reality behind the veil of ephemeral appearances, a real and stable thing underlying a world of copies, the current inflationary age eclipses and engulfs that model, and the result is imprinted on our interpretations of the apocalypse. For us today, and for the dominant economic model we call neoliberalism, the world consists of *resources* that agents, mainly individuals, but also collectives of individuals like corporations or states, use and manage. When the entire world is conceived as an ultimately expendable (albeit at the cost of our survival) resource, this is when the concept of sustainability comes into play.

Obviously, the idea behind sustainability is a noble one; indeed, if the prescriptions of sustainability were or had been until now followed, then the catastrophe of an ever-warming planet could be averted. But the dark side of sustainability is the insight it gives us into how the world is situated in the current medialogy: the world, once the transcendent, ineffable ground of appearances, has been relegated to the level of the copies, just one more, if greater, resource among equals. In Heidegger's famous formulation, like the great Danube whose waters have been locked behind a grid of hydroelectric dams, the world itself has been converted into a standing reserve.[12]

But what allows a ground as fundamental as the entire world to be subsumed by the logic of resources is how our medialogy frames reality. The ineffable, foundational yet common reality of the first inflationary age has been in turn subsumed in the new medialogy. Where everyday objects in the first were turned into copies of that massive, spectral thing, a reality independent of our individual perspectives, in the second age those fundamental things—souls, truth, God, the world—have disappeared, and their erstwhile copies—people, versions, faiths, resources—have taken on the status of things, dislodged from any common, transcendent ground.

We can use this schema to better understand the loss of interest in the commons that so obviously characterizes climate policies in the new medialogy; neoliberalism's all-out focus on the market agency of the individual as consumer simply has no room for a non-commodity that is nevertheless indispensable for the survival of all. This is why the policy recommendations in the discourse of sustainability often come dressed as commodity fetishes: carbon credits that wealthy companies or nations can purchase to offset their polluting ways, much as wealthy Catholics in the sixteenth century might have purchased indulgences to offset the pleasures of their sinful lives.

In a sense, the language of sustainability is the shadow indicator of our very inability to imagine any alternatives to capitalism as a global economic system; for the current medialogy, reality itself has the form of a commodity, which makes it all the easier for the elites controlling governments or markets to package and sell their own versions. To bastardize Stephen Colbert, reality has a well-known neoliberal bias.

This explains how a well-regarded architect and theorist in Italy like Giovanni Galli, in pointing to sustainability as the potential symbolic form of the twenty-first century, himself adopts the rhetorical stance of a climate change denier. He grounds his critical stance vis-à-vis the sustainability movement on the ostensibly philosophical, even hermeneutic argument that the seemingly urgent need for a politics of sustainability presupposes a static vision of being, one in which values are intrinsic to nature as opposed to invented by men. Understood this way, he argues, "products of a fossil origin (oil, coal, gas) don't have a value in themselves, but only insofar as they are made useful by and for the labor of mankind."[13] This much may seem obvious; but the conclusion he draws is eye-opening: "From this perspective, as the economist Julian Simon has argued, resources are inexhaustible."[14] What Galli doesn't mention is that Simon was employed by the Cato Institute until his death in 1998, an institute financed in large part by big business and, specifically big oil, with the purpose of producing policy papers in support of those industries.

What underlies such thinking, however, is both more specific and much, much more fundamental. The inexhaustibility of resources in this model is linked directly to the ungrounded nature of value. The world has been removed from its role as transcendental anchor of values, and now circulates like one more copy. But once such copies have turned into things in their own right, liberated from their subservience to an ultimate thing, they become, like Galli's and Simon's cynical definition of resources, inexhaustible, because their value is entirely defined by their consumers.

Climate denial, the self-annihilating, apocalyptic engine of our times, expresses in its purest form the power of our medialogy. Just as when the substance of a nation—once the ineffable thing to which symbolic copies (states) referred to—is turned into a hollow shell and shaken by ethnic substances, warring tribal alliances, or new racisms, in the new medialogy the entire world, once the ineffable ground of all existence, reveals itself as just one more resource. By turning copies into things and eradicating the transcendent ground projected by the first inflationary age, today's medialogy has effectively sidelined reality, and turned its naming rights over to the highest bidder.

Part Four

In Defense of Being

18

Minor Strategies

The inflationary media of the first and second age each inverted the medialogy of the prior age. Thus did the first inflationary age, by turning things into copies, transform an immanent domain of bodies and divine substance into a world of appearances masking an ineffable reality. Thus did the second reality invert that schema once more, importing those ineffable substances into the subjective realm, and turning what had been copies of those substances into ungrounded pieces of the real. Elites in each age were and have been agile at manipulating their respective medialogies, from imperial control of public media to promote the quiescent exchange of real privileges for symbolic honor in the seventeenth century, to the subversion of democratic governance by multinational corporations that benefit from the bolstering of technocratic bureaucracies in the face of rising fundamentalisms in the late twentieth century.

We have referred to the manipulation of the dominant medialogy by powerful elites as the major strategy, the hallmark of which is to establish a privileged interpretation of the reality contained by that medialogy, and exchange ostensible access to that reality for material investment and allegiance to the established power structure. In the case of the first inflationary age, the reality proffered comprised spectral values such as the eternal soul and a man's honor; in the second age, it comes in the form of subjective revelation, in which each individual becomes convinced of the fundamental truth of his or her own private belief system, body, or set of experiences.

The power of the major strategy lies in its inherent ability to coopt resistance. Denying the truth of a spectral, ineffable essence takes the form of a claim for a similar access to another truth, which can be combated as heresy or dismissed as fanaticism. Denying the truth of another's subjective claim to an embodied revelation of reality simply reiterates the structure and joins the field of competing private fundamentalisms. But there is another way, one that aligns itself with what philosophers have called the modern hermeneutic tradition because it emphasizes the foundational role of interpretation. For thinkers of this tradition, in fact, the *being* in human being is nothing other than humanity's incessant drive to interpret the world. As such, what we call defenders of being are precisely those who, against the dictates of the major strategy, refuse the cessation of interpretation demanded by ostensible access to unfiltered reality, and locate the essence of humans in their immersion in meanings and their ineluctable freedom to interpret these meanings anew. For the defenders of being, there is no unfiltered reality; reality is always filtered; in fact, reality or, rather, being is nothing other than the inevitable filtering of experience into knowledge.

From the onset of the first age of inflationary media, then, thinkers, artists, and activists have responded to media's framing in *minor*, analytic ways, by revealing the arbitrary exclusions that media's framing relies on, and cautioning against the pitfalls of paranoid reactions. These minor strategies don't counter the claims of the major strategies on their own terms, but instead start by taking them at their word, positioning readers and viewers in the very folds of those claims, in order to expose their non-sense. As we have argued, Miguel de Cervantes was acutely aware of how the media of his time manipulated the desires and identifications of audiences. His interlude *The Stage of Wonders* undermines the illusion of theater by confronting the comfortable conventions of blood purity and honor with the chaos of arbitrary class privilege. Today this function is performed by comedians like Stephen Colbert or cinematic subgenres of horror that explore how the media frames our perceptions, desires, and behaviors.

When Colbert roasted President Bush during his now infamous turn at the 2006 White House Press Forum, he praised him as "steady," a man who believes on Wednesday what he believed on Monday, regardless of what happened on Tuesday. Bush was steady because his crusading plans were reality-proof (since, as Colbert pointed out, reality has a well-known liberal bias). If there is something that can be said about Cervantes' character Don Quixote, it is that he is steady in the same way: reality proof. As one of us has argued elsewhere, this logic makes it possible to "read" the world in accordance with a pre-established set of notions: since Iraq is a terrorist state that produces weapons of mass-destruction with the intention of using them against the United States, the fact that there are no weapons of mass-destruction to be found in Iraq is irrelevant! Since the dust in the horizon is clear evidence that two armies are about to do battle, the fact that we can plainly see sheep instead of armed men is irrelevant! Don Quixote says that since he knows how things of war ultimately are, regardless of their appearance, how they look to others or even to himself is of no consequence.[1]

The means of contestation are carried in the media itself. The Arab Spring, the *indignados* of Spain, and the Occupy movement were all made possible by the rise of the same social media that corporations and governments can use to track consumer patterns and the movement of dissidents. These movements also reveal the growing discontent with traditional systems of political representation in the age of globalization. People are becoming increasingly conscious of the fact that economic policies are generated outside the traditional circuits of political representation, whether by global corporations or supranational institutions. New digital communities are emerging as a form of grassroots political action, creating a new public sphere at a time when the distinction between the public and the private is rapidly imploding. How entrenched elites respond is predictable, because these responses have been written into the very fabric of the first age of inflationary media. Identities formed as touchstones of resistance will be commoditized and incorporated into the acceptable framework, or vilified and excluded; specters of such exclusion will haunt cultural production; and elite interests will coalesce around fundamentalist fantasies of national identity whose sole purpose is to resist any weakening of the political and economic structures that function for their benefit. A critique adequate to the task of confronting these tactics must understand how the struggles of our own times are rooted in those of the first age of inflationary media.

To be sure, media technologies advance, and even advance at a relatively comparable pace, in other periods. As we have argued, however, in the two periods of inflationary media the transformations in how societies conceive of, produce, consume, and engage with media provoke a transformation in the dominant medialogy that is perceived as a crisis of reality. Societies no longer feel assured in their received truths, values, and beliefs. And of course the suspicion that "truth" is essentially unstable, manipulated, bought and sold, impossible, or even irrelevant precipitates other forms of crisis, most notably a *crisis of legitimacy*, as subjects contend with the perception that the principles they live by are arbitrary. Since these principles are predicated as the very foundation of social, economic, and political systems, subjects are left with the disturbing realization that the public realm (the realm of governance and politics) is just *theater*, a masquerade behind which there is nothing but the obscene struggle for power and recognition. This was in fact the end-point of the baroque culture industry, masterfully theorized in their own time, in very distinctive ways, by seventeenth-century authors like Baltasar Gracián and Miguel de Cervantes. We have much to learn from their insights into the first age of inflationary media, as we strive to understand our own.

19

Stranger than Fiction

When the Academy of Motion Picture Arts and Sciences issued its list of Oscar nominees in 2013, it unwittingly weighed in on a controversy that has bedeviled western thought for millennia. Three of that year's Best Picture nominees, including the film that eventually won best picture—*Lincoln*, *Zero Dark Thirty*, and *Argo*—raised questions about how accurately they portray history. In each case, the film's directors or screenwriters defended their choices by arguing that dramatic license permits artists to depart from historical fact in order to construct a better story. Their critics retort that these portrayals are not harmless, at best giving casual viewers and students a wrong idea of actual historical events and, at worst, swaying public opinion about controversial policies today.

Who is right? Does dramatic license trump the need for historical rigor, or should all dramatic manipulation stay within the borders of what historians can assert with confidence actually occurred? The Greek philosopher Plato gave us one side of the debate in the dialogue known as *The Republic*, in which Socrates outlines his plan for an ideal state. In such a state, he argues, "poetic imitators, beginning with Homer," should be given the boot, because they "imitate images of virtue and all the other things they write about and have no grasp of the truth."[1]

Plato's student Aristotle would eventually produce the poets' response. In his *Poetics* Aristotle argues that the difference between the historian and the poet is that "one relates what has happened, the other what may happen. Poetry, therefore, is a more philosophical and a higher thing than history: for poetry tends to express the universal, history the particular."[2] Where Plato banished poets for departing from historical truth, Aristotle restored them by pointing out that poets were concerned with even more important truths than those of history. Should today's Academy consider the same defense as it ponders the merits of its nominees' poetic renderings of history?

Tony Kushner, the Tony Award-winning playwright and the writer behind Stephen Spielberg's *Lincoln*, thinks so. For Kushner, because "history doesn't always organize itself according to the rules of drama," it is permissible to "manipulate a small detail in the service of a greater historical truth."[3] But in resorting to Aristotle's basic defense of poetry as expressing a greater truth, today's Oscar-hopeful poets are forgetting that we have a very different concept from that of our philosophical forebears for works of the imagination that depart from history. Today we call these works fictions, and the value of fiction has changed dramatically since the time when Renaissance scholars last resurrected the debates around poetry and history.

Fiction, or its Latin counterpart *fictio*, has also been around for a long time, but for the most part without the philosophical love shown to its cousin poetry. For ages the term stayed close to its etymological meaning of invention or pretense, and hence something simply not true. In the fourteenth century the Italian poet Giovanni Boccaccio explicitly used the term in his defense of poetry, but his arguments didn't differ substantially from the Aristotelian blueprint of poetry-as-greater-truth. Boccaccio uses the metaphor of the veil, admitting that poets "veil the truth with fiction," but then goes on to explain that they do so in order "to make truths which would otherwise cheapen by exposure the object of strong intellectual effort and various interpretation, that in ultimate discovery they shall be more precious."[4]

Today we have a very different set of expectations and interpretive skills we bring to bear when reading a book or viewing a film. Before cracking the page or settling down in a theater, we have already unconsciously decided whether we are reading a fiction or a non-fiction book, viewing a movie or a documentary, and we proceed to judge the experience based on those criteria. While we still value fiction, we tend to do so for very different reasons from those used by the ancients. We ask how effectively we were drawn into the story; how likeable the characters were. We are more concerned with a story being believable than being true. In other words, we understand we are there to be fooled, and we welcome the pretense, as long as it is a good one.

We are not saying that today's poet-historians should be entirely let off the hook. As many have pointed out, by embracing a "journalistic" approach, putting three historical advisers on payroll, and blending archival footage with dramatization, the makers of *Zero Dark Thirty*, *Lincoln*, and *Argo* invited the enhanced scrutiny. Rather, we should remember that in the modern world we have come to embrace fiction for its pretense, not despite it. While we still seek truths in the fiction we consume, these are far more likely to be truths about ourselves and how we see the world than about what actually happened at a given time or place. As Oscar Wilde once wrote, "Man is least himself when he talks in his own person. Give him a mask and he will tell you the truth."[5] How well a work of fiction inspires us to seek that kind of truth is a better gauge of its quality than how it recounts historical facts.

The problem of fiction bedevils us in even more potentially consequential ways than mere debates about historical accuracy in movies. Hearing arguments in late 2014 in a case pitting the government against Anthony Elonis, a man who posted rap lyrics online that contained language deemed personally threatening by his estranged wife, U.S. Supreme Court Chief Justice John Roberts asked whether the equally violent references made by the rapper Eminem to his own ex-wife in some of his songs should make him liable for prosecution. The government's lawyer answered that they should not, thus making the difference between what Eminem does and what Mr. Elonis did the line between artistic license and criminal conduct.

What is at stake in the Chief Justice's question goes to the heart of a specific way of using language that we call fictional. Fiction, as Joshua Landy has recently defined it, is "a verbal performance in which the events depicted never happened, and everyone knows they didn't."[6] A simpler version would be "untrue statements known to be untrue."

The problem with this formulation, as the Court discovered, is that with fiction it's not always the case that everyone knows it's fiction. In Elonis v. United States the test for whether a statement is merely a fiction and hence protected speech, or a "true threat" subject to prosecution, turns on how a reasonable person would interpret it. But just as Justice Roberts felt forced to ask whether the standard in a given case should be any reasonable person or, for instance, "a reasonable teenager on the internet,"[7] different schools of literary critics have ranged from arguing that discovering a given text's meaning relies on reconstructing its appropriate "context of reception" to asserting that texts posit their own "ideal readers."

In fact, over time, legal notions of what determines guilt have changed as much as have critical notions of what a text means. In the Middle Ages, guilt was often determined through "trial by ordeal," under the assumption that God would protect the truly innocent from feeling the full force of the pain inflicted on them. The "intent" of the accused meant so little that farm animals could be put on trial by the same methods. Medieval literary criticism, for its part, spelled out four different levels of meaning that a text could be read for, none of which depended on the author's intent.

In the Renaissance, critics became very concerned with how texts related to reality. While they understood from Aristotle that fictional texts would not need to represent things as they actually occurred, they also believed that such fictions should tell other, more philosophical truths than would a merely accurate rendering of facts. By making the value of realistic but untrue depictions depend on judgments about what ends those depictions served, critics implicitly began to assume that a text's ultimate meaning depends on its author's intent, such that a modern critic like the Cambridge professor Anthony Close could eventually argue that in literary criticism we "presuppose that what is meant is what was intended, because we are congenitally unable to do otherwise."[8]

The importance of intent, in other words, is an index of how established the practice of fiction is in a given society. The intent behind a text only becomes a question for a medialogy that values the practice of portraying untrue things as if they were true, and that distinguishes such practices from mere lying. Our present medialogy is very clearly one of those. Artists in our culture know the boundaries separating fictional from true language, and they explore and push those boundaries. When writing about things as if they were true but meaning something else, artists are employing the literary trope of irony. But they also know that for irony to be irony, it has to be signaled in their work by their choice of genre; by the use of other tropes such as hyperbole (think of Stephen Colbert); by the creation of different personae (think of him again); or by how they package, classify, or otherwise frame their words.

Justice Roberts interrupted the government lawyer's attempt to answer his question about Emimem's lyrics by posing a provocative answer of his own: is it not the case, he asked, that the reason we don't prosecute Eminem is "because Eminem said it instead of someone else?"

The short answer is yes: we grant artists that the apparent truths they write are not to be taken literally in part because they have convinced us, through their artistic choices and the cultivation of their personae, that they are artists and not sociopaths. Whether a reasonable person would feel threatened by their words depends in large measure on how well they have accomplished that task. But what about those who, systematically, perhaps, are incapable of distinguishing fiction from the reality it imitates all too well? In recent years psychiatrists have begun to identify a new condition they are calling Truman Show Syndrome, after the 1998 Jim Carrey movie about a man whose life is the subject of a television show without his being aware of it. The symptom of this syndrome is the patient's persistent belief against all evidence to the contrary that his or her life is the subject of a reality TV show, that his or her actions are being filmed 24 hours a day, and that his or her friends, relatives, and even closest family members are members of the cast, all of whom are in the know, and all of whom are conspiring to keep the patient in the dark about the true nature of his or her existence.

The problem of evidence rehearsed by Truman Show Syndrome is symptomatic of a culture-wide philosophical conundrum that emerged from the first age of inflationary media, which concerns the way we relate to what we call reality. The first thing to note is that the delusion itself mimics the basic structure of philosophical idealism's primal fantasy and ultimate vanishing point: solipsism, or a radical skepticism as to the existence of anything outside of my own mind. Once I accept the proposition that whatever I cognize is an idea, be it an idea proper or an idea of an external object, it becomes impossible to establish the existence of anything other than my ideas. In a similar move, those who suffer from Truman Show Syndrome or any similarly structured delusion already submit the very question of "external" evidence to the rules of their game.

The first point we can glean from the analogy between the basic structure of such theatrical delusions and the solipsistic conundrum of philosophical idealism is that sufferers of the former are for some reason *taking too seriously* the problem posed by the latter. In other words, while solipsism poses an irreducible difficulty once certain philosophical presuppositions have been accepted, even philosophers who accept those presuppositions do not usually for that reason alter their behavior to reflect the conundrum in which they find themselves trapped. For sufferers of the delusions, in contrast, what would seem a merely curious byproduct of modern philosophy's approach to the world has become an issue requiring active intervention.

The person suffering from a theatrical delusion is thus in the position of taking too seriously a primal presupposition of the modern world.[9] This presupposition is that I experience my existence as being constructed along a fissure between the world of a character and the world of the actor playing that character. Events in a character's world have no impact on the actor's world, and vice versa, because the frame separating those worlds has been, to use a term from the sociologist Erving Goffman, *keyed*.[10] This means that the ability of those actions within a given frame to change reality for spectators outside that frame has been suspended. While those actions remain fully comprehensible, they do not have the same effect on external spectators as they have on internal participants.

As we have seen, Michel Foucault famously speculated at the outset of *The Order of Things* that Cervantes' biting account of insanity in his character Don Quixote was really the critical commentary of one episteme, or historical structure of knowledge, on another: in this case Don Quixote represented the insertion into an episteme organized around the classificatory grid of knowledge of a consciousness that still judged the world in terms of resemblances. Foucault's reading thus presented Don Quixote as an example of insanity insofar as the knight fails to key the frames his contemporaries are keying already by second nature. But whereas for Foucault Don Quixote is a subject who has failed to adapt to the modern world's representational presupposition, for us he is a subject who has taken too seriously modernity's reigning metaphor.

Like the sufferer of Truman Show Syndrome, Don Quixote is convinced that everything that transpires in his world does so for his sake: namely, that it is the work of an evil enchanter who has bewitched him on several occasions, and has transformed his beloved lady Dulcinea del Toboso into a crass country wench. Any attempt on the part of others to lead Don Quixote out of his delusion is trumped by the fact that evidence against the delusion can be immediately marshaled in favor of the delusion. If others do not see what he does, it is because the enchanter has ensured that they do not. The enchanter, in other words, has taken on the role of theater director, that great master of illusions who ensures that the stagecraft comes off without a hitch.

Don Quixote's insanity, then, far from a failure to adapt to how we navigate interpersonal space in the modern world, is rather a case of a subject who has taken the theatrical nature of that interrelation all too seriously. At the dawning of the modern age Cervantes created a character who exemplifies the extreme of a new subjective spectrum: a character who failed to install at the core of his cognitive functioning that minimal distance between the world as it is for me and the world as it is independent of my perception that we see expounded by Descartes. Where normal modern subjects had learned by this time in cultural history to separate the roles they play as characters in their daily social and political dramas from the actor selves who represent those roles, and hence live their lives with a minimal degree of detachment from those roles, Don Quixote failed to grasp the fictional nature of the world and hence took his roles too seriously, thus projecting into his world a character who must prove to others at every step that his life is orchestrated and observed by that evil enchanter.

Theatrical delusions like Truman Show Syndrome give us a glimpse into the basic presuppositions of a cognitive structure common to the modern world, presuppositions shared by all of us even as they are deflected, ironized, or repressed by a minimal distance pried open by our implicit awareness of the fictional roles we play. That cognitive structure assumes a division of the world into various planes of existence, like the mutually encapsulated worlds of a character and the actor who plays him. This cognitive structure became dominant during the first age of inflationary media and expressed itself aesthetically in the play of appearances and perspective that achieved its extreme in baroque plastic arts and in philosophy in the form of modern philosophy, which placed knowledge of reality squarely in the hands of the human senses and then proceeded to undermine the ability of those senses to know anything other than themselves.

The philosopher at the dawn of modernity, in other words, stood on the stage of the world and wondered how, exactly—given that he must use the senses his character is provided with to scope out the nature of the world—he would ever come to know how the world *really is* beyond the confines of the stage. This question, taken too seriously, leads to Truman Show Syndrome; with the right amount of ironic detachment though, it has given us our dominant form of entertainment in the modern world: *fiction*. It makes sense, then, that now, in the second age of inflationary media with its attendant medialogy, we would see fiction fold back on itself as it has, from the dramatized realities occupying more than 50 percent of our television screens to the spread of a new psychiatric condition. In today's medialogy, the danger is precisely that we *take too seriously* representations that are in fact fictional, just as we tend to install in what are by nature copies the aura of a lost original.

Truth and Lies in Life and Art

The publication of the anonymous *Lazarillo de Tormes* in 1554 in Antwerp, Alcalá de Henares, and Burgos is a groundbreaking event in the history of print fiction. *Lazarillo* offers his readers a radically novel view of the world, a reframing of social reality from the bottom, from the perspective of the dispossessed. At the turn of the century, Mateo Alemán would publish a second picaresque novel, *Guzmán de Alfarache* (1599), which offers a reframing of the pícaro's life story from the watchtower position of the moralist, as the book's subtitle indicates: *Atalaya de la vida humana* or watchtower of human life. If *Lazarillo* justified the illicit practices of the pícaro and his "dishonorable" life-style as a victim of social injustice, Guzmán urges the pícaro to abandon his sinful ways and accept the social norms; and with them his God-given place in society. Just a few years later, medical doctor Francisco López de Ubeda would provide yet another reframing of the picaresque material. The novelty of his approach consists of his inclusion of two simultaneous frames: a narrative frame that records the shocking worldview and scandalous actions of a "free woman," the unrepentant pícara Justina; and an authorial frame that projects the diagnostic and admonishing judgment of the moralist.

In a well-known passage of Cervantes' masterpiece, don Quixote comes upon a group of convicts who are being escorted to the galleys (DQ I, 22), the most notorious of whom, Ginés de Pasamonte, reveals to him (and us) that he has written the story of his life. Don Quixote asks the convict whether his life story is complete to which the convict responds with a question of his own, *how could his story be complete if his life isn't?* Beyond the snarkiness of the convict's retort, we see a serious Cervantine probing concerning the complexity of the relation between life and storytelling, which, as Spadaccini and Talens have suggested, is directly tied to the early print phenomenon known as the *picaresque*. We could say that Ginés's statement "deconstructs" the frame of *Lazarillo de Tormes* and its literary brethren as it calls attention to the illusory nature of the structural identification of the authorial 'I' with the narrative 'I' and the 'I' of the protagonist in picaresque novels.

The impression that this is part of a Cervantine probing on the question of reality and its representation in life and art is further reinforced when Ginés reemerges in DQ II, 26 as a master puppeteer (Maese Pedro) whose own puppet show is misperceived by don Quixote as "reality" with disastrous consequences, as the knight-errant charges against the figures of the tableau in his attempt to right the wrongs of not only the "characters" but the "author" himself, whose mastery of the "artistic lie" is itself sub-standard. Don Quixote's complete identification, his giving his body to the "artistic lie" is a brilliant representation of the "mad reader or spectator" whose visceral identification with the theatrical illusion renders him incapable of judicious distance. This is precisely the kind of uncritical spectator that Lope de Vega has in mind when he refers to his own mass-audience as *vulgo* in his *Arte Nuevo de hacer comedias en este tiempo*. As in the previously discussed *Stage of Wonders*, Cervantes is inviting reflection on frames and framing techniques in what we call *art* and what we call *life*.

Cervantes' literary experiments with framing anticipate the artistic games of Diego de Velázquez, the (early) modern intellectual-painter par excellence. In his famous courtly paintings, for example, Diego de Velázquez represents the world of the court as a series of carefully framed scenes (or scenarios) in which models pose and courtly characters perform different roles, whether they are buffoons posing as Gods and legendary heroes, or members of the aristocracy and the royal family posing as aristocrats and royalty. The scandal of Velázquez's courtly portraits has to do precisely with the fact that clothing and other markers of social status are exposed as mere theatrical props. If taken seriously, this notion contradicts the official worldview of an aristocratic establishment that continues to promulgate and police laws to ensure the proper use of clothing in order to prevent the risk of social imposture that is often dramatized in picaresque narratives. His famous portrait *El bufón llamado don Juan de Austria* (The Buffoon Called don Juan de Austria) painted in 1632 or 1633 is a case in point.

While we may be tempted to dismiss Velázquez's theatrical games when applied to courtly buffoons (after all buffoons are carnivalesque characters to begin with), it would seem harder to dismiss the scandal of his royal portraits. Much has been written on Velázquez's *Las meninas* (1656) as a picture-puzzle that blurs the lines between inside and outside, that is, between the painting and the world that serves as its model or referent. For example, the mirror hanging on the back wall may reflect the King and Queen directly, or alternately, their pictorial image as represented on the canvas that spills out of the frame to our left. The viewer is incorporated into the represented world both as subject and object since we are "caught" in the gaze of most of the figures in front of us. They are shown observing us observing them. In fact, we can't help but feel as though the artist is actually studying us. We may even entertain the unsettling thought that, if somehow we were able to position ourselves in front of the canvas, we would be looking at our own image, rather than the portrait of the monarchs.

Commentators who have focused on the painting's air of dynamic spontaneity, with its resistance to "proper" centering and its in-your-face incompleteness, have often linked these aspects of Velázquez's painterly style to a "realistic," possibly even a "naturalistic" impulse that would have anticipated the nineteenth-century invention of the camera. According to this view, which can in fact be traced back to nineteenth-century critics, Velázquez's *Las meninas* would have offered the viewer a realistic "snapshot" of the royal court.

This notion may have inspired El Corte Inglés' recent version of *Las meninas*, an ingenious advertisement of clothing that turns the artist into a glamorous photographer while the other figures or "characters" that populated the courtly scene of Velázquez's painting are reimagined as members of a wedding party posing for pictures (or perhaps as models in a commercial with a wedding theme party). We will discuss this neo-baroque "updating" of the department store giant in our Epilogue. Here, we will simply make the point that, as an elaborate experiment in framing, Velázquez's *Meninas* has more in common with the type of epistemological explorations of the baroque stage concerning the complexity of the borders between reality and its representation than with notions of photographic transparency.

As a matter of fact, Velázquez's attention to the framing power of stages and, generally speaking, theatrically organized spaces can be traced back to his early work *Christ in the House of Martha and Mary* (1618). This interest continues after *Las meninas*, most notoriously in *Las hilanderas*, known in English as *The Tapestry Weavers* or *The Spinners*, which art historians have dated on or around 1657.

Christ in the House of Martha and Mary is generally thought of as a *bodegón* or still life in the tradition of Flemish paintings and engravings that combined biblical subjects with mundane objects displayed in domestic spaces. Here the biblical story is taken from the New Testament (Luke 10). When Christ visits the house of Martha, who immediately busies herself with meal preparations, her sister Mary listens to him attentively. Upset that her sister won't help in the kitchen, Martha complains to Jesus who in turn reminds Martha that Mary had made the wiser choice when she dropped all domestic chores in order to pay attention to his words. Velázquez's painting captures the moment of Christ's retort to Martha.

Up to this point there's general agreement among art critics. Yet things get tricky when it comes to describing Velázquez's framing of the scene against the foreground where two other female figures stand near the kitchen table. One of the females is busy at work even as she gazes in our direction, while the other stands right behind her with her index finger extended in the direction of the biblical scene to their left. Commentators agree that the background and foreground scenes are obviously connected, yet they have provided different interpretations of the material framing of the biblical scene. Is the scene reflected in a mirror as some suggest, or are we instead looking at a painting hanging on the wall? A third explanation that seems to have gained ground after the cleaning and restoration of 1964 is that the scene is framed by a hatch or opening in the wall.

Regardless of how we account for the actual framing of the biblical scene, it is clear that there is a theatrical imagination at work here. The figures of Christ, Martha, and Mary could just as well be characters in a religious play, conceivably offered as a life lesson to the present-day Martha in the foreground, and through her gaze to us, the viewers or spectators who inhabit a third space.

We find a similar arrangement of spaces in *Las hilanderas*, except that here the background is explicitly framed as a stage on which Athena confronts the mortal Arachne who has dared to challenge her. The weaving contest between the Goddess (disguised as an old woman) and Arachne wearing present-day clothing plays out in the foreground scene, which appears to be framed theatrically as well; the conventional recourse of the red curtain on the left adds to the theatrical feel. The viewer is addressed by one of the characters who looks straight at him or her from the right of the raised stage in the background. This figure is one of three women in present-day clothing witnessing Athena's confrontation with Arachne. They could very well be the spectators of a courtly play. For our part, we feel dragged into the theatrical space of the painting. We are obviously spectators of the two interrelated scenes, but we are also objects of the gaze of at least one of the painted figures.

As in the case of *Christ in the House of Martha and Mary*, the impression that we are somehow part of the scene is further reinforced by the directionality of the "reality bleed" effect of the painting. Thus, the Athena and Arachne figures in the background seem to literally spill out of the tapestries that frame the stage. In fact, commentators have often noted that it is difficult to tell whether these figures are inside or outside the tapestries lining up the wall. Remarkably, the spillage is not contained within the stage in the background. Rather, the thematic continuity between background and foreground suggests a cascading effect in the direction of the viewer; a continuation of the theatrical spillage beyond the material frame of the painting. We would argue that the space outside of the painting, the real space occupied by the viewer, is implicitly framed as another stage.

Thus, spectators are incorporated into the logic of the painting as active participants in the artistic game; they are invited to reflect on the medium itself and the porous nature of the boundaries between art and life, between theatrical stages and world stages. This is the aesthetic strategy that we associate with the "minor" baroque, as we look back to Velázquez and Cervantes in search for models on which to build an "ethical optics" in our own age of media saturation. To be sure, it is not just a matter of recognizing the function

Figure 20.1 Velázquez, *Las hilanderas*, courtesy of Wikimedia Commons.

of the media in making sense of life and art, but of seeing ourselves as part of that "media reality" and understanding our own libidinal investment under the frame's pressure, as in the above-mentioned episodes of *Don Quixote* and the previously discussed *Theater of Marvels*.

Cervantes and Velázquez's invitation to reflect on the medium and how our investments are determined by its frames has found receptive ears in our present medialogy. We mentioned earlier an interview published in *The New York Times Magazine* in 2004, in which Ron Suskind quoted an aide to then president George W. Bush (since then revealed to have been Karl Rove) who mocked him and other journalists for their allegiance to "the reality-based community."[1] The administration's apparent nonchalance about truth, along with its skill at using the media to influence the public's perception of world events, inspired the comedian Stephen Colbert to arm his right-wing alter-ego with lexical zingers like "truthiness" and that *non plus ultra* for all political debate, "reality has a well-known liberal bias."[2] When Colbert pushed his act to its extreme, roasting Mr. Bush and the Washington press corps in their presence, he was borrowing from Cervantes' repertoire to cross swords on a battlefield at least in part of Cervantes' making. The battle was over reality, and whose version of it would hold sway; the weapon was the irony that only fiction supports.

"The greatest thing about this man is that he's steady," Colbert said, standing in front of the President of the United States. "You know where he stands. He believes the same thing Wednesday that he believed on Monday... no matter what happened Tuesday." Colbert's routine mocked the administration's slippery relation to truth (what happened on Tuesday), and identified the president's famous "resoluteness" as the character trait that the administration relied on to sell its phony versions of reality. But the brilliance of Colbert's attack lay in *how* it was delivered. Colbert's body was inhabited by two conflicting realities, one in which "Colbert" was a right-wing pundit expressing his admiration for the president, and another that undermined the first by reveling in its inanities. The discomfort and hilarity of Colbert's act stemmed from his audience seeing how the fictions that had blurred into truths were expertly extracted and revealed for what they were.

As Cervantes realized in the context of the newly born mass culture of the Catholic, imperial, Spanish state, irony expertly wielded is the best defense against the manipulation of truth by the media. Its effect was and still is to remind its audience that we are all active participants in the creation and support of a fictional world that is always in danger of being sold to us as reality.

On January 12, 2012, the *New York Times* reported that Colbert's super PAC—which was called the "The Definitely Not Coordinating With Stephen Colbert Super PAC" before eventually settling on the name "Americans for a Better Tomorrow Tomorrow"—had filed just over $1 million with the Federal Elections Commission. In a statement on the organization's website, Colbert wrote, "We raised it on my show and used it to materially influence the elections—in full accordance with the law. It's the way our founding fathers would have wanted it, if they had founded corporations instead of just a country."[3] The super PAC and its money were then used to run campaign ads suggesting that Mitt Romney was a serial killer, as well as to support the presidential candidacy of failed republican candidate Herman Cain, once it was revealed that Cain's name was still on the ballot in South Carolina despite his having dropped out of the race. One memorable ad, ostensibly intended to demonstrate the PAC's independence from Colbert, featured a demonic rendering of the comedian with glowing green eyes, and an ominous voice-over asking, "Who is Stephen Colbert?"

As news sources have commented—and as Colbert has himself admitted when interviewed out of character—the intent of the super PAC performance was to point out the holes and inconsistencies in how campaigns are financed and run in the United States. By creating a fictional version of himself as the centerpiece to a legally real entity in order to reveal or at least bring into greater relief an underappreciated truth, Colbert was using one of the weapons Cervantes honed; for if politics is war by other means, Cervantine irony is the weapon of choice for the politics of a fictional world.

In what sense is the world fictional? A fictional world exists simultaneously at the levels of locally experienced life and superimposed, media representations of communities, nations, and the world in its entirety. The politics of a fictional world are one in which elites and sovereign powers exert control over individuals and communities in part by manipulating representations of them in the various media at their disposal. These representations are not directly of the individuals or communities—a hopelessly inefficient form of control—but of characters, that is, of people or groups, either real or invented, that larger agglomerations of individuals can identify with. As we identify with these representations, we implicitly perform as readers of fiction: we simultaneously treat them as true, and hence invest them with positive or negative emotions, and as untrue, and hence are able to disconnect them from our personal lives when necessary or when the identifications become too strong. Political representations in a fictional world portray us as if we were the character in a book or a movie. They show us ourselves relating to other people, to objects they want us to desire, to situations they want us to involve ourselves in.

The late Cambridge don Anthony Close once assailed critics who read Cervantes' work in a philosophical light for imposing "modern stereotypes and preoccupations" on a novel that, in his view, was written exclusively as a parody of the tales of chivalry predominant in the sixteenth century.[4] Other, philosophical interpretations fail to grasp that "we are essentially concerned in literary criticism with what literature means. We presuppose that what is meant is what was intended, because we are congenitally unable to do otherwise."[5] Close's Oxford ally P.E. Russell did him one better, asserting that Cervantes should not be considered to have "contributed anything of originality to the history of ideas."[6] The logic Russell used to support this claim was almost dizzying in its circularity, as it required him to stipulate as a standard for establishing that someone has had *a truly original idea* the presence of a contemporary who had expressed more or less *the same idea*.

But in truth Cervantes did contribute something of extraordinary importance to the history of ideas, and he did so when he made his writing be not about the objects, people, and events in a given setting, but about how those objects, people, and events are portrayed and interpreted in those settings, and about whose interests those portrayals and interpretations serve. When he did that, he also put into question the intent of the author, be it an internal authorial voice or, by extension, his own. It is therefore only in the fictional age that interpreting a book becomes not about revealing hidden meanings, historical truths, or eschatological consequences, but about deciphering "what literature means," and only from this perspective can "we presuppose that what is meant is what was intended, because we are congenitally unable to do otherwise."

The great Argentine writer Jorge Luis Borges understood Cervantes' role in this process when he created his fantastic parody of what he termed "the art of erroneous attribution" around two chapters of *Don Quixote* that had supposedly been penned anew, verbatim, by an early twentieth-century French author called Pierre Menard. Here's how he ends that so often-quoted story of quotations: "Menard (almost without intending to) has enriched the idle and rudimentary art of reading by way of a new technique: the technique of deliberate anachronism and erroneous attributions. That technique of infinite applications induces us to peruse the *Odyssey* as if it were posterior to the *Aeneid* and the book *Le Jardin du Centaure* by Madame Henri Bachelier as if were by Madame Henri Bachelier."[7]

Here Borges' sly mockery of literary criticism gets Cervantes better in some ways than do the most ardent Cervantes scholars. For both of these masters of Hispanic letters, the real target of their pens may have been something more along the lines of what the French Marxist philosopher Louis Althusser described with inimitable clunkiness when he wrote, in *Lenin and Philosophy* that, "one of the effects of ideology is the practical *denegation* of the ideological character of ideology by ideology."[8] When Colbert funds a super PAC to ask the question, "Who is Colbert," or Borges suggests as an example of erroneous attribution reading a work as if it were actually written by its own author, both are taking a page from Cervantes' invention, a page that multiplied itself with such ferocity that it became his work's driving trope and the soul of literary fiction to come. For if the world of fiction is born when we can claim to imagine every aspect of our existence being false, changed, other, while *we* remain the same, Cervantes made his fiction be about just that *we*, about how even as we laugh at the buffoon's antics or weep at the hero's awesome sacrifice, *we*'ve already drunk the Kool-Aid, *we*'re already part of the show.

Staging the Event

In their *Hermeneutic Communism* and elsewhere, Gianni Vattimo and Santiago Zabala have advanced a powerful philosophical distinction, derived from Heidegger, between "framed" and "hermeneutic" thought.[1] Their distinction is among the best modes of conceptualizing philosophical realism and its alternatives, not least because it draws attention to the material, medial underpinnings of thought in a similar way to how Heidegger himself alerted his readers to the way in which even purportedly "pure" forms of intuition like time and space (Kant) needed to be seen as always material, structured, embodied modes of existence.[2]

Framed thought, in brief, assumes the pre-established coherence of what is being thought as an object ready to be found in the world. Framed thinking always subordinates itself to that already-existent reality; hence, as Vattimo and Zabala have forcefully argued, framed thought's conduciveness to politically conservative projects and its allergy to the sort of anarchic, ground-shaking events that constitute being. Hermeneutic thought, in contrast, is characterized by an open attunement to the event of being, which it accomplished by consistently remaining attentive to the very framing functions that work to establish reality as pristine, pre-existing experience, and unproblematic at core.

Frames, of course, are material objects. The strange English translation of Heidegger's term *Gestell* in "The Question Concerning Technology" is *enframing*. As that translation runs, "Enframing means the gathering together of the setting-upon that sets upon man, i.e. challenges him forth, to reveal the actual, in the mode of ordering, as standing-reserve."[3] The *Gestell*, in other words, gathers together that which sets upon us and calls us forth and figures it as inert substance to be deployed by us. It turns the event-like nature of being into the quiescent discovery of reality. But *Gestell*, far from an obscure abstract philosophical concept, refers to material, physical things. *Gestelle* are real structures that hold things up. A bookshelf ordering and sustaining the collected knowledge in my living room is a *Gestell*. Likewise the wooden beams and studs under the plaster in the walls and ceilings of my house are its *Gestell*.

Heidegger's point is not that we ought to avoid structuring, but that we need to remain attuned to how we always structure, and avoid believing that this structured reality exists in that way independent of that structuring. Borges has a beautiful phrase that illustrates exactly the same point. In the epilogue to his story "Tlön, Uqbar, Orbis Tertius," Borges writes that reality is giving away before the fictional world of Tlön, and explains the catastrophe thus:

> Ten years ago whatever symmetry with the appearance of order—dialectic materialism, anti-Semitism, Nazism—was enough to bewitch men. How not to submit to Tlön, to the minute and vast evidence of an ordered world? It is useless to reply that reality is also ordered. Perhaps it is, but in accordance with divine laws—I translate: inhuman laws—that we will never perceive. Tlön may be a labyrinth, but it is a labyrinth woven by men, a labyrinth destined to be deciphered by men.
>
> The contact with and habits of Tlön have disintegrated this world. Enchanted by its rigor, humanity forgets and forgets again that it is a rigor of chess masters, not of angels.[4]

Borges' point in this cautionary tale is precisely how framing involves a fundamental forgetting of its own agency. The world is discovered already structured by the media through which we come to know it, but this discovery is accompanied by our forgetting the active role we had in structuring that reality. The dangers in such forgetting are rampant (and Borges' list of political consequences should remind us of the irony that insightful formulations of philosophical truths are not sufficient in themselves to ensure a life lived free of such bewitchment.)

Whereas in the technology essay Heidegger establishes the *Gestell* as a fundamental mode of *Technê* since the ancient Greeks, in "The Age of the World Picture" he focuses on a more specifically modern variation of the *Gestell*. Since more or less the seventeenth century, Heidegger argues, man

(European intellectual history) has adopted a mode of gathering being into a standing reserve that he calls the world as picture.[5] A picture also has a *Gestell*, which is its frame; and indeed, the frame has a crucial function in the world picture. The frame separates out the world from a subject viewing the world, and at the same time allows the subject to see himself as a potential object in that world as pictured. Thus the world as picture enables a particular kind of subjectivity, one in which Dasein pictures the world as an object lying in wait, and himself as exactly such an object moving among other objects. Dasein has an objective existence, can compare himself to other beings as objects, be valued as an object, and is calculable as an object.

This projection of Dasein into the picture requires a splitting into two beings: one outside the frame and one inside; and subsequently a forgetting: the conditions represented for the being inside the frame are assumed to be those of the being outside the framework. This division is immortalized in modern philosophy by Descartes' distinction between thinking things and extended things. But it is in Lacan's pithy characterization of the libidinal dimension of split subjectivity that we can best grasp the tendency to erase this distinction, when he describes the *ego cogito* as desperately trying to step into the always receding-shoes of the *ego sum*.[6]

But if we take seriously the notion that our being-in-the-world is structured by fundamental, material mediations, then we must ask why such a framing function, and precisely one with such a form, emerged at the moment when its essence is so clearly recorded in the history of philosophy. In *How the World Became a Stage*[7] one of us argued that the reason for the ascendency of this specific form of framing (which we call theatricality) was the extraordinary success and proliferation of a new mediatic form since the middle of the sixteenth century: the stage. Dramatic performances prior to the sixteenth century had, as with all such performances, relied on human bodies as media for the relation of stories and ideas; they had also used spaces such as town squares with so-called mansions constructed for the purposes of portraying allegorical places in the play. In Corpus Christi plays these could also be mobile, moving on carts through a town such that the embodied scenes of the passion could be viewed serially. But these media differed profoundly from the modern stage.

Although it was influenced by the reconstruction of classical theaters at the end of the fifteenth century, the stage did not need to be a permanent structure, as in the proscenium stages built in England or the detailed recreations of cityscapes or mythical settings that abounded in the monarchic courts of seventeenth century Europe. It could just as well be a plank of boards laid over some barrels with a curtain that could be drawn open or closed; or the spaces between city buildings that became the famous *corrales* of Madrid. What was essential is that the border of the plank or the line drawn by the curtain separates two ontologically distinct places: that of the audience and that of the diagetic space of the play. Furthermore, from the moment of its inception that diagetic space was capable of representing the space outside the bordering line, *including the space of the stage itself*, and hence including the very separation that engendered it. The represented space thus becomes viable as a habitat for a subject's own avatars, the objective representatives of Dasein that function to enable the specific form of mass "subjectifications" (*assujetissements*) that Foucault noted as a defining aspect of political modernity.[8]

Modernity's basic mode of framing, then, is the stage. The form of this medium quickly infiltrated every aspect of western experience: aesthetics (theater per se, but also painting and literature); philosophy (epistemology); and politics (the organization of states as agglomerations of symbolic representations of individuals). But it also helped structure what was perhaps the single most defining event of modernity: the encounter between Europeans and the new world.

As countless scholars have documented in great depth, European explorers faced enormous epistemological challenges when faced with the utter novelty of the American continent.[9] Lacking the language to categorize the geography, fauna, and flora of the new world, they necessarily resorted to models, stories, and metaphors from their own cultural repertoire and subsequently imposed these on the peoples they conquered as well. "Not in vain but with much cause and reason is this called the New World," wrote Vasco de Quiroga in 1535, "not because it is newly founded, but because it is in its people and in almost everything as were the first and golden ages."[10] This imposition naturally took the form of the emerging dominant medium, such that Europeans came to view the new world as another version of their own; the political structures they saw there as (flawed) variants of their own; the native inhabitants as lesser versions of themselves, needing their input and aid for improvement; and the very event of the encounter in the terms of colonization and conquest established by their own epic tradition. The entire conquest, in other words, played itself out on the stage of the European imagination.

By a century after the first contact that image of the new world had become a fixture in European culture, while relations with the continent continued to shape economic and political realities. As the period and confluences of styles known in cultural history as the Baroque rose to prominence in Europe, the American colonies both imported and adopted this movement into their own cultural sphere, and left their own imprint on the baroque mentality in Europe. As we will try to show in what follows, the framing function specific to early modern mentalities would work to produce one particular variant of baroque culture emphasizing and enabling greater centralization and control on the part of the nascent nation states and colonial powers. Simultaneously, hermeneutic possibilities emerged that would relativize and undermine the centralizing discourse of framed baroque culture. The event of the encounter, with all its disruptive possibilities, was a primary target for the baroque framing function; but that event would also fuel the hermeneutic questioning of the baroque frame.

Baroque aesthetics refers to a set of stylistic markers in the plastic, performing, and literary arts, including, but not limited, to *mise en abîme*, *trompe l'oeil, anamorphosis, coincidentia oppositorum*, hyperbole, heightened ornamentation, and in general, distortion or deformation. In a broader sense, the historical Baroque in Europe was characterized by a problem of thought[11] whereby the world is conceived of as a veil of appearances covering another reality that always recedes from accessibility. Given this basic problem of thought, the aesthetic tropes previously indicated are deployed as strategies for representing, engaging with, or attempting to circumvent the aporia attendant on that problem: namely, that as all knowledge of the world must pass through the senses, any reality thus attained could end up having the status of mere appearance.

As should now be clear, this problem of thought is an exact correlate of the framing function that emerges from a culture whose fundamental media are theatrical in form. The model is that of a spectator confronted with a theatrical spectacle. Given the representation facing the spectator, the question may arise whether what is being represented is true, but not whether something is being perceived as represented. This is the exact logical distinction deployed by Descartes in his *Meditations* between what can be doubted and what cannot be doubted, between corrigibility and incorrigibility, which in turn undergirds the distinction between extended and thinking substance. As Descartes reasoned, if I see a chimera, I may rightly doubt that what I am seeing is a chimera, but I cannot doubt that I am seeing something I take to be a chimera.[12]

Framed thought in the mode of theatricality tends toward a specific strategy of representation in baroque culture, that we are calling the major strategy. According to this strategy all appearances are epiphenomenal in regard to an ultimate reality that is for the present deferred. This strategy can and did in large part support a political theological project whereby current economic conditions and social status were equated with mere theatrical roles to be played during an ephemeral performance called life. Beyond that stage, of course, an eternal playwright-director awaits to judge how well we have played our roles.[13] Subjects are taught to expect disappointment (*desengaño*, meaning also disillusionment) in this world of appearances, but to hope for an ultimate *desengaño* or unveiling at the time of judgment. In the meantime they learn to conduct themselves according to the conventions of the play, from which they can be called at any time.

Unlike framed baroque thought, its hermeneutic counterpart, *the baroque minor strategy*, refuses to stake the world of appearances on an ultimate truth. Instead, it constantly reveals how the promised redemption is itself an effect of mediation. Rather than treat appearances as less than reality, the minor strategy inhabits appearances and shows them to be the stuff of reality. For the minor strategy, every reality is the interpretation of appearances, and the desire to forestall that process by reference to an ultimate reality is a cooptation of power whose agency the minor strategy seeks to reveal.

The previously discussed interlude by Cervantes, *The Stage of Wonders*, is an ideal example of the hermeneutic, minor strategy of the Baroque. The major, theatrical culture demanded of commoners in early modern Spain that they naturalize inequalities in status in exchange for a deferred but ultimate reality. In this case, Cervantes dramatizes the expected subservience of commoners to the King's soldiers. Such commoners clung fiercely to their identity as *cristianos viejos*, old Christians who had no blood impurities and hence could claim, despite their poverty, to be honorable. Actual conditions like poverty and their political subservience to nobles were figured in the framed baroque culture as mere appearances in contrast to the ultimate reality of their unblemished honor. In Cervantes' minor version, that ultimate reality is revealed to be the construct of the major strategy's framing function, and the villagers' honor is as imaginary as the soldiers' power is real.

The event of the encounter with the new world was readily converted into templates comfortable to European, framed thought, and the "guided culture" of baroque mass spectacle found a new home in the new world.[14] Nevertheless, the possibilities of hermeneutic critique enabled by the Baroque's minor strategies made room for the event-like nature of the encounter to resonate as well, shaking as it did the certainties of the framed culture. From the histories of chroniclers like the Bolivian Antonio de la Calancha to the sophisticated theological arguments of Sor Juana Inés de la Cruz to the synchretistic incorporation of indigenous figures into the baroque portals of the Cathedral of Potosí, new world baroque culture often produced a form of thought, literature, and art that distorted and undermined those of the framed major culture.

This is the primary reason for the coining in the mid-twentieth century by Latin American intellectuals of the term *neobaroque*. The term was probably first used by the Brazilian writer and concrete poet Haroldo de Campos, but it was later developed and given theoretical substance by the Cuban poet Severo Sarduy. The Argentine critic Ángel Guido was probably the first to articulate the Latin American baroque as a kind of response or resistance to the European baroque, an argument that resonated for generations of Latin American writers, including especially the Cuban baroque triumvirate of José

Lezama Lima, Alejo Carpentier, and Severo Sarduy, albeit each with markedly different arguments. Throughout all of this theoretical revision of baroque aesthetics, however, was an understanding of the Neobaroque as a kind of attempt at counter-conquest.[15] In the words of Mabel Moraña, "the logic of baroque disruption," which would appear to be an ahistorical marker, must be understood "with respect to the discourses that accompanied the entrance of Latin America into the successive instances of globalized modernity." This implies what she refers to as the "constitutive paradox of baroque aesthetics," namely, that it refers both to the imperial imposition of continental norms and forms of control and to the potential construction of "differentiated cultural identities."[16]

Santiago Zabala deploys an interpretation of a key term from Heidegger that he developed in his book, the *Remains of Being*: *Verwindung*. The point of Heidegger's emphasis on philosophy's need to *verwinden* (surpass) as opposed to *überwinden* (overcome) metaphysics is that philosophy's calling is not to clarify being but to generate it. As Zabala writes,

> this generation requires transformative thought that does not overcome (*überwinden*) metaphysics, but rather surpasses (*verwinden*) it. If metaphysics could be overcome entirely, there would not be a change of paradigms, as Kuhn pointed out, or a better understanding, as Schleiermacher demands, but rather a single paradigm with its unique knowledge. Although hermeneutic ontology facilitates the generation of Being by transgressing existing orders, such Being will always be at large, loose, and unpredictable as event.[17]

In Zabala's terminology, then, the *overcoming* of metaphysics that Heidegger ultimately warns against would be akin to positing the sort of ultimate reality that was deployed by the framed thought of the baroque major strategy. Being would here be replaced by an implacable reality, inured against the disruption of events and existential encounters by an illusion of a stability whose real function is to support exiting power structures. Surpassing or *verwinden*, on the other hand, implies, like the minor strategy, a refusal to posit an "other" side to metaphysics that would be its end, precisely because such a positing would reinstate the ultimate metaphysical trope.

It is of interest in this context to focus a bit more on Heidegger's term, *verwinden*. For while surpassing is perfectly acceptable and makes some sense, we would contend that one of its more colloquial meanings is even more apropos in the current context. That meaning is *to warp, deflect, or distort*. Like the baroque minor strategy, Heidegger's suggestion is that thought strive not for a final answer that would put to rest the errors of previous epochs, but rather that it linger with those errors and illusions, distorting their surfaces enough to reveal how the promised redemption of an interpretation-free existence is itself the ultimate play of mirrors. And this, indeed, is what baroque and neobaroque aesthetic works at their very best can do: distorting the world of appearances so as to remind us that there can be no greater illusion than that of a world free of appearances and interpretation.

22

The Architecture of Mourning

Braving flowing summer crowds to glimpse the endlessly flowing water at the center of the 9/11 Memorial Museum in the footprint of the former World Trade towers in New York City, we can share moments of stillness and awe, straining to imagine if not to see where the waters flow to, and placing our fingers in a few of the bottomless cutouts of the 2,983 names inscribed on the fountains' rims.

The Memorial is mesmerizing and beautiful; it is also unsettling, and not only for the reasons listed by Adam Gopnik in a thoughtful critique published in the *New Yorker*:

> The site contains more contradictions, unresolved and perhaps unresolvable, than any other eight acres in Manhattan. A celebration of liberty tightly policed; a cemetery that cowers in the shadow of commerce; an insistence that we are here to remember and an ambition to let us tell you what to recall; the boast that we have completely started over and the promise that we will never forget—visitors experience these things with a free-floating sense of unease.[1]

This cascade of contradictory impressions, Gopnik implies, themselves all flow from a primary source: the ill-suited nature of the Memorial itself for memorializing.

> Although officially described as "reflecting pools," they are not pools, and they leave no room for reflection. Wildly out of scale with the rest of the site in their immensity, they are subterranean waterfalls—two huge sinks spilling chlorinated water from their edges, which then flows up and over a smaller platform at their center, and down the drain, only to rise and be

recycled. Their constant roar interrupts any elegiac feeling that the list of engraved names of the dead which enclose them might engender.[2]

Indeed, the recourse to a massively mechanical installation—one of the architects admitted that the pumps might only last "thirty to forty years"— seems to belie the eternalizing premise that underlies the very idea of a memorial. But what if the source of these apparent contradictions is not the Memorial's flawed design, but our own contradictory and conflicted relation to the task of mourning? If this is the case, Michael Arad and Peter Walker's design could turn out to be disarmingly prescient, a unique insight into a struggle our age and culture has with time, memory, and loss.

What do we do when we mourn? The French psychoanalyst Jacques Lacan ventured an answer by turning to a literary patient, Hamlet, whose indelible influence on our culture stems, he claimed, from his inability to mourn. In his discussion of Hamlet and Laertes' conflict at Ophelia's grave he writes, "[t]he one unbearable dimension of possible human experience is not the experience of one's own death, which no one has, but the experience of the death of another."[3] Lacan describes the effect of this loss as the opening of "a hole in the real," and he locates in our rituals of mourning a community's attempt to repair that hole by, in essence, filling it up with words.

Still, he insists, "there is nothing of significance that can fill that hole in the real ... For it is the system of signifiers in their totality which is impeached by the least instance of mourning."[4] The least instance of mourning undermines the entirety of language. When faced with profound loss, words fail. Entirely. And yet, the work of mourning, despite its epic and foregone inadequacy, is not only undertaken by all cultures and communities, it is necessary. In its absence, madness blooms.

In mourning we fill with words, with meaning, a hole in the real. Yet the 9/11 Memorial inverts this formula. In the most literal sense it fills words, the names of the dead in this case, with voids—turning the litany of inscriptions so canonized by Maya Lin's Wall into hollow stencils, themselves echoing the roaring holes in the real that they silently border. Everything is inside out: instead of fixity paying tribute to a sacred list of names, fixed names frame and open out onto incessant loss, movement, churning.

This inversion is powerful, not because it locates something entirely unique in the disaster of 9/11, but because that disaster and our subsequent attempts to mourn it reveal a profound reversal in our relationship to time and loss. At least since the rise of modern nation states in the sixteenth century, western culture has made a practice of commemorating communal disasters by inscribing them in stone. In this sense, the Holocaust Memorials that after a generation of effort and consciousness-raising have been built in most of Europe's capitals—and here we think immediately of Rachel Whiteread's massive, tomb-like Nameless Library of inverted books that addresses the statue of Lessing across Vienna's Judenplatz—continue a lineage born of the statues commemorating victims of the bubonic plague that rose like mushrooms across the ravaged face of Europe's decimated cities in the seventeenth and eighteenth centuries.

What plague statues, like Holocaust memorials, are meant to do is to eternalize in stone the memory of the departed, thereby attesting to a confidence that, while bodies and events pass, the spirit, essence, or truth of those who are gone remains. Stone becomes, then, the next best emblem of what permanence we can muster in a passing world. That stone would be used to represent both permanence and passing, the inanimate reminder of an animate being, found its ideal expression in the same period that saw an explosion of such public art, the period that produced the famously "tortured" style we know today as baroque. Indeed, it was this style in sculpture that inspired Lacan to say of its material, stone, "to the extent that we…erect it, and make of it something fixed, isn't there in architecture itself a kind of actualization of pain?"[5]

It is no coincidence that this style emerged during the first age of inflationary media—when the scope of media's representation of the world outgrows the confines of their culture's prior notions of reality. This first age saw the mass production of books, the proliferation of perspective in painting, and the emergence of an urban mass culture centered around public theater. The exponential increase in exposure to these media began to attune European publics to thinking of the copies they encountered in books, painted images, and on stages as referring to ghostly, unchanging things hovering behind those copies—Plato's heaven of forms adapted to the modern media age.

Today, though, in the throes of our second age of inflationary media, this formula has been subjected to a curious reversal. Today our culture has lost faith in the eternal things that our copies were supposed to refer to, and instead we have begun to invest our desire for eternity in the copies themselves. This is the phenomenon Walter Benjamin referred to when he wrote, in his influential essay "The Work of Art in the Age of Mechanical Reproduction," "the technique of reproduction detaches the reproduced object from the domain of tradition. By making many reproductions it substitutes a plurality of copies for a unique existence. And in permitting the reproduction to meet the beholder or listener in his own particular situation, it reactivates the object reproduced."[6]

As we have argued, in our current media age, what were once mere copies—books, performances, specific events in time—have been "reactivated," turned into the originals underlying an infinite reproducibility and, as such, have become imbued with the authority and presence of original things. Consequently, our monuments, once tasked with memorializing something ephemeral by connecting a traumatic moment in time with the eternal soul of the departed, are now tasked with eternalizing the ephemeral itself.

Hence our struggle, a contradiction to be found in all modern memorials and museums dedicated to historical catastrophes, but one we feel is brilliantly attested to by the 9/11 Memorial Museum: while an eternal spirit is something we can represent, a disaster, a horror, a profound loss is not. It has been said of criticism that the only way to respond to a work of passion is through another work of passion. Perhaps the same must be said today of our attempts at public mourning: that the only way to memorialize great loss is with a work of loss.

23

Occupy and Resist

As we open the lens beyond spaces officially designated for public mourning, commemoration, or celebration, we would argue that today the production of both public and private spaces, including the very distinction between these two types of spaces, is itself a function (perhaps the primordial function) of our medialogy. Referring to the artistic developments of the early modern period, Philippe Braunstain famously wrote that subjectivity is born when the individual can see himself in perspective.[1] We would modify the statement slightly to focus the lens on the modern processes of production of space. We would propose that subjects are born when they see themselves *in space*, as they develop a sense of belonging to certain spaces and experience a sense of estrangement from other spaces.

As we suggested earlier, in the current medialogy, the production and regulation of space are tied to the economic fundamentals of the market society, most specifically, the protection of private property and global commerce. Yet, packets of resistance can and do emerge, even at the heart of first-world metropolitan centers, often linked to counter cultural, anti-capitalist, anti-globalization stands such as those that define the "occupy" movements in cities like Amsterdam, Paris, Milan, Berlin, Madrid, or Barcelona. Let's take the example of Barcelona where, according to city-government estimates, there are as of this writing about 300 known occupied buildings, ranging from abandoned apartments and private homes to banks, offices, movie theaters, factories, and even official buildings. In exploring the vibrant "okupa" movement in the Catalonian capital, we are struck by the remarkable degree of community-oriented thinking that drives organized occupations and also by the support that some notorious "okupa" groups have received from their socially integrated neighbors.

While the term "okupas" is applied to groups of squatters with very different backgrounds and individual and collective goals, their highly sophisticated graffiti and other forms of messaging, including direct public statements, reveal that most organized occupiers conceive of themselves and their activism as a life-affirming form of communal resistance that takes place outside and against the objectifying logic of the market society. We can say that "okupas" see themselves as in a world that has been turned over to profit-making machines which have enslaved humanity, leaving nothing but devastation and death in their wake; and like the other defenders we are discussing, the substance of their defense lies in their refusal to accept the designation of an ultimate, immutable reality as projected by the current medialogy.

In its inception, the occupy movement in Barcelona (as in other European metropolis) was inspired by the historical success of the autonomous neighborhood of Copenhagen known as Freetown Christiania (Fristaden Christiania) built on a squatted military area first occupied in 1971. Although the city of Barcelona has been an urban landscape of choice for international groups of organized squatters at least since the 1980s, the "okupa collective" as it is often called in the press has clearly sharpened its anti-globalization messaging in the new millennium, to the point that much of the mainstream media has come to identify the origins of the occupy movement in Barcelona with the anti-globalization protests of the early 2000s.

Today, while the okupa collective is anything but homogeneous, organized groups of occupiers cohere around anti-globalization themes in their denunciation of economic imperialism, corporate greed, and real estate speculation. Against the officially sanctioned and protected right of individual ownership and against the institutional high-jacking of the public sphere that have resulted in the proliferation of privately controlled spaces and spectacular (often carefully sanitized) public non-places, occupiers vindicate their and our right to the communal use of space. As one of the leading voices of the okupa movement in Barcelona said it: "[The occupy movement] is a singular form of political and public denunciation carried out by means of non-institutional action consisting of occupations of spaces as dwelling quarters and places for farming and social work."[2]

With their public art and their civic activism, occupiers hope to promote and pave the way for alternative lifestyles with a sustained focus on community, rather than the individual. As another member of the movement states, "The goal of an occupied house should be to offer the neighborhood opportunities for cultural and social activities that are not provided by public and private institutions....One of the messages we transmit is that the future does not have to be about the individual; that community association is the key to changing the world, and it does not have to depend on political parties."[3]

This kind of direct activism through occupation and communal utilization of abandoned spaces is often accompanied by elaborate forms of messaging aimed at transforming the skin of the city, so to speak. As another spokesman of the movement observed in a 2006 interview quoted in a mainstream Spanish newspaper, "The transformation of the city, conceived as a giant showcase, is at the root of the growing occupy movement."[4]

Occupiers see the need to transform the face of the city as part of a collective quest to "liberate" urban spaces from the economic and institutional powers that control the processes of production and utilization of space. And of course the notion of liberated space is symbiotically linked to the quest for communal liberation from enslaving economic and political powers.

A wonderful example of this drive to transform the epidermis of the city and to provide social services for the community is an occupied building of Calle Urgell known as La Carbonera. The rich imagery that covers the façade of the building, including broken chains and a hot air balloon that's just taking flight, is a compelling expression of the utopia of communal liberation that drives the occupy movement. Having been occupied for nearly two decades this emblematic building of the okupa movement in Barcelona is known for its vibrant community life. Over the years, this self-managed social center hosted all kinds of activities, from cooking competitions to art and theater classes and sewing workshops. The building also served as food and clothing recycling center. When the occupiers of La Carbonera were evicted in February of 2014, their neighbors came out in mass to protest the legal action and to denounce the activities of Barclays bank, the owner company that had pressed for the eviction, known in the local circles as Barclays Butcher for its extensive repossession program in Barcelona. News reports mention several protests, with one of them totaling about 1,500 participants who essentially collapsed much of the center of Barcelona for hours. The vice-president of the neighborhood association of Sant Antoni came out in support of the occupiers citing their impeccable respect for the norms of civic coexistence and their long-standing contribution to the communal life of the neighborhood.

The occupied complex known as Can Masdéu is another paradigmatic example of civic activism and community service. The occupation of Masdéu goes back to 2001 when a group of ecological activists took over the abandoned area. While the authorities attempted to evict the group three months after the original occupation, the okupas refused to leave and, with the decisive support of their neighbors, ended up negotiating an agreement with the Hospital de San Pau, the legal owner of the premises. At present, Masdéu serves as home for 27 people devoted to ecological farming. They share their farmland with their "integrated" neighbors and are known for facilitating community services and organizing activities such as yoga workshops and neighborhood dinners. As in the case of La Carbonera, Masdéu also functions as a clothing recycling center for the community.

The building known as Banc Expropiat, an abandoned bank in the neighborhood of Gracia, is another occupied space that has been serving as a center of social and cultural activities for years. The center has offered free language classes, art and culture workshops, and fitness classes, among other community services. But the oldest and most notorious occupation of Barcelona is the complex known among the locals as Kasa de la Muntanya, located in the outskirts of the famous park Güell designed by Antoni Gaudí. Kasa de la Muntanya has been occupied for over 25 years, despite a temporarily successful eviction that took place in 2001. The elaborate graffiti that convers the building is visible to the scores of local visitors and tourists who walk the grounds of the park Güell, including the exhortation that serves as okupa manifesto, which is accompanied by the anarchist symbol: OKUPA Y RESISTE. Above and below the roofline on which these words are displayed in giant characters, we can read two additional messages, this time in English: WE KNOW YOUR CAPITALIST PARADISE; WE LOOK FOR THE HELL OF FREEDOM.

Against the imposture of freedom that is "your capitalist paradise," with its sterilized non-places and its heavy editing of reality, the "we" of the okupa collective vindicates an un-sanitized version of freedom that we could indeed associate with the messiness of *being*. Given the location of the building and the choice of language, it seems clear that the target audience of the occupiers of Kasa de la Muntanya are the tourist crowds that file ceaselessly through park Güell. Indeed, in their notorious protests, the okupas of Barcelona have turned the accusation of terrorism, which is sometimes leveled against them, back against not only multinational corporations and the local and State institutions that protect their interests, but also against the legions of tourists for whose benefit the city has been transformed into a collection of plastinated "venues" and commoditized spaces; the very simulacrum of "capitalist paradise" that's evoked on the talking walls of Kasa de la Muntanya. VOSOTROS, TURISTAS, SOIS LOS TERRORISTAS (YOU, TOURISTS, ARE THE TERRORISTS) has become a common chant in anti-eviction protests.

Figure 23.1 Photograph by authors.

24

Empire of Solitude

As we conclude the writing of this book, the 2016 presidential primary season is in full bloom. One attribute of this year's contest that has not gone unnoticed by the press is the apparent insouciance with which the candidates, primarily the Republicans but at times Hillary Clinton as well, have gone about embellishing their records, denying the embellishment when confronted, and outright fabricating nonsensical facts, all without seeming to suffer any consequences when their lies are called out by the mainstream press. As Michael Barbaro wrote in the *Times*, "Today, it seems, truth is in the eyes of the beholder—and any assertion can be elevated and amplified if yelled loudly enough."[1]

How are we to understand this apparent growing disregard for reality, the ubiquitous presence in politics of an attitude or practice denoted so memorably by Stephen Colbert as "truthiness," in Webster's definition "the quality of preferring concepts or facts one wishes to be true, rather than concepts of facts known to be true"? Is this perhaps the result of the dismaying rise of cultural relativism, born in the twentieth century and now coming home to roost? Such was Dick Meyer's conclusion in a commentary he wrote in 2006 on the occasion of Merriam-Webster declaring Colbert's coinage the Word of the Year. Truthiness, Meyer writes, "is perfect for the times in every way. It is a fake word invented by a fake person, Stephen Colbert, the comedian whose character, Stephen Colbert, parodies cable news talk shows on his own cable show, 'The Colbert Report'." Truthiness, Meyer goes on to claim, "is the definitive cultural and comedic acknowledgement of moral relativism."[2]

If we take a second look, though, we should see right away that Republican presidential candidates are no more moral relativists than are the true believers of the Christian Right that they pander to. While they may be opportunists in their cooptation of certain political positions, those positions constitute the polar opposite of relativism. Truthiness has become such a convincing descriptor in early twenty-first century political life not because of a widespread realization that one's beliefs are culturally and historically determined, but because of a sharp increase in both the proportion of people who believe that their beliefs are direct expressions of reality, and the intensity with which they hold and defend those beliefs. Truthiness, in other words, is not an effect of the rise of relativism; it is an effect of the proliferation of fundamentalism. And fundamentalism is a symptom of today's medialogy.

As we have rehearsed throughout this book, the first age of inflationary media was formed by the new media's reproduction of things projecting ideal and ineffable versions of those things, which in turn generated a new concept of reality as independent of any given person's take on it but simultaneously beyond the grasp of any given person. In the history of philosophy, Immanuel Kant perhaps most fully realized this position in his transcendental idealism: humans could not know the world as it is in itself, but we could know there is one, and must be guided by regulative ideas and an understanding of the limitations of our knowledge to come to the right conclusions about the world and how we should act in it.

Naturally, it was always in the purview of thought leaders to encourage those conclusions through culture, philosophy, or the establishment of laws; but the basic model, the medialogy, included at its core a shared common reality. In the centuries leading up to Kant, states began to forge from specific shared symbols and practices (a royal seal, a common religious affiliation) the ineffable ideal of a national substance or identity. This idea of a national identity coincides with a national wealth or value, a thing at its core, that money and citizens are somehow copies of. This is the essential abstraction that enabled Rousseau's notion of la *volonté générale*, the sum of a citizenry's will, as the ultimate legitimacy of sovereignty.

Relativism, for its part, was always a potential byproduct of idealism. Hume's impressionism represented a kind of relativism to Kant, shocking enough to stir him from his self-described dogmatic slumber. Fichte radicalized that position out of Kantian thought, and Hegel brought it full circle to create the position of a subject founded on the knowledge of his own historical situatedness. But unlike relativism, what we now call fundamentalism is a symptom of the second age of inflationary media and its medialogy.

In the second age, starting gradually in the late nineteenth century but then accelerating exponentially with the arrival and broad adoption of digital media, the materiality of prior medial forms begins to absorb the aura, to use Benjamin's term, of the new media's projection of reality. In other words, while initially functioning in a similar way by framing content and projecting a concept of reality beyond the screen of the frame and excluding content at the margins, the new medialogy is already once removed from the reality concept implied by the first medialogy. Its prima facie content is now the level of the material media that preceded it: books, bodies, images, and identities are injected with the aura of the real and endowed with a special authenticity. Objects that had become copies of an ineffable real emerge as things in themselves with no further regression required. They are already real and hence require no transcendent reference to ground them. This reification of what had been relegated to the status of copies is the basis for an unconscious fundamentalism that spreads to all walks of life.

In such a medialogical context, the state as the copy of national substance loses that anchoring in the real and becomes a groundless thing, a hollow shell that dissolves into diverse ethnic and religious identifications. Individuals cease to experience themselves as partial perspectives of a shared common ground, and instead start to conceive of themselves as the direct expressions of a particular identity that becomes all important. In the conditions of the new medialogy, the individual is an unanchored island of solitude connecting via the media to others he or she conceives of as conjoined members of a community with unfettered access to the truth. And as these fellow travelers are always apparently in the minority, others are demonized as at best deluded, at worst, agents of a sinister plot.

But in truth, neoliberalism, the economic model of the new medialogy, profits from this state of affairs. The medialogy's concept of reality, where erstwhile copies are now things, promotes an endless war of unanchored identities; the notion of the commons abandoned, a new commons develops, not "underlying" those identities but "above" them, unseen, siphoning off profits at unprecedented levels on a global scale. Terrorist fundamentalists strengthen rightwing isolationists, who demonize immigrants and hence further reify national, ethnic, and religious difference. Governments aren't weakened, though; rather, the constant threat of an irrational other strengthens "democratic" regimes that are little else than symbolic cover for oligarchies whose purpose is the creation and maintenance of rules leading to greater syphoning power.

Stability becomes the failsafe: Greek debt is not forgiven, but neither does Greece exit the Eurozone; instead, a stable path of maximum extraction is maintained. Whether they are Eurocrats in Brussels or legislators taking their cues from business executives in the United States, the formal show of democracy veils decision-making that is incestuously orchestrated to extract maximum profits while maintaining stability. As Karthik Ramanna writes in the *Times*,

> On any specific rule-making issue, there are usually a handful of business executives—often fewer than 50—who are truly experts on the subject. They also have the greatest stakes in the outcome. They meet with regulators in genteel isolation, obligingly offering direction for regulation. The rules of the game that emerge reflect their interests.... Those who might oppose them are sometimes not even aware of the regulatory proceedings. What arises in aggregate is a system of rules that looks as if it was produced by a quilt of special interests. Society as a whole bears the costs of this subtle subversion of capitalism.[3]

The default tendency toward stability on the part of the states creates a structure that exacerbates the economy of extraction, efficiently passing profits up the pyramid while pushing losses down. Currency trading markets, so large as to surpass in value the gross national product of the world's major economies combined,[4] produce fluctuations in the value of national currencies that national banks must react to by decreasing or increasing the money supply, hence inflating or devaluing their currencies:

> The banker bureaucrats then judge their performance not on how much money they won or lost but on how well they fulfilled the policy goal. If they lose money, the loss is blamed on the market, not on them. The taxpayers,

knowing or not, must pay the bill; it is part of the price of government. In this way the government subsidizes currency trading and speculation. Without government intervention, there would be painfully little profit in such endeavors. The more government banks struggle to control the currency market, the more money can be made in currency speculation since the government is virtually always trying to move against the market.[5]

High-frequency trading has created another venue by which those with the greatest access extract the greatest profits. As computers get faster and faster, automatically programmed buy-and-sell orders have become so finely tuned that the distance traveled by electronic signals, once considered to be essentially irrelevant given that such signals travel near the speed of light, has become a factor in competition between trading firms. Now real estate in lower Manhattan or across the river in New Jersey can translate to great advantages and increased profits for the companies that can afford it.

This picture is, again, reminiscent of the "reality" revealed in the movie *The Matrix* when the virtual reality program that humanity is plugged into is disrupted: thousands of isolated minds each plugged into its own screen, all feeding a system none of them is aware of. And make no mistake about it: the system of global capital benefits from humanity not realizing its common ground or its common plight. In this sense, sociopolitical phenomena like the rise of right wing, xenophobic parties, and candidates in the United States and Europe; the apparently ubiquitous threat of terror attacks, often committed by home-grown extremists; or the dramatic rise in school shootings in the United States since the nineties are not disparate cases, examples of a world devolving into chaos. Rather, they are tightly interconnected pieces of a machine that is functioning with great precision, even as it multiplies death and destruction.

Think about a terror organization like the inaptly named Islamic State—inapt because it has neither the attributes normally associated with a state nor is its organizing principle Islam in any theologically recognizable form. In fact, what ISIS most resembles is an online community dedicated to a particularly noxious perversion—like those frequented by the so-called cannibal cop who fantasized online about killing and eating women—the difference being that its members take the next step and carry out the grim fantasies they encourage in one another. This phenomenon, whereby group dynamics permit the overriding of borders determined by norms of social acceptability, was first theorized by the Stanford psychologist Mark Granovetter in the 1970s, as he tried to explain why otherwise law-abiding citizens would, in the context of a riot, commit acts of violence that they would individually find appalling under normal circumstances. What he argued was that the "thresholds" separating members of the group from such actions could be collectively lowered by the proximity of these members to others whose own thresholds were respectively lower. In other words, a few agitators with extremely low violence thresholds could influence a next layer, who in turn would influence a larger group with far higher thresholds, etc. But whereas the phenomena Granovetter was describing were localized, what we can now see is the same process liberated by the possibilities of virtual space.

This is what, as Malcom Gladwell argues in a recent piece in the *New Yorker*, explains the dramatic increase in school shootings since the nineties, and in particular since the tragedy at Columbine High School in Colorado in 1999. News of the massacre of thirteen fellow students by duster-sporting outsiders Eric Harris and Dylan Klebold was interspersed at the time with television ads for an innovative martial arts film starring a duster-sporting Keanu Reeves as a kung fu wielding member of a cyber-revolutionary group intent on freeing humanity from the all-encompassing virtual reality program that has it in their grips. Who could have foreseen the irony that these two figures would become internet legends themselves, inspiring dozens of isolated young men over the next two decades to lower the thresholds keeping them from enacting their revenge fantasies, convincing them that their own psychic reality was the true, the revealed, the one?

Indeed, this is what we're missing when we point out the racist discrepancy involved in denoting any violence perpetrated by Muslims as terrorism while refusing to use the same term for the shootings committed by non-Muslim white males, despite their often explicitly racist and misogynist reasoning in the manifestos they leave behind. Yes, these are essentially the same as the acts of terror committed by ISIS, but not merely because of the hate that inspires them. They are structurally congruous acts because they are symptoms of a medialogy in which disparate islands of solitude meet in a virtual space to commiserate and share their fantasies, thereby lowering the threshold to enacting these fantasies and hence creating a new reality. What Gladwell writes of the two-decade long epidemic of school shootings is equally true of the growth of ISIS and al-Qaeda before it: they are like "slow-motion, ever-evolving"[6] riots unfolding over years instead of hours, and over the whole globe instead of a few city blocks.

This theory also helps us solve the puzzle of why radicalization fails to track accurately with socio-economic oppression. Many of the young men who kill and blow themselves up come from well-established middle class families. Their allegiance to radical groups is similar to the adherence of the other, isolated non-Muslim white men to the cult of the black duster. They believe it is about history, religion, and culture, but it is not; it is about an entirely constructed identity whose online proponents proffer it as a solution to all their pain.

This is not to say that there aren't real social and cultural factors underlying the fragmentation of groups according to ethnic and religious identity. France's failure to offer equal opportunity for the full economic integration of its citizens is absolutely central to the sense of exclusion, of being strangers in their own nation, that so many young men of African and Near Eastern decent growing up in the *banlieue* feel. As George Packer reports, "*Banlieue* residents joke that going into Paris requires a visa and a vaccination card."[7] And this is true of young people who are French, born in France, and speak only French. But again, it is vital to note that the alienation of the *banlieue* is not founded on a positive, historical identity. As Andrew Hussey has put it, "The kids in the *banlieues* live in this perpetual present of weed, girls, gangsters, Islam .... They have no sense of history, no sense of where they come from in North Africa, other than localized bits of Arabic that they don't understand, bits of Islam that don't make sense."[8]

The *banlieue* as a brewer of extremism is a test case of the new medialogy. Categories such as class, nation, religion, or ethnicity have all migrated from the position of copies referring to ineffable substances, and are now self-sustaining, self-referential identities floating free of any history other than fragmentation and alienation. This is the ground of fundamentalism. Not a return to the substantial reality of the past, but the frantic desires of an unmoored present. Fundamentalism is fragmentation.

But what is true of the new medialogy's production of terrorism in all its forms is also true of its more gentrified version, the nativism of right wing politics in the United States and Europe. As some commentators, in particular Evan Osnos and Thomas Edsall, have noted, Donald Trump's popularity in the race for the 2016 Republican presidential nomination was primarily an effect of his nationalism, a position that mirrors and follows on the growth of formerly fringe parties of the European anti-immigrant right such as the *Front National* in France. As Edsall writes, citing Ivo Daalder, the president of the Chicago Council on Global Affairs, "Just as the 'disaffected, lower educated/ working-class native folks' in Europe 'are fueling the rise of the Front National, UKIP and other parties,' similar constituencies are drawn to the Trump campaign in the United States." Daalder continues: "These are the folks who have lost out, at least in their perception, to globalization and immigration— they feel threatened by cheaper labor abroad and migrants at home."[9] And the irony is that they *have* lost out to globalization; but by focusing their animus on immigrants seeking to better their own lives, working class followers of right wing politics in fact work to strengthen the forces of globalization by reinforcing support of "centrist" governments on the part of those who are most disturbed by extremist messaging.

The logic of this political manipulation dates to the first inflationary age, when the media of the time generated and propagated the myth of the seducer in order to buttress and inflate an illusory value, that of honor, the effect of which was to increase adherence to the Spanish state and elites by those who benefitted the least from its policies. Now, and in an analogous way, fear of outsiders buttresses and inflates another illusory value, the "real" of Sarah Palin's famous "real America," that sense of who "we" white, Christian, U.S. or European citizens are, in the face of the threatening influx of other kinds of people. Indeed, this logic goes even further, in that faced with the internal threat of extremist politics, potentially critical forces align to support the lesser of two evils, such as when left-leaning Democrats in the United States forego supporting a socialist candidate like Bernie Sanders in favor of an electable Wall Street confidant like Hillary Clinton. Finally, it is also a logic of distraction. Just as Barack Obama was resoundingly criticized by Republicans for citing climate change rather than terrorism as the real threat to humanity (which, of course, it is), rank-and-file citizens can more comfortably focus on the visible threat of a militant other than on the invisible but far more ubiquitous damage our way of life is inflicting on the planet as a whole.

This is why we agree with Slavoj Žižek when he wrote, in the aftermath of the Paris attacks of November 2015, "The greatest victims of the Paris terror attacks will be refugees themselves, and the true winners, behind the platitudes in the style of *je suis Paris,* will be simply the partisans of total war on both sides. This is how we should *really* condemn the Paris killings: not just to engage in shows of anti-terrorist solidarity but to insist on the simple *cui bono* [sic] (for whose benefit?) question."[10] But does it solve the problem to ask *qui bono* when our very notion of reality and the desires it supports remain unchanged? Do we not run into the very problem so eloquently analyzed by Žižek himself when he points out that the structure of ideology today is such that awareness is not enough, that we know very well what we are doing but we do it anyway? Does not the current medialogy demand a different response, one that Žižek himself theorized in his very first book, when he argued that the effective step required not merely seeing through the illusion but also realizing how one's desire itself is implicated in that illusion?

Indeed, articulating and arguing for a position can seem fruitless, since today's medialogy is able to package any such position, no matter how urgent, into yet another portable reality, complete with its own interest group, marketing, and product line. It does not escape us that in order for these very lines we are now writing to have any potential impact we will depend on exactly the same mechanisms provided by the very medialogy we are attempting to elucidate. That said, what is certainly not enough is to double down on truth, as if the ills of today's medialogy were an effect of relativism instead of its opposite, fundamentalism. And if the fundamentalists (at least of the Christian variety) have a mantra, WWJD, what would Jesus do? (although we suspect that whatever the historical Jesus would do, it would have very little similarity to what today's fundamentalists think he would do), we prefer to replace that with a mantra of our own: WWCD, or what would Cervantes do?

The reason we see Cervantes as a model of what we call the defenders of being is that he had a privileged vantage on the medialogy created by the first inflationary age. From that vantage he developed a special insight into how the media frame not only what we see, but what we want to see. And his response was not to deny that reality, not to stake a different claim to truth, but to depict himself, his contemporaries, us, in the act of being formed by that medialogy. By showing us not a different version of the world but how the world can produce so many versions of itself, Cervantes created a form of cultural production, which we now call fiction, which has the power to attune minds to actively *reading reality* as opposed to passively receiving it. While the reality created by Cervantes' medialogy was different, as we have tried to show in the course of this book, his fundamental strategy is still sound, and it is one shared by other defenders of being.

Defenders of being are not better people; they are not prophets whom we should follow blindly. Indeed, some of them have made atrocious choices in their own lives and should not serve as models for anyone. No, defenders of being are simply those whose creations, in whatever media they use, have the capacity to attune us to the ways in which the medialogy produces our sense of reality and generates our desires. They are writers and thinkers and artists whose work causes us to see outside the frame, and inspires us to imagine other ways of thinking, being, and desiring.

Only a short time after Cervantes, the German mathematician and philosopher Gottfried Leibniz wrote,

> If someone looks attentively at more pictures of plants and animals than another person, and at more diagrams of machines and descriptions and depictions of houses and fortresses, and if he reads more imaginative novels and listens to more strange stories, then he can be said to have more knowledge than the other, even if there is not a word of truth in all that he has seen and heard.[11]

We continue to believe that Leibniz's words hold a special wisdom. Literature, art, and philosophy have the capacity to teach us to think differently, precisely and especially when they are not captive to a strictly representationalist or objectivist logic. Hence our almost obnoxiously simple yet totally urgent prescription: more humanities!

Reading literature and viewing art and thinking and writing about these experiences is the vital and indispensable foundation for any possible liberation from today's medialogy and the self-destructive traps of desire it engenders. This is not a reductively idealistic prescription, too far removed from the real dangers that threaten us. We know that we are destroying the environment, but we continue to do nothing. Encouraging narrow, technologically, and instrumentally oriented education is clearly not solving the problem, and is most likely contributing to it. Global fragmentation continues to rise, and our responses make the situation worse. Current educational practices are clearly doing nothing to solve these problems either; yet, in less time than it takes the oceans to rise a meter, an entire generation could be introduced to the humanities and the practices of interpretation that characterize them. A new generation of people more likely to be reflective, more likely to see how their own desires and actions impact the world, could arise.

We know we are preaching to the choir, but the choir needs to become more strident. The choir needs to stop being embarrassed about its interests and methods, stand up proudly, and insist that there is no such thing as an adequate education, at any level, that does not include humanistic inquiry. The humanities are not a luxury, not just a shiny patina to make our bleak lives prettier; they are vital to our very survival as a species. Without them we will continue on our present course, each with his own reality in hand, self-contained fiefdoms in an empire of solitude, doomed, like in the prophetic closing words of García Márquez's great novel, "because races condemned to one hundred years of solitude did not have a second opportunity on earth."[12]

Epilogue

Our medialogy's framing of the *world as resource* is itself anchored in the mechanistic view of the universe that emerged in the 1500s and 1600s in natural philosophy and new science circles. As Carolyn Merchant has noted, the reduction of the cosmos to mere "mechanism" allows for a reading of the world as inert, passive matter, subject to immutable mathematical laws. This explains why new scientists such as Bacon and Glanvill conceived of their own scientific activity as a dissection of nature aimed at rendering visible the springs of its motion in the service of man. While this objectifying view of the world and the version of instrumental reason that goes with it were by no means uncontested in the 1600s and beyond,[1] they quickly became *fundamentals* within the emerging discourse of capitalism. Today, we are witnessing a radicalization of this worldview in the direction of individual possession. It's no longer a matter of the world being read or dissected as humanity's resource. Instead, our medialogy promises the world to you personally, neatly wrapped in an individualized version of reality: Your World, Your Resource, Your Reality!

The familiar discourse of the tourist industry provides endless illustrations of this notion. A long-running theme in commercials associated with the Virgin Islands, for example, makes use of the traditional song *this land is your land, this land is my land … this land was made for you and me*. While the familiar lyrics may seem harmless enough, in the context of a commercial directed to potential tourists, the *you* in "your land" names the tourist visitor while the *I* in "my land" has to be thought of not as the actual people who inhabit the land, but rather in terms of the framing presence of the tourist industry that has converted it into a commoditized resource. This is, in essence, the act of dispossession, which—as we mentioned earlier—the okupas of Barcelona and their sympathizers routinely protest in most explicit terms when they take to the streets to chant: "Vosotros turistas, sois los terroristas."

As we focus our attention on the frame (as Cervantes and Velázquez taught us to do), we can see that it is not just the land that's being commoditized (turned into a series of plastinated *venues*), but the people who are themselves part of the attraction as *authentic natives*, and also the tourists as *consumers*, as the whole world is converted into an endless stream of spectacle-resources for the benefit of global corporations.

Daniel Cooper Alarcón has studied the production of Mexicanness as part of the conversion of Mexico into a tourist resource in *The Aztec Palimpsest. Mexico in the Modern Imagination*. He perceptively concludes that "the greatest tourist construct of all time is the concept of authenticity,"[2] which is the ultimate sign of the *Disneyfication* of the land (he specifically refers to the EPCOT effect in his discussion of the theme park Mexico Mágico and other tourist attractions); or as Guy Debord would put it, the "banalization" of the world, its conversion into timeless spectacle. As Debord writes in *Society of the Spectacle*: "Tourism— human circulation packaged for consumption, a by-product of the circulation of commodities—is the opportunity to go and see what has been banalized. The economic organization of travel to different places already guarantees their *equivalence*. The modernization that has eliminated the time involved in travel has simultaneously eliminated any real space from it."[3]

Indeed, the commercial discourse of the tourist industry encapsulates the view of the world that defines our current medialogy: an endless stream of spectacle-resources. As Debord states: "In societies dominated by modern conditions of production, life is presented as an immense accumulation of spectacles. Everything that was directly lived has receded into a representation . . . . The spectacle is a concrete inversion of life, an autonomous movement of the non-living . . . . The spectacle is not a collection of images; it is a social relation between people that is mediated by images."[4] Debord seems to evoke here the zombie masses that populate our apocalyptic fantasies while drawing a sharp distinction between what is or was "directly lived" and the "representation" into which lived experience would have receded in the society of the spectacle.

Throughout our book, we have looked at this distinction from a different perspective, a baroque perspective. As baroque writers and artists often remind us, the borders between reality and its representations are difficult to draw except in the most abstract of terms. In *Don Quixote*, for example, the very distinction between reality and appearance is "exposed" as an effect of the representation, which is why the focus is on different modes of representation (different literary and artistic genres and, generally speaking, different types of discourse) and their framing of reality. We also talked about Velázquez's treatment of frames and framing techniques in picture-puzzles that invite mental oscillation. In following their lead one more time, we would like to close our discussion with an invitation to engage in just this kind of baroque *game of frames* as we examine a couple of examples of paradigmatically neo-baroque representations from our medialogical context in connection or in conversation with their imagistic referents in the historical baroque. Our comparative commentary is meant to offer a "grounded," "embodied," or "situated" (and thus thoroughly Cervantine) response to the question that drives Richard Sherwin's discussion of the need for visual literacy (for us, reality literacy) in the age of the digital baroque: "Who and what do we become when we live on the screen, when we internalize the screen's optical code as our own?"[5]

The first example is from the notoriously controversial artwork of Damien Hirst, who is known for his animal exhibits featuring butterfly art (made with real butterflies) and aesthetically arranged dissections such as the 1993 Turner Prize Winner, an installation consisting of bisected cows preserved in a formaldehyde solution.

The description of this installation in the *Guardian Unlimited* is a dramatic illustration of our treatment of nature as raw matter or mere resource exploitable for profit: "Damien Hirst, Mother and Child, Divided, 1993 Steel, GRP, composites, glass, silicon sealants, cow, calf, formaldehyde solution; dimensions variable © the artist."[6] Yet the composition on which we would like to focus here is *For the Love of God*, a molding made from an eighteenth-century skull, encrusted with nearly 9,000 diamonds, which was reportedly sold for a hundred million dollars. The ironic overtones of the work's title become exceedingly evident when we hear Hirst explain his vision for the project: "I just want to celebrate life by saying to Hell with death .... What better way of saying that than by taking the ultimate symbol of death, and covering it in the ultimate symbol of luxury, desire and decadence? [This] will be the ultimate two fingers up to death."[7] In his declaration of intentions concerning his yet unfinished sculpture, Hirst invited us to consume his art piece as a celebration of life predicated on a reversal of the cultural tradition that saw in human skulls reminders or symbols of death.

Within the baroque tradition that we associate with the *major strategy*, the skull was of course meant to turn spectators away from the pursuit of wealth and other potentially deadly deceptions, which would have distracted them from the search for true life, as in the well-known series of vanitas painted by Juan de Valdés Leal.

By contrast, Hirst places the diamonds as symbols of luxury, desire, and decadence on the side of life. As one of us has argued in a different context, "Hirst's obscenely expensive skull is no longer the placeholder of the spiritual

Figure E.1 Valdés Leal, *Finis Gloriae Mundi*, 1672, courtesy of Wikimedia Commons.

truth of the cosmos or the stain in the picture that reveals our true face hidden behind layers of worldly deceptions. Rather, it is…a tribute to the commodification of life and death in our culture industry, a celebratory totem of the illusion manufactured by the economic and political forces of global capitalism—the cynical promise of a universal triumph of wealth and luxury over suffering and death."[8]

The second example operates a similar postmodern or neo-baroque reversal on the baroque *minor strategy* brilliantly exemplified in Velázquez's *Las meninas*.

Figure E.2 Velázquez, *Las meninas*, 1656, courtesy of Wikimedia Commons.

In its "tribute" to Velázquez's iconic painting, the department store giant El Corte Inglés made it a point to replicate as many aspects of the original artwork as possible. Yet, as we examine these images side by side, we can see a few differences. For starters, El Corte Inglés has no use for dwarfs. This is clearly an element of the original that just doesn't translate to the commercial context of the "updated" version. The same can apparently be said about members of the clergy, as the nun and the priest of the original are replaced with secular figures in the version of El Corte Inglés. The back of the canvas that appears in the original as a partially visible object is gone, replaced in the new version with the partial image of a photographer's umbrella, which makes sense in the new context in which the painter himself is replaced by a photographer.

But this is where things get truly interesting. As we take stock of the presence of the painter in the original and compare it with the photographer in the pastiche, it becomes clear that this is not just a matter of a practitioner of one craft versus another. Something has been lost in translation: ownership itself. The ownership that was firmly located in the towering image of the painter (this is my world-view, enter at your own risk/gain!) is nowhere to be found in the figure of his replicant. Indeed, in the original, the artist appears thoroughly immersed in the intellectual act of painting; he is studying us as he reloads. The photographer, on the other hand, is not shown in the act of photographing. With his body slightly turned to the right and the objective of the camera pointed way from us, he looks like one more clothing model holding the camera as a prop. There's no sense of creative activity emanating from him or the camera that he is awkwardly holding, and therefore no sense of ownership of the discursive situation. So if the photographer is not it, who is the owner of this worldview, we might ask? As it turns out, in his own painting, Diego de Velázquez provided the key to unlocking the mystery of the lost ownership: the frame! And of course what we find there in the pastiche is corporate messaging in English and Spanish, *welcome where the fashion is art, your best shopping,* and the corporate logo itself: *El Corte Inglés.*

El Corte Inglés's version of *Las meninas* alienates the artist from his own creation by erasing his authorial presence, and this erasure affects the spectator as well. If in Velázquez's original painting the spectator was invited and challenged to participate in the artistic game and asked to reflect on the porous borders between reality and its representations and the meaning-producing effects of framing techniques, the new spectator of the advertising pastiche of El Corte Inglés is re-constructed as mere resource. In this context, the phrase "welcome to where the fashion is art" must be interpreted as its actual opposite: "welcome to where art is fashion"; that is, where art is swallowed up by the fashion industry, re-constructed as a resource, like the rest of the world with you in it, and turned into $.

Isn't this precisely what Hirst's exhibitions literally do? Isn't his notorious one-hundred-million-dollar art piece *For the Love of God* the infinitely reproducible dead-nature that keeps on giving? You can buy a 3D print of Hirst's diamond encrusted skull for $12,000 and keep on celebrating life the way it is meant to be celebrated as defined by our medialogy.[9] Indeed, Hirst's skull has the right to be unlimited and so do you, at least for as long as your wallet holds.

Against these familiar forms of commodification of nature, life, art, and even education (as we discussed in Chapter 12), our proposal is to reclaim the visionary legacy of the *minor* baroque in order to promote *reality literacy*, for, without the ability to read reality and see the frames that bind us, we are copper tops in the Matrix, prey for those hundred dollar bills that swallow us up with our family and friends in the Direct TV commercial. So to ask Sherwin's question one more time: "Who and what do we become when we live on the screen, when we internalize the screen's optical code as our own?" We become props on the stage of wonders, crowds of consumer-spectators, and infinitely reproducible embodiments of the corporate logo: zombie masses.

Notes

Introduction

1   Regis Debray used the term "médiologie," translated into English as "mediology," to refer to the function of *medium* in the transmission of culture. As he writes: "Transmitting meanings in culture, to come back to the outline of a knowable subject, still seems at this time to be a theme whose implications have not yet been explored and pinned down. It floats alongside, or outside, the routines of several disciplines of study that by now benefit from well-honed arguments and premises, such as sociology, the history of thought, genetics, and epidemiology. When it comes to the mediological question of *how meanings are materially transmitted*, however, these disparate fields show no congruence of focus. My intention is to contribute to finding a firm and proprietary foundation for a mediology, to make it an object of thought [...] It meant asking that an original sector of research be identified and dedicated to the facts of cultural transmission as an object of study in its own right" (*Transmitting Culture*, vii–viii). While we are also concerned with the material dimension of the medium, our focus is not how culture is transmitted per se, but the ways in which media frame and thus determine a given conception of reality. Specifically, we examine and compare the medialogy of the present with that of the early modern period, epochs that we have identified as ages defined by inflationary media.

2   Egginton, *World, passim.*

3   Shields, *passim.*

4   Benjamin, "Work," *passim.*

5   Pariser, *passim.*

6   Sherwin, 11.

7   Ibid., 171.

Chapter 1

1 Suskind, http://www.nytimes.com/2004/10/17/magazine/faith-certainty-and
   -the-presidency-of-george-w-bush.html
2 See Egginton, *Theater, passim.*
3 Gállego, 54.
4 *Lazarillo*, prologue, our translation.
5 Sherwin, 15.
6 Ibid.
7 Ibid.
8 Vattimo and Zabala, 28.
9 Quoted in Colbert, 12.
10 Ibid., 13.
11 Ibid.
12 Borges, *Obras* I, 439, our translation.

Chapter 2

1 Vesely, 110.
2 See Castillo and Egginton, "The Perspectival Imagination."
3 Radice, 41; Orgel and Strong, 63–64.
4 As Panofsky explains, Dürer insisted on the limits of theoretical rules in humans'
   attempts to represent "the infinite complexity of God's creation." He felt that
   human theory was "sorely limited, not only by the inequality of individual gifts
   and tastes, but also by the finiteness of human reason as such: 'For, the lie is
   inherent in our very cognition'" (Panofsky, *Life and Art*, 12).
5 See John North's book *The Ambassadors' Secret* for a fascinating history of the
   painting and its almost inexhaustible meanings.
6 For a history of the technique as well as relations to literary wit, see Gilman,
   The Curious Perspective, 16–49; Castillo and Egginton, "The Perspectival
   Imagination"; Castillo, *A(Wry) Views*, 1–3.
7 See Panofsky for an authoritative history of perspective.
8 Foucault, 4.
9 Ibid., 48–49.

10   Ibid., 4.
11   Ibid., 64.
12   Heidegger, *The Question*, 131.
13   Foucault, 48.
14   Ibid.

Chapter 3

1   Carr, *passim*.
2   Cervantes, *Retablo*, 222, our translation.
3   Ibid.
4   Ibid.
5   Ibid.

Chapter 4

1   The article was originally published in Florida by the *Orlando Sentinel* and reproduced in the science page of the *Buffalo News* on October 21, 2007.
2   Van Wert, 206.
3   Baudrillard's concept of the *simulacrum* is perhaps best captured in the following quote: "Today abstraction is no longer that of the map, the double, the mirror, or the concept. Simulation is no longer that of a territory, a referential being, or a substance. It is a generation by models of a real without origin or reality: a hyperreal. The territory no longer precedes the map, nor does it survive it. It is nevertheless the map that precedes the territory—precession of simulacra— that engenders the territory ....It is no longer a question of imitation, nor duplication, nor even parody. It is a question of substituting the signs of the real for the real, that is to say of an operation of deterring every real process via its operational double, a programmatic, metastable, perfectly descriptive machine that offers all the signs of the real and short-circuits all its vicissitudes" (*Simulacra and Simulation*, 1–2).
4   Baudrillard, *Simulacra and Simulations*, 12–13.
5   Quoted from Disney World website, since changed.
6   Disneyworld exemplifies Marc Augé's notion of *non-place*: "If a place can be defined as relational, historical and concerned with identity, then a space that

cannot be defined as relational, or historical, or concerned with identity will be a non-place ... [S]upermodernity produces non-places, meaning spaces which are not themselves anthropological places and which ... do not integrate the earlier places: instead these are listed, classified, promoted to the status of 'places of memory', and assigned to a circumscribed and specific position" (*Non-Places: Introduction to an Anthropology of Supermodernity*, 77–78).

7   Van Wert, 203–204.

8   The expression comes from Manuel Aguirre's *The Closed Space: Horror Literature and Western Symbolism* (1990). Aguirre theorizes modernity as a Western drive to realize the entropic dreams of reason in the perfectly secured citadel: *the closed space*.

9   Baudrillard, *Simulacra*, 12.

10   Debord, 6.

11   Ibid., 9–10.

12   Gracián, *Criticón* I, 8.

13   See the Introduction by Nicholas Spadaccini and Jenaro Talens to the collection *Rhetoric and Politics. Baltasar Gracian and the New World Order* (1997).
     The following quote is illustrative of the type of questions that have recently emerged around the work of Baltasar Gracián and its (post)modern reception: "A few years ago, when Gracián's *The Art of Worldly Wisdom* appeared on one of the best-seller lists of the New York Times, we speculated on the possible reasons for its success. Even if for two active Hispanists, as we are, this success could be read as a symptom of the healthy state of Spanish Golden Age literature and culture, it seemed a little odd to find the Spanish Jesuit's name among other 'mass-cultured' authors. Out of such situation there arose a number of questions, including the following obvious ones: What does a seventeenth-century Jesuit thinker mean to a postmodern reader here and now, at the end of the millennium? Do his writings have any value, outside of their pure historical and/or archeological interest?" (xii).

14   Debord, 13–16.

Chapter 5

1   He didn't say the line during the campaign. The quotation is originally from his 2008 book, *Think Big: Make It Happen in Business and Life*. We quote it from the website http://www.politico.com/magazine/story/2015/08/the-absolute -trumpest-121328#.Vc4RDRw4JfM (accessed June 2, 2016).

2   http://www.nbcnews.com/tech/innovation/campaign-launched-against-harmful
    -sex-robots-n427751 (accessed June 2, 2016).

3   True Companion website, http://www.truecompanion.com/home.html (accessed
    June 2, 2016).

4   Weatherford, 75.

5   Ibid., 107.

6   Ibid., 180.

7   Ibid., 201.

8   http://www.cnn.com/2015/11/16/opinions/waldman-paris-trump-iowa-voters
    /index.html (accessed June 2, 2016).

Chapter 6

1   Interview aired on March 7, 2013. http://www.cc.com/video-clips/uldxcb/the
    -colbert-report-john-sexton

2   Von Hagens, "Anatomy and Plastination," 36.

3   For a definitive study, see Adler and Adler, *The Tender Cut, passim.*

4   Egginton used the term in this blog post: http://arcade.stanford.edu/blogs
    /character-fundamentalism (accessed June 2, 2016).

5   Cervantes, *Entremeses.* Ed. Nicholas Spadaccini, 154–155.

6   Jennifer Rubin, *Washington Post,* http://www.washingtonpost.com/blogs
    /right-turn/post/gop-should-not-fall-into-the-trap-of-being-proudly
    -ignorant/2011/03/29/gIQA1glFSK_blog.html (accessed June 2, 2016).

Chapter 7

1   Nebrija, *Gramática de la lengua castellana,* http://www.filos.unam.mx
    /LICENCIATURA/Pagina_FyF_2004/introduccion/Gramatica_Nebrija.pdf
    (accessed January 1, 2015).

2   Cervantes, *DQ* II, 65.

3   José María Aznar, "Seven Theses on Today's Terrorism," http://www3
    .georgetown.edu/president/aznar/inauguraladdress.html (accessed June 2, 2016).

4   Lozano, 52.

5 Parsley, quoted in *Mother Jones*, http://www.motherjones.com/politics/2008/05 /mccains-pastor-problem-video (accessed June 2, 2016).

6 George W. Bush, 2003 State of the Union Address, http://whitehouse .georgewbush.org/news/2003/012803-SOTU.asp (accessed June 2, 2016).

7 Colbert, 13–14.

8 Ibid., 12.

Chapter 8

1 Hume, 166.

2 Ibid., 117.

3 Ibid.

4 Ibid., 84.

5 Gracián, *El héroe*, 12.

Chapter 9

1 Goodrich, "Visiocracy," 508.

2 As Goodrich puts it, "The blindness of justice is emblematic .... The simple point is that the eye of the spirit, the interior eye, has precedence over the exterior ...." Goodrich, *Legal Emblems and the Art of Law*, 16.

3 Yankah, "The Truth About Trayvon."

4 Shelton, "The 'CSI Effect': Does It Really Exist?" http://www.nij.gov/journals/259 /pages/csi-effect.aspx (accessed June 2, 2016).

5 Ibid.

6 Kevin Jon Heller, "The Cognitive Psychology of Circumstantial Evidence," *Michigan Law Review*, 106 (2006): 241–306, 245–246

7 Goodrich, *Legal Emblems and the Art of Law*, xvii.

8 Goodrich, "Visiocracy," 499.

9 Ibid., 508.

10 Nelson, 24.

11 Richard Kagan, *Lawsuits and Litigants*, 31; quoted in Byrne, 49.

12 Quoted in Byrne, 49.

Chapter 10

1   Cálderon de la Barca, *El alcalde de Zalamea*, I, 857.
2   Nelson, 149.
3   Cull, 620. Quoted in Nelson 149.
4   For a fuller discussion, see Egginton, *How the World Became a Stage.*
5   Nelson, 149.
6   Calderón de la Barca, *El alcalde de Zalamea*, III, 937–938. Quoted in Nelson, 153.
7   Lope de Vega, *Fuenteovejuna*, v, 736–739.
8   See Alexander Samson and Jonathan Thacker's discussion in their chapter "Three Canonical Plays," 122.
9   Dixon, 159.
10 Derrida, 256.
11 Goodrich, "Visiocracy," 516.
12 Davis, 9.
13 Heller, 1.
14 Sherwin, 23.

Chapter 11

1   Maravall, *Teatro y literatura*, 117.
2   Yi-Fu Tuan, 133. Much of the discussion in this chapter was originally published as David Castillo, "Monumental Landscapes in the Society of the Spectacle: From Fuenteovejuna to New York," in Castillo and Nelson eds., *Spectacle and Topophilia.*
3   Barthes, *Mythologies*, cite.
4   Schama, 61.
5   Rainey, 69.
6   American Airlines website, http://hub.aa.com/en/nr/pressrelease/huge-mural -at-american-airlines-jfk-terminal-blends-global-skylines-making-the-world -smaller
7   Lorca, 113.

Chapter 12

1   Lewis, cite. (http://utotherescue.blogspot.com/2014/02/beyond-program
    -closings-more.html).

2   Sandel, 10–11.

3   Bakan, 2.

4   Chomsky, https://www.jacobinmag.com/2014/03/the-death-of-american
    -universities/

5   Eagleton, "The Slow Death of the University." http://chronicle.com/article/The
    -Slow-Death-of-the/228991/

6   Rawlings, https://www.washingtonpost.com/posteverything/wp/2015/06/09
    /college-is-not-a-commodity-stop-treating-it-like-one/

7   Fear, http://futureu.education/uncategorized/neoliberalism-comes-to-higher
    -education/

8   See Corey Robin's article in *Salon*: http://www.salon.com/2015/08/29/higher
    _educations_real_censors_what_were_missing_in_the_debate_over_trigger
    _warnings_and_coddled_students/

Chapter 13

1   Evgeny Morozov. "The Perils of Perfection." *The New York Times. Sunday Review.*
    March 2, 2013. http://www.nytimes.com/2013/03/03/opinion/sunday/the-perils
    -of-perfection.html?_r=0

2   Gelder, 161.

3   Lovecraft, 346.

4   See Castillo, *Baroque Horrors*, especially Chapter 1.

5   McCarthy, 130.

6   Ibid., 177.

7   Ibid., 222.

8   For more on Zayas's brand of domestic terror, see Chapter 3 of *Baroque Horrors*.

9   Marie-Hélene Huet, 87.

10 Quoted in Del Río Parra, 24.

11 Quoted in Daston and Park, 203.

12 Quoted in Del Río Parra, 24.

13 Castillo, *Baroque Horrors, passim.*

14 Benedict, 180.

Chapter 14

1 Gelder, 146.

2 http://www.rollingstone.com/politics/news/the-great-american-bubble
   -machine-20100405

3 *Dracula*, quoted by Arata, 166.

4 Arata provides further evidence of this suggested equivalence between
   Harker and Dracula in the following passage: "The text's insistence that these
   characters are capable of substituting for one another becomes most pressing
   when Dracula twice dons Harker's clothes to leave the Castle. Since on both
   occasions the Count's mission is to plunder the town, we are encouraged to
   see a correspondence between the vampire's actions and those of the travelling
   Westerner. The equivalence between these two sets of actions is underlined by
   the reaction of the town's people, who have no trouble believing that it really is
   Harker, the visiting Englishman, who is stealing their goods, their money, their
   children. The peasant woman's anguished cry—'Monster, give me my child!'
   (ibid., 60)—is directed at him, not Dracula" (170).

5 Ibid., 166.

6 Moretti, 149.

7 Grahame-Smith, 192.

8 Del Toro, 206–207.

9 Ibid., 86.

10 Ibid., 213.

11 Zayas, 287.

12 Castillo, *Baroque Horrors*, 118.

13 http://www.miamiherald.com/2012/06/04/v-fullstory/2832770/fear-anxiety
   -drive-zombie-craze.html

14 Ibid.

15 Ibid.

16 While the notion of the post-human can be traced back to different (and often conflicting) theorizations, such as those of Robert Pepperell (*The Posthuman Condition: Consciousness Beyond the Brain*) and Katherine Hayles (*How We Became Posthuman. Virtual Bodies in Cybernetics, Literature and Informatics*), this concept has been recently associated with the zombie phenomenon; see the multiauthored volume *Better Off Dead: The Evolution of the Zombie as Post-Human*, edited by Deborah Christie and Sarah Juliet Lauro.

17 As Slavoj Žižek writes in *The Ticklish Subject*: "The horizon of social imagination no longer allows us to entertain the idea of an eventual demise of capitalism [...] everybody tacitly accepts that capitalism is here to stay" (218). Incidentally, Žižek has also drawn the analogy between zombie and vampire fantasies and class antagonism. After an extended reading of Graham-Smith's novel, he writes, "One could venture the hypothesis that horror movies register the class difference in the guise of the difference between vampires and zombies. Vampires are well-manned, exquisite, and aristocratic, and they live among normal people, while zombies are clumsy, and attack from the outside, like a primitive revolt of the excluded." Žižek, *Trouble in Paradise*, 64.

18 Roth, 5.

Chapter 15

1   Conde, 296; our translation.

2   Ibid., 311.

3   Ibid., 241.

4   Ibid., 222.

5   González Pérez de Tormes, 167; our translation.

6   Ibid., 83.

7   Ibid., 192.

8   Ibid., 195.

9   See Castillo's discussion in Chapter 4 of *(A)Wry Views*.

10 González Pérez de Tormes, 307.

11 Ibid., 195; our translation.

12 Peisner, 55.

13 Luhmann, 67.

Chapter 16

1   Schmid, 95.
2   Ibid., 96.
3   Ibid., 97.
4   Ibid.
5   Reilly, 71–72.
6   Ford, *passim.*
7   Kant, 152.
8   Browning, 27.
9   Lacan, *Ecrits*, 671–702.

Chapter 17

1   Pinker, *passim.*
2   Kristof, http://www.nytimes.com/2015/10/01/opinion/nicholas-kristof-the-most-important-thing-and-its-almost-a-secret.html
3   Revelations, 17:3, http://biblehub.com/revelation/17-3.htm
4   Clark, *Thinking With Demons*, 326.
5   Klein, 2.
6   Should the provisions of the Paris Agreement produced by the 2015 United Nations Climate Change Conference Paris be ratified and adhered to, there is a chance that temperatures could be held to less than 2°C above preindustrial levels.
7   Ibid., 13.
8   Ibid., 15.
9   Ibid., 18.
10 Patterson, 268.
11 Ibid., 357.
12 Heidegger, *Question*, 325.
13 Galli, 19, our translation.
14 Ibid.

Chapter 18

1 Castillo, "Don Quixote and Political Satire: Cervantine Lessons from Sacha Baron Cohen and Stephen Colbert," 174–175.

Chapter 19

1 Plato, 1205.

2 Aristotle, 68–69.

3 Maureen Down, "Oscar for Best Fabrication," NYT, Feb 16, 2013, http://www.nytimes.com/2013/02/17/opinion/sunday/dowd-the-oscar-for-best-fabrication.html

4 Boccaccio, 60.

5 Wilde, 389.

6 Landy, 3.

7 Adam Liptak, "Chief Justice Samples Eminem in Online Threats Case," NYT Dec 1 2014, http://www.nytimes.com/2014/12/02/us/chief-justice-samples-eminem-in-online-threats-case.html

8 Close, 249.

9 See Farrell's discussion of Don Quixote's paranoia and its relation to the modern world. Farrell, esp. 36–37.

10 The theory is expounded in his *Frame Analysis*. It is also a crucial aspect of Costa Lima's theory of *fictionality*, which underlies much of the present argument.

Chapter 20

1 Suskind, http://www.nytimes.com/2004/10/17/magazine/faith-certainty-and-the-presidency-of-george-w-bush.html

2 Quoted from Stephen Colbert's appearance at the 2006 White House Correspondents' Dinner.

3 Quoted in Maslin Nir.

4 Close, *Romantic*, 249.

5 Ibid.

6 Russell, *Cervantes*, 105.

7 Borges, 450, our translation.

8 Althusser, 118.

Chapter 21

1   Vattimo and Zabala, *passim.*

2   Heidegger, *Sein und Zeit* 31.

3   Heidegger, *Question*, 325.

4   Borges, "Tlön, Uqbar, Orbis Tertius," *Obras Completas* I, 442–443, our translation.

5   Heidegger, "Die Zeit des Weltbildes," *passim.*

6   Lacan, *Ecrits*, 516.

7   Egginton, *How the World Became a Stage, passim.*

8   Foucault, *Surveiller et Punir, passim.*

9   For a selection of seminal writings on the subject, see Lois Parkinson Zamora and Monika Kaup, eds. *Baroque New Worlds.*

10 Quoted in Kadir, 14.

11 Egginton, *The Theater of Truth*, introduction.

12 Descartes, *Meditations*, 25–26.

13 The classic version is Pedro Calderón de la Barca's interlude *El gran teatro del mundo.*

14 Rama, *La ciudad letrada, passim.*

15 According to Parkinson Zamora, the Cuban theorists of the Neobaroque, Carpentier, Lezama Lima, and Sarduy, "came increasingly to understand the Baroque as a postcolonialist strategy, as an instrument of *contraconquista* (counterconquest), to use Lezama Lima's term, by means of which Latin American artists might define themselves *against* colonializing structures" Lois Parkinson Zamora, *The Inordinate Eye*, 120. Gonzalo Celerio takes this term from Lezama for the title to his book *Ensayo de contraconquista*, in which he declares the New World Baroque as a kind of counterconquest. *Ensayo de contraconquista*, 75.

16 Moraña, "Baroque/Neobaroque/Ultrabaroque: Disruptive Readings of Modernity," 241–282, 242.

17 Zabala, 81.

Chapter 22

1 Gopnik.
2 Ibid.
3 Lacan, Hamlet and Mourning, 37–38.
4 Ibid.
5 Lacan, The Ethics of Psychoanalysis, 60.
6 Benjamin, 231.

Chapter 23

1 Braunstein, 536.
2 https://7vagones.wordpress.com/2014/10/04/las-casas-ocupas-de-barcelona/
3 Ibid.
4 http://elpais.com/diario/2006/12/09/espana/1165618815_850215.html

Chapter 24

1 Michael Barbaro. "Candidates Stick to Script, If Not the Truth, in the 2016 Race." *The New York Times*, November 7, 2015. http://www.nytimes.com/2015/11/08/us/politics/candidates-stick-to-script-if-not-the-truth-in-2016-race.html?_r=0.
2 Dick Meyer, "The Truth of Truthiness," http://www.cbsnews.com/news/the-truth-of-truthiness/
3 Ramanna, "Ruling from the Shadows," *New York Times*, November 21, 2015: http://www.nytimes.com/2015/11/22/opinion/sunday/ruling-from-the-shadows.html?ref=opinion
4 Weatherford, 254.
5 Ibid., 262.
6 Gladwell, 35.

7   Packer, 63.

8   Quoted in ibid., 64.

9   Edsall, "Euro-Trump," *New York Times*, Nov. 18, 2015, http://www.nytimes
.com/2015/11/18/opinion/campaign-stops/euro-trump.html?action=click&pgty
pe=Homepage&clickSource=story-heading&module=opinion-c-col-left
-region&region=opinion-c-col-left-region&WT.nav=opinion-c-col-left-region

10   Žižek, http://inthesetimes.com/article/18605/breaking-the-taboos-in-the-wake
-of-paris-attacks-the-left-must-embrace-its

11   Leibniz, 355.

12   Gárcia Márquez, 383.

Epilogue

1   See Bono, "Perception, Living Matter," *passim*.

2   Cooper Alarcón, 174.

3   Debord, 94.

4   Ibid., 7.

5   Sherwin, 174.

6   "20 Years of Turner Prize-Winners," in *Guardian Unlimited Art Index*.

7   *The Observer*, May 21, 2006.

8   Castillo, *Baroque Horrors*, 122.

9   https://www.1stdibs.com/art/prints-works-on-paper/damien-hirst
-love-god-lenticular-3d/id-a_575962//?utm_medium=pla&utm
_source=google&utm_term=none&utm_content=personalized-ship/&gcli
d=Cj0KEQiA96CyBRDk5qOtp5vz8LkBEiQA6wx8MKNMrngE5CUPD
_AhjNmJunAvWB2WCAphRvSyKmMpsN4aAi1D8P8HAQ

Bibliography

Note on sources: we list here published works and films that we have cited in the text. Internet sources such as online newspapers are cited in the endnotes and do not appear in this list except in the case of online versions of established works.

Abraham Lincoln Vampire Hunter (2012). Dir. Timur Beckmambetov.

Abre los ojos (1997). Dir. Alejandro Amenábar.

Adams, John (ed.). *The Living Dead*. San Francisco: Night Shade Books, 2008. Print.

Adler, Patricia and Peter Alder. *The Tender Cut: Inside The Hidden World of Self-Injury*. New York University Press, 2011. Print.

Adorno, Theodor and Max Horkheimer. *Dialectic of the Enlightenment*. New York: Continuum, 1998. Print.

Aguirre, Manuel. *The Closed Space: Horror Literature and Western Symbolism*. Manchester: Manchester University Press, 1990. Print.

Alarcón, Daniel Cooper. *The Aztec Palimpsest. Mexico in the Modern Imagination*. Tucson: University of Arizona Press, 1997. Print.

Alemán, Mateo. *Guzmán de Alfarache*. Ed. Benito Brancaforte. 2 Vols. 2nd edn. Madrid: Cátedra, 1981. Print.

Alighieri, Dante. *The Divine Comedy*. Trans. Clive James. New York: Norton, 2013. Print.

Alighieri, Dante. *Vita Nova*. Trans. Andrew Frisardi. Evanston, IL: Northwestern University Press, 2012. Print.

Althusser, Louis. "Ideology and Ideological States Apparatuses (Notes towards an Investigation)." *Mapping Ideology*. Ed. Slavoj Žižek. London: Verso, 1994 100–140. Print.

Althusser, Louis. *Lenin and Philosophy and Other Essays*. Trans. Andy Blundin. New York: Monthly Review Press, 1971. Print.

Anonymous. *Lazarillo de Tormes*. Ed. Joseph Ricapito. 9th edn. Madrid: Cátedra, 1981. Print.

Arata, Stephen. "The Occidental Tourist: Dracula and the Anxiety of Reverse Colonization." *The Horror Reader*. Ed. Ken Gelder. New York: Routledge, 2000. 161–172. Print.

Argo (2012). Dir. Ben Affleck.

Aristotle. *Poetics*. Trans. Francis Fergusson. New York: Hill and Wang, 1961. Print.

Augé, Marc. *Non-Places: Introduction to an Anthropology of Supermodernity*. Trans. John Howe. London: Verso, 1995. Print.

Bakan, Joel. *The Corporation: The Pathological Pursuit of Profit and Power*. New York: Free Press, 2004. Print.

Barthes, Roland. *Mythologies*. Trans. Annette Lavers. New York: Hill and Wang, 1972. Print.

Baudrillard, Jean. *Simulacra and Simulation*. Trans. Sheila Faria Glaser. Ann Arbor: Michigan University Press, 1994. Print.

Benedict, Barbara. *A Cultural History of Early Modern Inquiry*. Chicago: University of Chicago Press, 2001. Print.

Benjamin, Walter. "The Work of Art in the Age of Mechanical Reproduction." *Illuminations*. Ed. Hannah Arend. Trans. Harry Zohn. New York: Schocken Books, 1969. Print.

Bishop, Kyle. *American Zombie Gothic: The Rise and Fall (and Rise) of the Walking Dead in Popular Culture*. Jefferson, NC: McFarland and Company, 2010. Print.

Boccaccio, Giovanni. *Boccaccio on Poetry; Being the Preface and the Fourteenth and Fifteenth Books of Boccaccio's* Genealogia Deorum Gentilium *in an English Version with Introductory Essay and* Commentary. Trans. Charles Grosvenor Osgood. New York: Liberal Arts Press, 1956. Print.

Bono, James. "Perception, Living Matter, Cognitive Systems, Immune Networks: A Whiteheadian Future for Science Studies." *Configurations* 13 (2005): 135–181. Print.

Borges, Jorge Luis. "Pierre Menard, autor del Quijote." *Obras Completas* I. Buenos Aires: Emecé, 1994a. Print.

Borges, Jorge Luis. "Tlön, Uqbar, Orbis Tertius." *Obras Completas* I. Buenos Aires: Emecé, 1994b. Print.

Borges, Jorge Luis. "The Aleph." *The Aleph and Other Stories*. New York: Penguin Classics, 2004. Print.

Braunstein, Philippe. "Toward Intimacy: The Fourteenth and Fifteenth Centuries." *A History of Private Life*. Vol. 2. Ed. Georges Duby. Cambridge: Belknap-Harvard University Press, 1988. 535–630. Print.

Brooks, Max. *World War Z. An Oral History of the Zombie War*. New York: Crown, 2006. Print.

Browning, John. "Survival Horrors, Survival Spaces: Tracing the Modern Zombie (Cine)Myth." *Zombie Talk: Culture, History, Politics*. Eds. David Castillo et al. New York: Palgrave Macmillan, 2016. 9–32. Print.

Buffy the Vampire Slayer. WB Television Network Series. Dir. Joss Whedon.

Byrne, Susan. *Law and History in Cervantes' Don Quixote*. Toronto: University of Toronto Press, 2013. Print.

Calderón de la Barca, Pedro. *El alcalde de Zalamea*. Ed. Valbuena Briones. Madrid: Cátedra, 1990. Print.

Calderón de la Barca, Pedro. *El gran teatro del mundo*. http://www.cervantesvirtual .com/obra/el-gran-teatro-del-mundo-0/ (accessed June 2, 2016).

Calderón de la Barca, Pedro. *La vida es sueño*. Ed. Ciríaco Morón. 20th edn. Madrid: Cátedra, 2004. Print.

Carr, Nicholas. *The Glass Cage: Automation and Us*. New York: Norton and Co, 2014. Print.

Castillo, David. *Baroque Horrors: Roots of the Fantastic in the Age of Curiosities*. Ann Arbor: The University of Michigan Press, 2010. Print.

Castillo, David. "Monumental Landscapes in the Society of the Spectacle: From Fuenteovejuna to New York." *Spectacle and Topophilia: Reading Early Modern and Postmodern Hispanic Cultures*. Eds. David Castillo and Bradley Nelson. Nashville: Vanderbilt University Press, 2012. 3–18. Print.

Castillo, David. "Baroques Landscapes: The Spectacle of America." *America Scapes: Americans in/and Their Diverse Sceneries*. Eds.Ewelina Banka, Mateusz Liwinski and Kamil Rusitowicz. Lublin: Wydawnictwo KUL, 2013. 227–240. Print.

Castillo, David. "Monsters for the Age of the Post-human." *Writing Monsters: Essays on Spanish and Latin American Literatures and Culture*. Eds. Adriana Gordillo and Nicholas Spadaccini. *Hispanic Issues On Line* (HIOL), 2013.

Castillo, David. "Don Quixote and Political Satire: Cervantine Lessons from Sacha Baron Cohen and Stephen Colbert." *Approaches to Teaching Cervantes's Don Quixote*. Eds. James Parr and Lisa Vollendorf. New York: Modern Language Association of America, 2015. 171–177

Castillo, David. *(A)Wry Views: Anamorphosis, Cervantes and the Early Picaresque*. West Lafayette, IN: Purdue University Press, 2001. Print.

Castillo, David and William Egginton. "The Perspectival Imagination and the Symbolization of Power." *Indiana Journal of Hispanic Literature* 8 (1996): 75–93. Print.

Castillo, Moisés. "Lope de Vega, inventor de América: *El Nuevo Mundo descubierto por Cristóbal Colón*." *Bulletin of the Comediantes* 54 (2002): 57–90. Print.

Celerio, Gonzalo. *Ensayo de contraconquista*. México: Tusquet, 2001. Print.

Cervantes, Miguel de. *Don Quixote de la Mancha*. 2 Vols. Ed. John J. Allen. Madrid: Cátedra, 1998. Print.

Cervantes, Miguel de. "El retablo de las maravillas." *Entremeses*. Ed. Nicholas Spadaccini. Madrid: Cátedra, 1982. Print.

Cervantes, Miguel de. "El retablo de las maravillas." http://miguelde.cervantes.com /pdf/El%20Retablo%20de%20las%20Maravillas.pdf (accessed June 2, 2016).

Cervantes, Miguel de. "La elección de los alcaldes de Daganzo." *Entremeses*. Ed. Nicholas Spadaccini. Madrid: Cátedra, 1982. Print.

Cervantes, Miguel de. *Los trabajos de Persiles y Sigismunda*. Ed. Carlos Romero Muñoz. Madrid: Cátedra, 1997. Print.

Cervantes, Miguel de. *Novelas ejemplares*. 2 Vols. Ed. Harry Sieber. Madrid: Cátedra, 1990. Print.

Choderlos de Laclos, Pierre. *Les Liaisons Dangereuses*. Paris: J. Rozez, 1869. Print.

Christie, Deborah and Sarah Juliet Lauro. *Better Off Dead: The Evolution of the Zombie as Post-Human*. New York: Fordham University Press, 2011. Print.

Clark, Stuart. *Thinking with Demons: The Idea of Witchcraft in Early Modern Europe*. Oxford: Oxford University Press, 1999. Print.

Close, Anthony. *The Romantic Approach to 'Don Quixote': A Critical History of the Romantic Tradition in 'Quixote' Criticism*. Cambridge: Cambridge University Press, 1978. Print.

Colbert, Stephen. *America Again: Re-Becoming the Greatness You Never Weren't*. New York: Grand Central Publishing, 2012. Print.

Collins, Suzanne. *The Hunger Games*. New York: Scholastic Inc., 2008. Print.

Conde, Víctor. *Naturaleza muerta*. Palma de Mallorca: Dolmen, 2009. Print.

Costa Lima, Luiz. *The Control of the Imaginary Reason and Imagination in Modern Times*. Minneapolis: University of Minnesota Press, 1988. Print.

Covarrubias, Sebastián de. *Emblemas morales*. Madrid: Juan de la Cuesta, 1610. Print.

Creed, Barbara. *The Monstrous-Feminine: Film, Feminism, Psychoanalysis*. New York: Routledge, 1993. Print.

CSI: Crime Scene Investigation. CBS TV Series.

Cull, John T. "Hablan poco y dicen mucho: The Function of Discovery Scenes in the Drama of Tirso de Molina." *Modern Language Review* 91 (1996): 619–634. Print.

Dangerous Liaisons (1988). Dir. Stephen Frears.

Daston, Lorraine and Katherine Park. *Wonders and the Order of Nature, 1150–1750*. New York: Zone Books, 1998. Print.

Davis, J. Madison., "He Do the Police in Different Voices: The Rise of the Police Procedural." *World Literature Today* 86 (2012): 9–11. Print

Dawn of the Dead (1978). Dir. George Romero.

Debord, Guy. *The Society of the Spectacle*. London: Rebel Press, 2005. Print.

Debray, Regis. *Transmitting Culture*. Trans. Eric Rauth. New York: Columbia University Press, 1997. Print.

Del Río Parra, Elena. *Una era de monstruos. Representaciones de lo deforme en el Siglo de Oro español*. Madrid: Iberoamericana, 2003. Print.

Del Toro, Guillermo and Chuck Hogan. *The Night Eternal*. New York: HaperCollins Publishing, 2011. Print.

Derrida, Jacques. *Acts of Religion*. London and New York: Routledge, 2001.

Descartes, René. *Meditations on First Philosophy*. 3rd edn. Trans. Donald A. Cress. Indianapolis and Cambridge: Hackett Publishing Co., 1993. Print.

Díez-Borque, José María. *El teatro en el siglo XVII*. Madrid: Taurus, 1988. Print.

Díez-Borque, José María. *Sociología de la comedia española del siglo XVII*. Madrid: Cátedra, 1976. Print.

Dixon, Victor. "'Su majestad habla, en fin, como quien tanto ha acertado': la conclusión ejemplar de *Fuente Ovejuna*." *Criticón* 42 (1988): 157–168. Print.

Egginton, William. "Crime Shows: CSI Hapsburg Spain." *Genealogies of Legal Vision*. Eds. Peter Goodrich and Valerie Hayaert. London: Routledge, 2015. 243–258. Print.

Egginton, William. *How the World Became a Stage*. Albany: SUNY Press, 2003. Print.

Egginton, William. "Staging the Event: The Theatrical Ground of Metaphysical Framing." *Being Shaken*. Eds. Michael Marder and Santiago Zabala. New York: Palgrave, 2014. 177–185. Print.

Egginton, William. *The Theater of Truth: The Ideology of (Neo)Baroque Aesthetics*. Palo Alto: Stanford University Press, 2010. Print.

Egginton, William and David Castillo. "The Rules of Chanfalla's Game." *Romance Languages Annual* 6 (1995): 444–449. Print.

Elizabeth (1998). Dir. Shekhar Kapur.

Ex Machina (2015). Dir. Alex Garland.

Fernández Gonzalo, Jorge. *Filosofía zombie*. Barcelona: Anagrama, 2011. Print.

Ford, Martin. *Rise of the Robots: Technology and the Threat of a Jobless Future*. New York: Basic Books, 2015. Print.

Forrest Gump (1994). Dir. Robert Zemeckis.

Foucault, Michel. *The Order of Things: An Archaeology of the Human Sciences*. New York: Pantheon Books, 1970. Print.

Foucault, Michel. *Surveiller et Punir*. Paris: Gallimard, 1975. Print.

Fuenteovejuna. Radiotelevisión Española (RTVE), 1972.

Gállego, Julián. *Visión y símbolos en la pintura española del siglo de oro*. Madrid: Cátedra, 1987. Print.

Galli, Giovanni. *Sostenibilità e potere*. Genova: Sagep, 2015. Print.

García Lorca, Federico. *Poeta en Nueva York*. México: Porrúa, 1986. Print.

García Márquez, Gabriel. *One Hundred Years of Solitude*. Trans. Gregory Rabassa. Harold Bloom's Modern Classics. Philadelphia: Chelsea, 2003.

Gelder, Ken. "Introduction to Part 5." *The Horror Reader*. Ed. Ken Gelder. New York: Routledge, 2000. 145–147. Print.

Gilman, Ernest. *The Curious Perspective. Literary and Pictorial Wit in the Seventeenth Century*. New Haven: Yale University Press, 1978. Print.

Giroux, Henry. "Neoliberalism, Corporate Culture, and the Promise of Higher Education: The University as a Democratic Public Sphere." *Harvard Education Review* 72 (2002). 425–464. Print.

Gladwell, Malcom. "The Thresholds of Violence: How School Shootings Catch On. *The New Yorker*, October 19, 2015. http://www.newyorker.com /magazine/2015/10/19/thresholds-of-violence

González, Házael. *La muerte negra. El triunfo de los no muertos*. Palma de Mallorca: Dolmen, 2010. Print.

González, Házael. *Quijote Z*. Palma de Mallorca: Dolmen, 2010. Print.

González Pérez de Tormes, Lázaro. *Lazarillo Z: Matar Zombies nunca fue pan comido*. Barcelona: Debolsillo, 2010. Print.

Goodrich, Peter. *Legal Emblems and the Art of Law*. Cambridge: Cambridge University press, 2014. Print.

Goodrich, Peter. "Visiocracy: On the Futures of the Fingerpost." *Critical Inquiry* 39 (2013): 498–531. Print.

Gopnik, Adam. "Stones and Bones: Visiting the 9/11 Memorial and Museum." *The New Yorker*, July 7, 2014. http://www.newyorker.com/magazine/2014/07/07/ stones-and-bones

Gracián, Baltasar. *El criticón*. Madrid: Aguilar, 1944a. Print.

Gracián, Baltasar. *El héroe. Obras completas*. Madrid: Aguilar, 1944b. Print.

Gracián, Baltasar. *Oráculo manual y arte de prudencia. Obras completas*. Madrid: Aguilar, 1944c. Print.

Gracián, Baltasar. *The Art of Worldly Wisdom. A Packet Oracle*. Trans. Christopher Maurer. New York: Double Day, 1992. Print.

Grahame-Smith, Seth. *Abraham Lincoln Vampire Hunter*. New York: Grand Central Publishing, 2010. Print.

Grahame-Smith, Seth. *Pride and Prejudice and Zombies*. Philadelphia, PA: Quirk Productions, 2009. Print.

Greer, Margaret. *María de Zayas Tells Baroque Tales of Love and the Cruelty of Men*. University Park: Pennsylvania State University Press, 2000. Print.

Hayles, Katherine. *How We Became Posthuman. Virtual Bodies in Cybernetics, Literature and Informatics*. Chicago: University of Chicago Press, 1999. Print.

Heidegger, Martin. "The Age of the World Picture." *The Question oncerning Technology and Other Essays*. Trans. William Lovitt. New York: Harper Collins, 1982.

Heidegger, Martin. "Die Zeit des Weltbildes." *Holzwege*. Frankfourt: Vittorio Klostermann, 2003. Print.

Heidegger, Martin. *Sein Und Zeit*. Tübingen: Max Niemeyer Verlag, 1986. Print.

Heidegger, Martin. "The Question Concerning Technology." *Basic Writings*. Ed. David Krell. New York: HarperCollins Publishers, 1993. Print.

Heller, Kevin Jon. "The Cognitive Psychology of Circumstantial Evidence." *Michigan Law Review* 106 (2006): 241–306, 245–246.

Her (2013). Dir. Spike Jonze.

Hobbes, Thomas. *The Leviathan*. London: Penguin Classics, 1985. Print.

House of Cards. Netflix TV Series.

Huet, Marie-Hélene. "Introduction to *Monstrous Imagination*." *The Horror Reader*. Ed. Ken Gelder. New York: Routledge, 2000. 84–89. Print.

Hume, David. *Enquiry Concerning the Principles of Morals*.

Inception (2010). Dir. Christopher Nolan.

Into the Wild (2007). Dir. Sean Penn.

Jackson, John B., *A Sense of Place, a Sense of Time*. New Haven: Yale University Press, 1994. Print.

Kadir, Djelal. *Questioning Fictions: Latin America's Family Romance*. Minneapolis: University of Minnesota Press, 1986. Print.

Kagan, Richard. *Lawsuits and Litigants in Castile, 1500–1700*. Chapel Hill: University of North Carolina Press, 1981. Print.

Kant, Immanuel. *Critique of the Power of Judgment*. Ed. Paul Guyer. Trans. Paul Guyer and Eric Matthews. Cambridge: Cambridge University Press, 2000. Print.

King, Stephen. *Four Past Midnight*. New York: Viking, 1990. Print.

King, Stephen. *Needful Things*. New York: Viking, 1991. Print.

Kiskila, Martha, Guillem Griera and Marialenia Savvaidi. "Las casas ocupas de Barcelona." https://7vagones.wordpress.com/2014/10/04/las-casas-ocupas-de -barcelona/ (accessed June 2, 2016).

Klein, Naomi. *This Changes Everything*. New York: Simon and Schuster, 2014. Print.

Kristeva, Julia. *Powers of Horror: An Essay on Abjection*. Trans. León Roudiez. New York: Columbia University Press, 1982. Print.

La piel que habito (2011). Dir. Pedro Almodóvar.

Lacan, Jacques. *Ecrits*. Trans. Bruce Fink. New York: Norton, 2002. Print.

Lacan, Jacques. *The Ethics of Psychoanalysis 1959–1960: The Seminar of Jacques Lacan.* Ed. Jacques-Alain Miller. Routledge, 19 Nov 2013.

Lacan, Jacques. *The Four Fundamental Concepts of Psychoanalysis.* Ed. Jacques-Alain Miller. Trans. Alan Sheridan. New York: Norton, 1981. Print.

Lacan Jacques, Jacques-Alain Miller and James Hulbert. *Desire and the Interpretation of Desire in Hamlet.* Yale French Studies, No. 55/56, Literature and Psychoanalysis. The Question of Reading: Otherwise. (1977), pp. 11–52.

Lacan, Jacques. "L'instance de la lettre dans l'inconscient depuis Freud." *Ecrits.* Paris: Seuil, 1966. Print.

Land of the Dead (2005). Dir. George Romero.

Landy, Joshua. *How to Do Things with Fictions.* New York: Oxford University Press, 2012. Print.

Law and Order. NBC TV Series.

Leibniz, Gottfried. *New Essays on Human Understanding.* Trans. and ed. by Peter Remnant and Jonathan Bennett. Cambridge: Cambridge University Press, 1982. Print.

Lincoln (2012). Dir. Steven Spielberg.

López de Ubeda, Francisco. *La pícara Justina.* Ed. Bruno Mario Damiani. Madrid: Turanzas, Potomac MD, Studia Humanitatis, 1982. Print.

Loureiro, Manel. *Apocalipsis Z.* Dolmen: Palma de Mallorca, 2007. Print.

Lovecraft, H.P. "The Call of Cthulhu." *The 13 Best Horror Stories of All Time.* Ed. Leslie Pockell. New York: Warner Books, 2002. 346–378. Print.

Lozano, Cristóbal. *Historias y leyendas.* 2 vols. Ed. Joaquín Entrambasaguas. Madrid: Espasa-Calpe, 1955. Print.

Luhmann, Niklas. "Globalization or World Society. How to Conceive of Modern Society." *International Review of Sociology* 7 (1997). http://www.generation-online .org/p/fpluhmann2.htm

Luna, Miguel de. *Historia verdadera del rey don Rodrigo.* Ed. Luis F. Bernabé Pons. Granada: Universidad de Granada, 2001. Print.

Machiavelli, Niccolò. *The Prince.* Ed. Philip Smith. New York: Dover Thrift Editions, 1992. Print.

Maravall, José Antonio. *Teatro y literatura en la sociedad barroca.* Barcelona: Crítica, 1990. Print.

Maravall, José Antonio. *Culture of the Baroque: Analysis of a Historical Structure.* Minneapolis: University of Minnesota Press, 1986. Print.

Marin, Louis. "Disneyland: A Degenerate Utopia." *Glyph.* Vol. 1. Baltimore: John Hopkins University Press, 1977. Print.

Martín, Manuel. *Noche de difuntos del 38.* Palma de Mallorca: Dolmen, 2012. Print.

Matheson, Richard. *I am legend*. New York: Gold Medal Books, 1954. Print.

McCarthy, Cormac. *The Road*. New York: Vintage Books, 2006. Print.

Medrano, Julián de. *La silva curiosa*. Ed. Mercedes Alcalá Galán. New York: Peter Lang, 1998. Print.

Merchant, Carolyn. *The Death of Nature: Women, Ecology, and the Scientific Revolution*. San Francisco: Harper and Row, 1980. Print.

Migoya, Hernán. *Una, grande y zombie*. Barcelona: Ediciones B, 2011. Print.

Milne. A.A., *Winnie-the-Pooh*. New York: Puffin Modern Classics, Penguin Group, 2005. Print.

Monleón, José. *A Specter Is Haunting Europe. A Sociohistorical Approach to the Fantastic*. Princeton: Princeton University Press, 1990. Print.

Moraña, Mabel. "Baroque/Neobaroque/Ultrabaroque: Disruptive Readings of Modernity." *Hispanic Baroques: Reading Cultures in Context*. Eds. Nicholas Spadaccini and Luis Martín-Estudillo, Hispanic Issues 31. Nashville, TN: Vanderbilt University Press, 2005. 241–282. Print.

Moretti, Franco. "Dialectic of Fear (Extract)." *The Horror Reader*. Ed. Ken Gelder. New York: Routledge, 2000. 148–160. Print.

Mozart, Wolfgang Amadeus and Lorenzo Da Ponte. *Don Giovanni*. http://www .murashev.com/opera/Don_Giovanni_libretto_Italian_English (accessed July 8, 2016).

Nebrija, Antonio de. Gramática de la lengua castellana (1492). http://www.filos .unam.mx/LICENCIATURA/Pagina_FyF_2004/introduccion/Gramatica_Nebrija .pdf (accessed June 2, 2016).

Nelson, Bradley J. *The Persistence of Presence: Emblem and Ritual in Baroque Spain*. Toronto: University of Toronto Press, 2010. Print.

North, John. *The Ambassadors' Secret: Holbein and the World of the Renaissance*. New York: Bloomsbury, 2005.

Orgel, Stephen and Roy C. Strong. *Inigo Jones, the Theatre of the Stuart Court: Including the Complete Designs for Productions at Court for the Most Part in the Collection of the Duke of Devonshire Together with Their Texts and Historical Documentation*. London: Sotheby Parke-Bernet, 1973. Print.

Packer, George. "The Other France: Are the Suburbs of Paris Incubators of Terror?" *The New Yorker*, August 31, 2015. http://www.newyorker.com /magazine/2015/08/31/the-other-france

Panofsky, Erwin. *The Life and Art of Albrecht Dürer*. Princeton, Princeton University Press, 2005. Print.

Pariser, Eli. *The Filter Bubble*. New York: Penguin, 2012. Print.

Parkinson Zamora, Lois and Monica Kaup, eds. *Baroque New Worlds: Representation, Transculturation, Counterconquest.* Durham: Duke University Press, 2012. Print.

Parkinson Zamora, Lois and Monica Kaup, eds. *The Inordinate Eye: New World Baroque and Latin American Fiction.* Chicago: University of Chicago Press, 2006, Print.

Parsley, Rod. *Silent No More.* Lake Mary, FL: Charisma House, 2005. Print.

Patterson, James and Michael Ledwidge. *Zoo.* New York: Grand Central Publishing, 2014.

Peisner, David. "Blood, Sweat, & Zombies." *Rolling Stone*, October 24, 2013. Print.

Pepperell, Robert. *The Posthuman Condition: Consciousness Beyond the Brain.* Portland, OR: Intellect Books, 2003. Print.

Pinker, Steven. *The Better Angels of Our Nature: Why Violence Has Declined.* New York: Penguin, 2011. Print.

Plato. *Complete Works.* Ed. John M. Cooper. Indianapolis, IN: Hackett Publishing, 1997. Print.

Pocahontas (1995). Dir. Eric Goldberg and Mike Gabriel.

Powers, Scott. "Disney's Secret Garden." *Buffalo News*, October 21, 2007. Print.

Revolution. NBC Series. Created by Eric Kripke.

Radice, Mark A. *Opera in Context: Essays on Historical Staging from the Late Renaissance to the Time of Puccini.* Portland, OR: Amadeus Press, 1998. Print.

Rainey, Reuben. "Hallowed Grounds and Rituals of Remembrance: Union Regimental Monuments at Gettysburg." *Understanding Ordinary Landscapes.* Eds. Paul Groth and Todd Bressi. New Haven: Yale University Press, 1997. 67–80. Print.

Rama, Angel. *La ciudad letrada.* Texas: Ediciones del norte, 1984. Print.

Reilly, David. "The Coming Apocalypses of Zombies and Globalization." *Zombie Talk: Culture, History, Politics.* Ed. David Castillo et al. New York: Palgrave Macmillan, 2016 63–91. Print.

Rice, Anne. *Interview with the Vampire.* Book 1 of *The Vampire Chronicles.* New York: Random House, 1976. Print.

Ringu (1998). Dir. Hideo Nakata.

Rodríguez de la Flor, Fernando. *Barroco: Representación e ideología en el mundo hispánico (1580–1680).* Madrid: Cátedra. 2002. Print.

Rodríguez de la Flor, Fernando. "On the Notion of a Melancholic Baroque." *Hispanic Baroques: Reading Cultures in Context.* Eds. Nicholas Spadaccini and Luis Martín-Estudillo. Nashville: Vanderbilt University Press, 2005. 3–19. Print.

Rojas Zorrilla, Francisco de. *Del rey abajo, ninguno.* Ed. Brigitte Whittmann. Madrid: Cátedra, 2007. Print.

Roth, Veronica. *Divergent*. New York: Katherine Tegen Books, 2011. Print.

Russell, P.E. *Cervantes*. Oxford: Oxford University Press, 1985. Print.

Samson, Alexander and Jonathan Thacker. "Three Canonical Plays." *A Companion to Lope de Vega*. Eds. Alexander Samson and Jonathan Thacker. London: Tamesis, 2008), 119–30. Print.

Sandel, Michael. *What Money Can't Buy: The Moral Limits of Markets*. New York: Ferraus, Straus and Giroux, 2012. Print.

Schama, Simon. *Landscape and Memory*. London: Harper Collins, 1995. Print.

Schmid, David. "The Zombie as Neoliberal Symptom." *Zombie Talk: Culture, History, Politics*. Eds. David Castillo et al. New York: Palgrave Macmillan, 2016 92–107. Print.

Schramm, Percy. *Las insignias de la realeza en la Edad Media española*. Madrid: Instituto de Estudios Políticos, 1960. Print.

Schrecker, Ellen. *The Lost Soul of Higher Education: Corporatization, The Assault on Academic Freedom, and the End of the American University*. New York: The New Press, 2010. Print.

Scream (1996). Dir. Wes Craven.

Sheldrake, Philip. *Spaces for the Sacred: Place, Memory, and Identity*. Baltimore: The Johns Hopkins University Press, 2001. Print.

Shelton, Donald. "The 'CSI Effect': Does It Really Exist?" *NIJ Journal* 259. http://www.nij.gov/journals/259/csi-effect.htm

Sherwin, Richard. *Visualizing Law in the Age of the Digital Baroque: Arabesques and Entanglements*. New York: Routledge, 2011. Print.

Shields, David. *Reality Hunger: A Manifesto*. New York, Knopf, 2010.

Sisí, Carlos. *Los caminantes*. Dolmen: Palma de Mallorca, 2009. Print.

Spadaccini, Nicholas and Jenaro Talens. *Rhetoric and Politics: Baltasar Gracián and the New World Order*. Minneapolis: University of Minnesota Press, 1997. Print.

Standage, Tom. *Writing on the Wall: Social Media. The First 2000 Years*. New York: Bloomsbury, 2013. Print.

Stoker, Bram. *Dracula*. Eds. Nina Averbach and David Skul. New York: W.W. Norton, 1997. Print.

Tatort. ARD TV Series.

The Book of Eli (2010). Dir. Allen Hughes and Albert Hughes.

The Madness of King George (1994). Dir. Nicholas Hytner.

The Mask (1994). Dir. Chuck Russell.

The Matrix (1999). Dir. Larry Wachowski and Andy Wachowski.

The Night of the Living Dead (1968). Dir. George Romero.

The Ring (2002). Dir. Gore Verbinski.

The Terminator (1984). Dir. James Cameron.

The Truman Show (1998). Dir. Peter Weir.

The Vampire Diaries. CW Television Network Series. Produced by Kevin Williamson and Julie Plec.

The Walking Dead. AMC Network Television Series. Produced by Frank Darabount.

Tirso de Molina. *El burlador de Sevilla*. Ed. Alfredo Rodríguez López Vázquez. Madrid: Cátedra, 2007. Print.

Torquemada, Antonio de. *Jardín de flores curiosas*. Ed. Giovanni Allegra. Madrid: Castalia, 1982. Print.

True Blood. HBO Series. Produced by Alan Ball.

Tuan, Yi-Fu. *Topophilia. A Study of Environmental Perception, Attitudes, and Values*. New York: Columbia University Press, 1990. Print.

Twilight (2008). Dir. Catherine Hardwicke.

Vanilla Sky (2001). Dir. Cameron Crowe.

Van Wert, William. "Disney World and Posthistory." *Cultural Critique* 32 (Winter 1995–1996): 188–191. Print.

Vattimo, Gianni and Santiago Zabala. *Hermeneutic Communism: From Heidegger to Marx*. New York, Columbia University Press, 2014. Print.

Vega y Carpio, Félix Lope de. *El arte nuevo de hacer comedias en este tiempo*. Ed. Juan Manuel Rozas. http://www.cervantesvirtual.com/obra-visor/arte -nuevo-de-hacer-comedias-en-este-tiempo–0/html/ffb1e6c0-82b1-11df-acc7 -002185ce6064_2.html (accessed June 2, 2016).

Vega y Carpio, Félix Lope de. *El caballero de Olmedo*. Ed. Francisco Rico. 12 edn. Madrid: Cátedra, 2004. Print.

Vega y Carpio, Félix Lope de. *El Nuevo Mundo descubierto por Cristóbal Colón*. Ed. Robert Shannon. New York: Iberica, 2001. Print.

Vega y Carpio, Félix Lope de. *El villano en su rincón*. Ed. Juan María Marín. Madrid: Cátedra, 1968. Print.

Vega y Carpio, Félix Lope de. *Fuenteovejuna*. Ed. Juan María Marín. Madrid: Cátedra, 2001. Print.

Vega y Carpio, Félix Lope de. *Lo fingido verdadero (Acting is Believing)*. Ed. and trans. Michael McGaha. San Antonio, TX: Trinity University Press, 1986. Print.

Vega y Carpio, Félix Lope de. *Peribáñez y el comendador de Ocaña*. Ed. Juan María Marín. Madrid: Cátedra, 1995. Print.

Vesely, Dalibor. *Architecture in the Age of Divided Representation: The Question of Creativity in the Shadow of Production*. Cambridge, MA: MIT Press, 2004. Print.

Von Hagens, Gunther. "Anatomy and Plastination." *Catalogue. Anatomy Art. Fascination Beneath the Surface.* Heidelberg: Institute of Plastination, first printing 2000. 11–38. Print.

Vonnegut, Kurt. *Mother Knight.* New York: Fawcett Publications, 1961. Print.

Weatherford, Jack. *The History of Money.* New York: Crown, 1998.

White Zombie (1932). Dir. Victor Halperin and Edward Halperin.

Williamsen, Amy. "Challenging the Code: Honor in María de Zayas." *María de Zayas: The Dynamics of Discourse.* Eds. Amy Williamsen and Judith Whitenack. Madison: Fairleigh Dickinson University Press, 1995. 170–191. Print.

Zabala, Santiago. The *Remains of Being: Hermeneutic Ontology after Metaphysics.* New York: Columbia University Press, 2009. Print.

Zayas, María de. *Desengaños amorosos.* Ed. Alicia Yllera. Madrid: Cátedra, 1983. Print.

Zero Dark Thirty (2012). Dir. Kathryn Bigelow.

Žižek, Slavoj. "How Did Marx Invent the Symptom?" *Mapping Ideology.* Ed. Slavoj Žižek. London: Verso, 1994. 296–331. Print.

Žižek, Slavoj. *The Sublime Object of Ideology.* London: Verso, 1989. Print.

Žižek, Slavoj. *The Ticklish Subject. The Absent Center of Political Ontology.* London: Verso, 1999. Print.

Žižek, Slavoj. *Trouble in Paradise: From the End of History to the End of Capitalism.* London: Penguin, 2015. Print.

Index

Note: The letters 'f' and 'n' following locators refer to figures and notes.

AAU (Association of the American
    Universities) 114
Abentarique, Abulcácim Táriq 67
abnormality 124–5, 126
Abraham Lincoln Vampire Hunter (Dir.
    Timur Bekmambetov) 131
Abraham Lincoln Vampire Hunter
    (Grahame-Smith) 130–1
Abre los ojos (Dir. Alejandro Amenábar)
    27
absolutism 12, 78, 101
abstraction 36, 41, 99, 208, 228 n.3
Academy of Motion Picture Arts and
    Sciences 169, 170
actor/character relationship 1, 11, 174–6
Adam 143
ads (commercials) 15, 74, 77, 99, 106, 116,
    179, 183–4, 212, 219–20, 224–5
Aeneid 185
aesthetics 6, 11, 40, 61, 125, 175, 181, 190,
    191, 194, 195, 221
Africa 132, 134, 150, 213
âge classique 22
agency 137, 188, 192
agenda 40
"Age of the World Picture, The"
    (Heidegger) 24, 188
Aguirre, Manuel 229 n.8
AIDS 150
Alarcón, Daniel Cooper 220
Alcalá de Henares 177
Alderman of Zalamea, The (Calderón de la
    Barca) 12, 13, 91, 99
Alemán, Mateo 177
alienation 41, 108, 126, 213, 224
Alighieri, Dante 18
allegory 17, 40, 44, 100, 129, 131, 144, 189
Almodóvar, Pedro 29, 30
Alpujarras rebellion 66

Al Qaeda 68, 213
alter ego 45, 182
Althusser, Louis 186
altruism 75, 87
Ambassadors, The (Holbein) 19, 21f
*America Again: Re-Becoming the Greatness
    We Never Weren't* (Colbert) 14
American Airlines 107–8
American Crossroads 74, 78
American determination 105
American dream 56, 155
American exceptionalism 14, 69, 73
Americanization 130–1
American Revolution 4
American values 39, 105
American Zombie Gothic (Bishop) 135
Amsterdam, occupy movement 201
anachronism 185
anamorphosis 21, 191
anarchy 187, 204
Anatomy Art exhibitions 61
Andrew W. Mellon foundation 111
animal/animality 109, 129, 133, 158, 172,
    216, 221
antagonism 101, 235 n.17
anti-capitalism 201
anti-elitism 62–3
anti-eviction protests 205
anti-freedom terror 13
anti-globalization 201, 202
Antigone 128
anti-immigration 214
anti-intellectualism 62–3
antiquity 122, 123
anti-Semitism 188
anti-smarts 62
Antwerp 177
anxiety 124, 126, 135, 149
apariencia 92, 93

Apocalipsis Z (Loureiro) 141
apocalypse
    biblical context 156
    catastrophic consequences 156–7,
        158
    discourse of sustainability 159–60
    elites' influence 157–60
    and globalization 150–1
    and new medialogy 159–61
    in popular culture 60, 123, 124, 133,
        135–8, 141–3, 146, 148–9, 152, 158
    postmodern ideology 156
    skepticism 158
    zombie 133, 135, 136, 138, 141–2, 148,
        151, 152, 220
Apocalypse Now (Dir. Francis Ford
    Coppola) 13
appearance 4, 27, 30, 97, 149, 158, 159,
    165, 167, 175, 188, 191, 192, 193,
    195, 221
Apple 15, 74
Aquinas, Thomas 97–8
Arab Spring 167
Arachne 181
Arad, Michael 198
Arata, Stephen 130, 131, 234 n.4
archetypes 128
architecture 1, 17, 21–2, 37, 92, 100, 125,
    197–200
Argentina 185, 193
Argo (Dir. Ben Affleck) 169, 171
aristocracy 5, 78, 100, 123–4, 129, 130,
    133, 136, 178, 235 n.17
Aristotle 169–70, 172
Armageddon 151
Arnauld, Antoine 23
art 3, 23, 25, 29, 40, 61, 77, 111, 125, 133,
    175, 177–86, 191, 193, 199, 203,
    204, 212, 216–17, 221–2, 224–5
*Arte Nuevo de hacer comedias en este
    tiempo* (Vega y Carpio) 12, 178
art history 11, 180
artifice 4, 30, 40
artificial intelligence 44, 47, 49
artificiality 4, 35, 40, 60, 61, 112
Art of Worldly Wisdom, The (Gracián) 5,
    40–1, 229 n.13

Asia 157
Athena 181
audience 5, 12, 13, 19, 30, 31, 32, 55, 56, 82,
    92, 105, 138, 166, 178, 183, 190, 205
Augé, Marc 228–9 n.6
aura 2, 3, 93, 176, 209
Auschwitz 68
Austin, Jane 136
authenticity 3–4, 61, 209, 220
autonomy 151, 152, 153, 154, 202, 220
Aznar, José María 68
*Aztec Palimpsest. Mexico in the Modern
    Imagination, The* (Alarcón) 220

Bachmann, Michelle 62
Bacon 41, 219
Bakan, Joel 112
banalization 37, 220
Banc Expropiat, occupation of 204
banking revolution 50–1
Banksy 38
banlieues 213
Barbaro, Michael 207
Barcelona, occupy movement 201–5,
    219–20
Barclays bank 203–4
baroque
    aesthetics 11, 40, 191, 194, 195
    architecture 1, 17, 21–2, 125
    desengaño 11–12, 40
    digital 6, 221
    fantasies 121–6, 145
    frame 187–95, 221
    guided culture of 5, 40
    literature 11–12, 27, 40, 121–6, 132,
        133, 220–1
    major strategies 11, 31, 165–6, 181,
        192, 193, 194, 222
    minor strategies 11, 31, 165–8, 181,
        192–5, 223, 225
    new world 193–4, 238 n.15
    painting 3, 19–22, 27, 125, 133, 175,
        177–86, 220–1
    spectacle 6, 101
    theater 27–33, 99–100, 101, 106,
        179–80, 187–95
baroque horrors 121–6

Baroque Horrors (David Castillo) 68–9
Barthes, Roland 101
Baseball as a Road to God: Seeing Beyond
       the Game (Sexton) 60
Baudrillard, Jean 37, 39, 228 n.3
Bechdel, Alison 116
Beck, Glenn 63
Beckford, William 125
behavior 31, 41, 69, 75–7, 80, 82,
       112, 125, 133–4, 138, 152, 158,
       166, 174
behavioral disorders 61
being 29, 30, 112, 160, 166, 187–9, 194,
       205, 216
being-in-the-world 189
belief 11, 13, 15, 31–3, 55, 56, 73, 96, 116,
       137, 165, 168, 173, 208
belonging 31, 91, 132, 201
Benedict, Barbara 125
Benengeli, Cide Hamete 67
Benjamin, Franklin 77
Benjamin, Walter 3, 200, 209
Berlin, occupy movement 201
Better Angels of our Nature, The (Pinker)
       155
Bible 60
bills of exchange 51, 53
Bird, Elizabeth 135
Bishop, Kyle 135, 149
bitcoins 53–4
Black Death 144
Black Death: The Triumph of the Undead
       (González) 144
black magic 46, 126, 132
blockbusters 12, 128, 133, 137, 139
blood markets/blood culture 128–31
blood purity and honor 32, 90, 166, 193
Boccaccio, Giovanni 18, 170
bodegón (still life) 180
body, the 2–3, 10, 60, 61, 83, 92, 128, 131,
       133, 138, 144, 145, 147, 154, 165,
       178, 183, 189, 199, 209, 224
body politic 100–1
Body Worlds (von Hagens) 61
Book of Eli, The (Dir. Hughes brothers)
       60, 62
Book of Revelations 156

Borges, Jorge Luis 15, 36, 185–6, 188
Bosse, Abraham 101, 102f
bourgeois/bourgeoisie 76–7, 100, 129
Braunstain, Philippe 201
Brazil 157, 193
Brook, Max 134
Brooklyn Bridge 108
Browning, John Edgar 152
Brunelleschi, Filippo 10, 18
Bruno, Giordano 17, 123
Brussels 210
bubonic plague 199
Buffy the Vampire Slayer (TV series) 128
bureaucracy 79, 165, 210
Burgos 177
Bush, George W. 9, 69–70, 166, 182–3
butterfly art 221
Byrne, Susan 83

cable TV 5, 153, 207
Cain, Herman 183–4
Calancha, Antonio de la 193
Calderón de la Barca 12, 27, 28, 91, 93
California 39, 157
"Call of Cthulhu, The" (Lovecraft) 122
Cambridge University 172, 184
Campanella 66
Campos, Haroldo de 193
Canada 36
Can Masdéu, occupation of 204
cannibalism 132, 134, 136, 137, 153, 211
Canterbury Tales (Chaucer) 18
capitalism 73, 77, 108, 124, 129, 135, 147,
       150, 153, 154, 160, 199, 204, 205,
       210, 219, 235 n.17
carbon credits 159
Cardozo Law School 80, 95
Carpentier, Alejo 194, 238 n.15
Carr, Nicholas 30
Carrey, Jim 173
Carson, Ben 54
cash-driven society 53, 77–8, 112
Castilian language 65
Castilla, Francisco de 65–6
Castillo, Alonso del 67
Castillo, David 65, 68–9
Castle of Otranto, The (Walpole) 125

cataclysm 133, 156
Cathedral of Potosí 193
Catholic Church/Catholics 5, 12, 60, 66, 93, 100, 159, 183
Cato Institute 158, 160
CBS 158
CDC (Centers for Disease Control and Prevention) 134
Celerio, Gonzalo 238 n.15
censorship 79
centrism 214
certainty 117, 125, 155, 156, 193
Cervantes, Miguel de 3, 12, 22, 23, 24–5, 27, 31, 32, 45, 62, 67, 68, 144, 166–7, 168, 174–5, 177, 178, 181–6, 193, 215–16, 220
Chanfalla 32, 33
characters 1, 10, 11, 18, 24–5, 29, 32, 37, 38, 51, 61, 78, 92, 126, 128, 129, 136, 137, 166–7, 170, 174–81, 183, 184, 186, 204, 207, 234 n.4
Charles V 66
Chaucer, Geoffrey 18
Chicago 107
Chicago Council on Global Affairs 214
China 36, 56
Choderlos de Laclos, Pierre 44
choice 5, 40, 70, 116, 137, 169, 172, 173, 180, 184, 202, 205, 216
Chomsky, Noam 112
Christianity/Christians 12, 17, 29, 31–2, 62, 65–70, 116, 124, 143, 156, 193, 208, 214, 215
Christie, Agatha 97
Christ in the House of Martha and Mary (Velazquez) 180–1
citizen/citizenship 15, 38, 39, 41, 62, 100, 106, 154, 208, 212–15
cityscapes 105–7, 190
Civil War 130
class 76, 91, 213
    lower 51
    middle 213
    race and 116
    ruling 123
    upper 53, 54
    working 214

class differences 116, 129, 147, 166, 235 n.17
class interests 76
climate change 156–61, 214–15, 236 n.6
climate change denial 160–1
Clinton, Hillary 207, 214
Close, Anthony 172, 184–5
Close, Glenn 44
closed space 39, 229 n.8
CNN 5, 54
coincidentia oppositorum 191
Colbert, Stephen 14, 60, 63, 67, 70, 71, 160, 166, 172, 182–4, 186, 207
Colbert Report, The (TV series) 63, 207
Colbert Super PAC 183–4, 186
collective histories 13
collective spectatorship 82, 104
collective unconscious 135
colonial age/colonialism 36, 50, 69–70, 101–5, 124, 130–1, 132, 135, 136, 191, 238 n.15
Colucci, Alejandro 142
Columbine High School shootings (1999) 212
Columbus, Christopher 69, 103
comedia 91–3
comedia de capa y espada 91
comedia de honor 91
comedia nueva 12, 13
comedias de enredo 13
coming-of-age fantasies 128
commemoration 106, 199, 201
commercials. *See* ads
commodity 15, 39, 41, 111, 112, 114, 115, 160, 167, 205, 219
commodity fetishism 15, 159
commodity-spectacles 35–41
Commoner in his Corner, The (Vega y Carpio) 99
commons 159, 209–10
communal disasters 199
communal interests 14, 138, 201–5
communication 1, 36, 53, 136, 153
community services 204
Conde, Víctor 142, 143
Conrad, Joseph 121
consciousness 46–50, 136, 174, 199

conservatism 62, 63, 75, 113, 116, 117, 124, 187
consumerism/consumption 5, 15, 36, 38, 61, 73, 74, 115, 116, 128, 135, 137, 144, 146, 150, 152–4, 159, 160, 167, 220, 225
contingency 39
conversion 29, 31, 52, 113, 220
Copenhagen 202
Copernicus 17
copy(ies) 1–3, 10, 11, 15, 40, 43–56, 60, 61, 116, 145, 147, 158–61, 165, 176, 199–200, 208–9, 213
Córdoba, Cabrera de 83
Cornell, Drucilla 95
Cornell University 114
corporal punishment 87–90, 88f, 89f
corporate culture 113
Corpus Christi plays 189
corrales 91, 190
corruption 69, 79, 82–3, 97
cosmic fear 62, 122, 123
cosmos 17, 100, 219, 223
counterconquest 194, 238 n.15
counter-culture 67, 201
counterreformation 62
courtly love 44–7, 50
courtly paintings 178–9
courtly theater 28–9, 181
courtrooms, visual media in 81–2
Covarrubias, Sebastián de 66, 83, 84f, 85f, 86f, 87, 88f, 89–90, 89f, 92, 95, 96f, 97, 125
Craven, Wes 9
Creon 128
crime/criminality 12, 46, 79–81, 91, 92, 132–3, 155, 171
crime shows 12, 79–90, 91
    defined 80
criminal justice system 79–81
    visual aspect of 81–2
crisis of reality 1–4, 5, 6, 9–10, 23, 25, 168
cristianos viejos 193
Criticón (Gracian) 40
Crown, the 12
CSI (TV series) 80–1, 91
CSI effect 79, 80

Cuba 193–4, 238 n.15
Cuban revolution 112
Cull, John T. 92
cultural history 40, 175, 191
cultural production 3–4, 5, 22, 79, 146, 150, 167, 216
cultural relativism 207
culture/cultural 6, 36, 199–200, 204, 208
    baroque 5, 6, 27, 101, 168, 191, 192, 193
    consumer 5
    curiosity 125
    history and 24, 36, 40, 156, 175, 191, 198, 213
    identity 105, 194
    language and 65
    media 9, 10
    otherness 62
    political 65, 149
    postmodern 40
    rituals 66
    spectacular 6, 13, 31, 40, 193
    transmission 226 n.1
    western 9, 124–5, 130, 191, 199
    zombie 133, 136, 137, 138, 146, 149
culture industry 141, 146, 147, 150, 168, 223
culture wars 11
curiosity 18, 125, 126
currency/currency market 15, 36, 44, 51–4, 77–8, 210–11
"cutting." *See* self-mutilation
cybersex 44
cynicism 137, 145, 146–7, 160, 223

Daalder, Ivo 214
daily life 9, 18
Dante, Alighieri 18, 45
Danube 159
Da Ponte 43
Dark Days, The (Loureiro) 141
Dark Night of the Soul (St John of the Cross) 44–5
Dasein 189, 190
Davis, J. Madison 97
Dawn of the Dead (Dir. George Romero) 135

dead, the
    living 135, 145, 154
    public mourning for 197–200, 201
    return of 133–4, 143
    walking 133–6, 138, 141
"dead things" 142–3
death
    commodification of 223
    and destruction 202, 211
    entre-deux-morts state 127
    living 127–8, 133
    and mourning 197–200, 201
    suffering and 223
    symbolic/real 127–8
    symbol of 221–2
    unnatural 149
"Death of American Universities" 112–13
Debord, Guy 40, 41, 220
Debray, Regis 226 n.1
Decameron (Boccaccio) 18
decision-making 114, 137, 210
deconstruction 178
"Deconstruction and the Possibility of
    Justice" 95
defamiliarization 67
defenders of being 166, 215–16
deformation 191
dehumanization 28–9, 146
de la Cruz, Sor Juana Ines 12, 193
delinquency 79
Del rey abajo, ninguno (Rojas Zorrilla)
    99, 106
del Toro, Guillermo 131
democracy 59, 73, 74, 99, 113, 165, 210, 214
demons 130, 148, 156
denialism 5, 74, 137, 158, 160
Derrida, Jacques 95
Descartes, René 175, 189, 192
desengaño (disillusion) 11–12, 40, 123,
    132, 192
desire 18, 24, 28, 44–5, 46, 48, 49, 50, 54,
    59, 76, 77, 83, 87, 124, 129, 130,
    132, 153, 156, 166, 184, 192, 200,
    213, 215, 216, 217, 221, 222
deus ex machina 93
deviance 82, 125
Diaries (Columbus) 103

die Neuzeit (modernity) 24
Diesel, Vin 139
digital communities 167, 211–12, 213
digital technologies 2, 6, 30, 53, 81, 106,
    209, 221
disbelief 33
Dis-illusions of Love (Zayas) 132
Dismaland 38
Disneyfication 220
"Disneyland: A Degenerate Utopia"
    (Marin) 39
Disney productions 101
"Disney's Secret Garden" (Powers) 35
Disneyworld 35–41, 108, 228 n.6
distortion 147, 191, 193, 195
Divergent (Roth) 137
Divine Comedy (Dante) 45
Dixon, Victor 95
documentary 105, 170
dollar 36, 52, 54, 71, 77, 78, 99, 112, 114,
    221, 225
Dolmen 141, 144
Don Giovanni (Mozart and Da Ponte) 43
Don Quixote (Cervantes) 12, 22, 24–5,
    67–8, 145, 182, 185, 221
Don Quixote (character) 22, 24–5, 145,
    166–7, 174–5, 177–8, 237 n.9
doubles 24, 38, 228 n.3
Doyle, Arthur Conan 97
Dracula (character) 126, 130, 131, 234 n.4
Dracula (Stocker) 129–30, 132
Dracula (TV series) 128
dramas de honor. See honor plays
Duke University 116
Dürer, Albrecht 19, 20f, 227 n.4
dystopian societies 137

Eagleton, Terry 112–13
eccentricity 126, 145
"economic repressed" 123, 124, 129, 130,
    132
economy 5, 6, 11, 40, 41, 50–3, 59, 71, 73,
    74, 77, 99, 106, 112–14, 123, 124,
    129, 130, 131, 132, 135, 146, 147,
    150, 151, 153, 154, 156, 157, 159,
    160, 167, 168, 191, 192, 201, 202,
    203, 209, 210, 213, 220, 223

Ecuador 157
Ediciones Debolsillo 144
Edsall, Thomas 214
education
    commodification/corporatization of
        111–15, 225
    and corporal punishment 87–90
    environmental 217
    as a marker of identity 62
egalitarianism 99
ego cogito 189
ego sum 189
El bufón llamado don Juan de Austria
    (Velazquez) 178–9
El Corte Inglés 179, 224–5
Election of the Majors of Daganzo, The
    (Cervantes) 62
electronic media 2, 10, 53
elites 4, 5, 6, 14, 59, 71, 114, 136, 157–8,
    160, 165, 167, 184, 214
Elizabeth (Dir. Shekhar Kapur) 28–9
Elonis, Anthony 171
Elonis v. United States 171–2
Emblemas morales (Covarrubias) 83, 84f,
    85f, 86f, 88f, 89f, 92
emblems/emblematics 80–5, 87–90, 91,
    92–3, 95, 97, 199, 203
embodiment 38, 92, 93, 128, 166, 187, 189,
    221, 225
Eminem 171, 173
Emmanuel, Rahm 157
emotions 18, 75, 76, 97, 104, 138, 184
empire 65, 79, 97, 130
End of the Oregon Trail Interpretive
    Center 105–6
England 36, 38, 100, 103, 190
English language 65, 141, 149
*Enquiry Concerning the Principles of
    Morals* (Hume) 75
Ensayo de contraconquista (Celerio) 238
    n.15
entertainment 176
entertainment and leisure industry 61
entre-deux-morts 127
environmental damage 135, 147, 158, 217
Epcot (Experimental Prototype
    Community of Tomorrow) 35–6,
    38, 108, 220

ephemerality 28, 158, 192, 200
epistemes 22, 174
epistemology 27, 126, 179, 190
equality 83, 99, 128, 213
erroneous attribution 185–6
eschatology 156, 185
eternal spirit 200
eternity 147, 200
"ethical optics" 6, 181
ethics 74, 114, 115
Eurocrats 210
Europe/European 1, 17, 19, 21, 23, 38,
    50–2, 69, 79, 125, 143, 156, 189,
    190–1, 193, 199, 202, 211, 214
Eurozone 210
exceptionalism 14, 32, 39, 55
exchange 22, 36, 50–1, 54, 99, 114, 165,
    193
exclusion 10, 14–15, 38, 121, 123, 166,
    167, 213
Ex Machina (Dir. Alex Garland) 47, 48–9,
    50
experience 2, 10, 18, 23, 24, 36, 38, 43, 52,
    60, 61, 76, 92, 106, 108, 115, 116,
    126, 165, 166, 170, 174, 184, 187,
    190, 197, 198, 201, 209, 216, 220
experiment 19, 27, 30, 46, 178, 179
exploitation 36, 52, 83, 105, 106, 108, 112,
    129, 130, 131, 136, 137, 147, 151,
    221
expressionism 123
extraction 51, 52, 131, 150, 210–11
extreme rhetoric 59, 112, 125, 175
extremism 211, 213, 214

Fajardo, Saavedra 66
'Fall of the House of Usher, The' (Poe) 133
Falwell, Jerry 69
fantasy 44, 47, 50, 59–62, 76, 105, 106,
    122, 123, 125, 128, 130, 132–5,
    137–8, 141, 145, 148, 151, 152, 154,
    158, 167, 173, 185, 211–13, 220,
    235 n.17
fashion industry 179, 224–5
fear 68, 82, 83, 104, 105, 122, 124, 125,
    129, 135, 148, 150, 152, 156, 214
Fear, Frank 115
Felipe II 93

female figures 180–1
Ferdinand and Isabella 66, 93, 95, 100
Ferdinand III 93, 94f
Fernández Gonzalo, Jorge 146
Festival book 87, 93, 94f
fetishism 15, 159
feudal system 50, 93
Fichte 208–9
fiction
    definitions of 170, 171, 216
    dramatization of 169–76
    and poetry 170
    problem of 171
    and reality 145, 173, 216
    and truth 170, 171, 172, 183, 184
Filosofía zombi (Fernández Gonzalo) 146
"filter bubble" 5
final destruction 143, 155
finitude 76
First World War 52
Florence Cathedral 10
folk tales/folklore 129, 134
forced role-enactment 30
Ford, Martin 151
forgetting 31, 170, 188, 189
Forrest Gump (Dir. Robert Zemeckis) 62
For the Love of God (Hirst) 221, 225
Foucault, Michel 22–5, 174, 190
Four Past Midnight (King) 122
Fox News 5, 73
fragmentation 213, 217
Frame Analysis (Goffman) 237 n.10
frames/framing techniques 10, 15, 23, 25,
    31, 38, 59, 65, 66, 69, 74, 75, 92,
    97–8, 100, 105, 108, 121, 123, 159,
    166, 167, 172, 174, 177–86, 187–95,
    198, 209, 216, 220, 221, 224, 225,
    226 n.1
France/French 36, 45, 51, 101, 111, 125,
    185, 186, 198, 213, 214
Franco, Francisco 101, 144
freedom 6, 13, 14, 69–70, 73–8, 82, 105,
    106, 114, 115, 153, 166, 204, 205
free role-play 30
Freetown Christiania 202
French Revolution 4
frescos 21–2
Front National (France) 214

Fuenteovejuna (TV series) 100–1, 106
Fuenteovejuna (Vega y Carpio) 12, 93–4,
    99, 101, 106
Fuji TV building, Tokyo 107
functionality 13
fundamentalism 3, 10, 59–62, 69, 73,
    111–17, 165, 166, 167, 208–10, 213,
    215
Fun House (Bechdel) 116
future 36, 71, 75, 106, 111, 135, 136, 151,
    156, 157, 203

Galileo 122
Gállego, Julián 11
Galli, Giovanni 160
games 27, 30, 46–7, 77, 78, 141, 173, 178,
    179, 181, 210, 225
game of frames 221
Garden of Curious Flowers (Torquemada)
    126
Garland, Alex 47
Gaudí, Antoni 204
Gelder, Ken 121, 129
Gentleman from Olmedo, The (Vega y
    Carpio) 99
Georgetown University 68
Germany/German 19, 24, 29, 36, 52, 53,
    68, 147, 216
Gestell 187–9
Gettysburg 106
Gingrich, Newt 14, 15
Giroux, Henry 113, 149
Gladwell, Malcom 212, 213
Glanvill 41, 219
glass cage 30
global capitalism 15, 50, 124, 130, 135,
    147, 150, 151, 153, 160, 211, 223
globalization 15, 65, 106, 147, 150–1, 167,
    194, 214
global warming 156–60, 214
goals 17, 40, 68, 114, 122, 202, 203, 210
God 12, 14, 18, 23, 28, 44, 46, 59–60, 69,
    70, 73, 91, 95, 98, 122, 123, 124,
    159, 172, 177, 178, 181, 221, 225,
    227 n.4
Goffman, Erving 174
gold 2, 50–3
Goldman Sachs 129

gold standard 52, 53, 103
Góngora, Luis de 12
González, Házael G. 144
González Pérez de Tormes, Lázaro 144
Goodrich, Peter 80, 81–2, 95–6
Google Ngram viewer 149
Gopnik, Adam 197
Gothic fictions 125, 126
governance 76, 95, 113, 165, 168
Goya, Francisco de 121, 123
Gracia, Barcelona 204
Gracián, Baltasar 4, 5, 40–1, 77–8, 168,
    229 n.13
Grahame-Smith, Seth 130–1, 136
Granada 66–7
Granovetter, Mark 212
Grasso, David 116
grass-roots 167
Great Recession 129
Greece/Greek 4, 169
    ancient 188
    debt crisis 210
greenhouse emissions 157
Grimm, Fred 134–5
grotesque 35
ground zero 77, 148
Guardian Unlimited 221
Guido, Ángel 193
guilt 79, 80, 95, 172
gusto (pleasure) 83, 87, 142
Guzmán de Alfarache (Alemán) 177

Halperin, Edward 132, 133
Halperin, Victor 132, 133
Hampton, Christopher 44
Hannity, Sean 63
hard boiled 97
Harker (character) 130, 234 n.4
Harris, Eric 212
Hayles, Katherine 235 n.16
HBO 124
Heartland Institute 158
Hegel 209
hegemony 66
Heidegger, Martin 23–4, 25, 159, 187–9,
    194–5
Heller, Kevin Jon 81

Her (Dir. Spike Jonze) 49–50
here and now 12, 105, 229 n.13
heresy 59, 165–6
Hermeneutic Communism (Vattimo) 187
hermeneutics 160, 166, 187, 191, 192–4
heroes 17, 24, 41, 67–8, 97, 101, 138–9,
    144, 145, 178, 186
heterogeneity 36
high-frequency trading 211
Hillcoat, John 123
Hirst, Damien 221–2, 225
historical accuracy 169, 171
historical plays 12, 13, 71, 101
historical truth 71, 169–70, 185
history
    art 11, 180
    and culture 24, 36, 40, 156, 175, 191,
        198, 213
    of ideas 185, 226 n.1
    life and 39, 40
    making of 68
    naturalization of 101, 103–4
    poetry and 169–71
history wars 67, 68
Hobbes, Thomas 101, 102f
Hogan, Chuck 131
Holbein, Hans 19–21, 21f
Hollywood 101, 139
Holocaust Memorials 199
Homer 169
homogeneity 36, 202
homosexuality 124, 144
honor, notion of 13, 14, 32, 46, 47, 50, 91,
        93, 99, 123, 165, 166, 193, 214
honor code 13, 46, 47, 54
honor plays 12–13
horror fiction 9, 60, 122, 123–4, 134
horror films 29–30, 35, 134, 149, 166
horror plays 92
horror vacui 62, 123
House of Cards (TV series) 78
How the World Became a Stage
        (Egginton) 189
humanities 111, 113, 114, 115, 216, 217
human life/nature 22, 23, 28, 29, 30, 40–1,
        75, 132, 147, 177
Hume, David 74–7, 208

Hunger Games, The (book and movie) 137, 138
Hussey, Andrew 213
hybridity 124–5, 126
hyperbole 172, 191
hyperinflation 52–3
hyperreal 37, 228 n.3

I Am Legend (Matheson) 149, 152
Iberian Peninsula 17, 65, 67, 122
idea 11, 19, 22, 23–4, 51, 75, 82, 93, 116, 135, 159, 173, 185, 198, 208, 235 n.17
idealism 3, 4, 46, 103, 173–4, 199, 208, 217
identity(ies)
    cultural 105, 167, 194
    and differences 22, 23
    ethnic 209, 210, 213
    historical 15, 105, 213
    individual 46, 49, 138, 213
    national 3, 10, 15, 105, 167, 208, 209–10, 213
    religious 68, 193, 209, 213
    social 31, 32, 33
ideologies 13, 53, 59, 99, 105, 112, 115, 147, 156, 186, 215
"If I Never Knew You" (song) 104, 105, 106
ignorance 27, 62, 122, 158
image/imagery 3, 5, 6, 10, 11, 13–14, 19, 23, 28, 35, 36, 37, 38, 39, 55, 66, 67, 77, 79, 81, 82–3, 91–3, 97, 98, 101, 105–7, 112, 123, 128, 130, 142–3, 147, 153, 169, 179, 191, 199, 203, 209, 220, 224
imagination 37, 39, 48, 76, 81, 82–3, 99, 105, 124, 125, 127, 129, 134, 142, 152, 170, 180, 191, 193, 220, 235 n.17
Imperial and Cesarean History of Charles V (Mexía) 66
impressionism 11, 29, 136, 178, 181, 197, 208
Inception (Dir. Christopher Nolan) 27
Indignados movement 167
individualism 41, 77, 82, 106, 116, 159, 219

individuals rights 76
Industrial Revolution 50, 127
ineffability, idea of 3, 10, 50, 59–63, 116, 117, 159, 160–1, 165–6, 208, 209, 213
inequalities 193, 227 n.4
Infanta Margarita 22
inflationary media
    first age of 1–2, 3–4, 5, 11, 15, 17, 45, 50, 53, 74, 116, 121, 147, 158, 166, 167, 168, 173, 175, 199, 208
    second age of 2–3, 6, 10, 15, 62, 116, 159, 165, 176, 200, 209
information technology 2, 29, 36, 61, 151, 153
Innocence Punished (Zayas) 132–3
installation 198, 221
intelligence 47, 62, 63
intent/intention 18, 46, 87, 97, 114, 124, 136, 167, 172, 184, 185, 212, 221, 226 n.1
internet 5, 49, 60, 147, 153, 171, 212
interpellation 13, 31, 82
interpretation 23, 28, 61, 80, 82, 92, 105, 106, 113, 116, 124, 125, 131, 151, 156, 159, 165, 166, 170, 171, 180, 184, 185, 192, 194, 195, 217, 225
Into the Wild (Krakauer) 60
intuition 187
inversion 87, 199, 220
iPhone 5 15, 74, 106, 116
Iraq 167
Iraq war 13, 69–70, 112
Ireland 113
irony 15, 29, 61, 62, 67, 136, 142, 143, 150, 157, 172, 176, 183, 184, 188, 212, 214, 221
Isabella and Ferdinand 66, 93, 95, 100
Islam 66–7, 68, 69, 211, 213
Islamic State (IS) 56, 68–9, 211–13
Italy/Italian 18, 36, 50, 111, 160, 170

Japan 36
Jarhead (Dir. Sam Mendes) 13
Jesus 59, 70, 143, 156, 180, 215
Jews 17, 66, 68
JFK airport 107–8

Jindal, Bobby 63
Jonze, Spike 49
Judenplatz Holocaust Memorial 199
Judeo-Christian tradition 124, 143
justice 31, 70, 73, 75–6, 79–83, 91–8,
    171–3, 177
Justiniano, Bernardo 66

Kagan, Richard 83
Kant, Immanuel 151, 152, 187, 208–9
Kapur, Shekhar 28
Kasa de la Muntanya, occupation of 204,
    205
Kennedy, John F. 56, 70
Kepler 17
keying/keyed 174
King, Stephen 74, 122
Kirkman, Robert 146
Klebold, Dylan 212
Klein, Naomi 156–7
knowledge 1, 2, 4, 22, 24, 25, 28, 41, 59,
    76, 77, 121, 122, 126, 130, 142, 150,
    151, 153, 156, 166, 174, 175, 188,
    191, 194, 208–9, 216
Koran 61
Kristof, Nicholas 155
Kurzweil, Ray 47
Kushner, Tony 170

Lacan, Jacques 28, 127–8, 153, 189, 198,
    199
La carbonera, occupation of 203, 204
Land of the Dead (Dir. George Romero)
    136, 137, 138
Landy, Joshua 171
language 2, 22, 23, 36, 46, 48, 59, 65–6, 69,
    70, 76, 82, 108, 111, 141, 149, 160,
    171–2, 190, 198, 204, 205
Las Hilanderas (Velazquez) 180, 181,
    182f
Latin America/Latin American 53, 193–4,
    238 n.15
Lazarillo de Tormes 12, 144, 146, 177,
    178
*Lazarillo Z: Killing Zombies Was Never a
    Piece of Cake* (González Pérez de
    Tormes) 144

left-wing politics 116, 214
Legal Emblems and the Art of Law
    (Goodrich) 81
legitimacy 31, 32, 70, 73, 75, 79, 81–2, 83,
    97, 101, 208
legitimacy crisis 168
Leibniz, Gottfried 216
Le Jardin du Centaure 185
Lenin and Philosophy (Althusser) 186
Les Liaisons Dangereuses (Choderlos de
    Laclos) 44
Leviathan (Hobbes) 101, 102f
Lewis, Philip 111
liberal bias 160, 166, 182
liberal democracy 74
liberalism 59, 69, 76–7, 116
liberation 5, 15, 52, 160, 185, 203, 212,
    216–17
lies, truth and 177–86, 207
life
    and art 177–86, 192
    celebration of 221–2, 225
    commodification of 223, 225
    community 201–5
    and death 29, 221–3
    death in 133
    as a dream 28
    earthly 28
    and history 39–40
    meaning of 60
    still 142, 180
Life is a Dream (Calderón) 27–8
life stories 12, 177
lifestyle 126, 138, 158, 177, 203, 215
Lights of Dawn (Torre) 87, 87f
Lima, Costa 237 n.10
Lima, José Lezama 193–4
Limbaugh, Rush 63, 147
Lin, Maya 198
Lincoln (Dir. Steven Spielberg) 169, 170,
    171
linear perspective 10, 19
Línea Z series 141, 144
literary criticism 172, 185
Living Dead, The (Adams) 134
Locke, John 74
London 20, 107, 130

Lorca, Federico García 108
Los Caminantes: Hades Nebula (Sisí) 141
Loureiro, Manel 141
Lovecraft, H. P. 122
Lozano, Cristóbal 68, 69
Luhmann, Niklas 147, 151
Luna, Miguel de 67
Luther, Martin 5

Machiavelli, Niccolò 5
Madness of King George, The (Dir.
    Nicholas Hytner) 28, 29
Madrid
    bombing (2004) 68
    corrales 190
    crime shows 91
    Occupy movement 201
Madrid Academy 12
mainstream media 9, 202, 203, 207
major strategies 11, 31, 165–6, 166, 181,
    192, 193, 194, 222
Maldives 157
Malkovich, John 44
manifest destiny 103, 104
Maravall, José Antonio 5, 31, 40, 99, 125
marginalized groups 4, 12, 66
Marin, Louis 39
Márquez, García 217
Martín, Manuel 145–6
Martin, Treyvon 80
martyrdom 29, 31
Marx, Karl 129, 153, 156, 186
mask 4, 29–30, 92, 105, 106, 116, 130, 153,
    165, 171
Mask, The (Russell) 29
mass-culture 40, 146, 147, 229 n.13
mass-production 11, 39, 41, 128, 146
materiality/materialism 2, 10, 12, 30, 63,
    74, 92, 115, 137, 145, 165, 177, 180,
    181, 183, 187, 188, 189, 199, 209,
    226 n.1
Matheson, Robert 149, 152
Matrix sagas (Dir. Wachowski brothers)
    27, 35–6, 133, 154, 211
Maya Lin's Wall 198
McCain, John 69
McCarthy, Cormac 123

McLuhan, Marshall 9
meaning 13, 22, 40, 60, 61, 92, 98, 100,
    123, 124, 127, 142, 150, 154, 166,
    170, 172, 185, 192, 195, 198, 225,
    226 n.1, 227 n.5, 229 n.6
meaninglessness 61, 123
means of production 153
media developments 1–2, 167–8
media explosion 62
media facts 73–4, 182
medialogy, definition of 1, 226 n.1
media reality 182
media revolution 1, 9–10, 53
media saturation 9, 181
Meditations (Descartes) 192
Medrano, Julian de 122–3, 126, 145
memento mori 133
memorials 106, 197–200
Menard, Pierre 185
Meninas (Velazquez) 22, 23, 179–80,
    223–5, 223f
Merchant, Carolyn 219
Merian, Matthaeus 81
Messianic 69–70
metanarrative 101
metaphor 36, 105, 129, 130, 131, 135, 149,
    150, 151, 170, 174, 190
metaphysics 11, 194
metonymy 50, 92, 101
Mexía, Pedro 66
Mexico 36, 54, 56, 220
Mexico Mágico 220
Meyer, Dick 207
Miami Herald, The 134–5
Michigan State University 115
microcosm 10
Middle Ages 12, 17, 19, 44, 59, 92, 93, 156,
    172
Middle East 117
Migoya, Hernán 144–6
Milan 51, 201
Milne, A. A. 14
minor strategies 11, 31, 165–8, 181, 192–5,
    223, 225
Minotauro 141
mise en abîme 191
misogyny 43, 212

MIT 113
modernity 24, 59, 99, 100, 132, 174, 176,
    190, 194, 220, 229 n.6, 229 n.8
modern science 59
modern state 5, 40, 41, 69, 106, 189
modern theater 10, 11
modern world 39, 40, 171, 174, 175, 176,
    237 n.9
Moliere 43
monarchy 12, 28, 29, 54, 66, 79, 82, 93,
    99–101, 144, 179, 190
money 2, 44, 50–3, 74, 78, 129, 183, 208,
    210–11, 234 n.4
monsters 10, 121–6, 128–33, 135, 141,
    144, 146, 147, 149, 150, 155, 234 n.4
monuments/monumental sites 71, 101,
    105–6, 108, 200
morality 75–7, 87
moral philosophy 40, 74, 77, 78
moral relativism 207–8
Moraña, Mabel 194
Moretti, Franco 131
Mother Night (Vonnegut) 29
motifs 92, 143, 144
mourning 197–200, 201
moveable stage machinery 92
moveable type 1, 23
Mozart 43
MSNBC 5
multinational corporations 2, 15, 76, 112,
    130, 151, 159, 165, 167, 183, 205,
    220
murals 107–8
Muslims 17, 66–8, 116, 212
myth 14, 33, 36, 43, 50, 54, 62, 66, 67, 69,
    101, 104–6, 145, 146, 190, 214
Mythologies (Barthes) 101

naked-emperor politics 56
Nameless Library 199
National Gallery, London 20
national identity 3, 10, 15, 105, 167, 208,
    209–10, 213
nationalism 14, 214
nation-building 65, 66
Nation Like No Other, A (Gingrich) 14
nation state 2, 10, 15, 99, 191, 199

natural law 125
nature
    and art 40
    commodification of 225
    early modern notions of 59, 100
    rebirth of 143
Nazism 29, 188
Near East 213
Nebrija, Antonio de 65
necromancy 132–3
Necrópolis (Sisí) 141
Needful Things (King) 74
Nelson, Bradley 82, 93
neobaroque 30, 142, 179, 193, 194, 195,
    221, 223, 238 n.15
neoconservatives 62
neoliberalism 112–17, 150, 155–6, 159,
    209
"Neoliberalism, Corporate Culture, and
    the Promise of Higher Education:
    The University as a Democratic
    Public Sphere" (Giroux) 113
Netherlands 157
New Art of Making Plays in Our Time, The
    (Vega y Carpio) 12
new media 2, 4–5, 9, 11, 23, 32, 159, 161,
    189, 208, 209, 213, 214
news reports 5, 73, 107, 126, 134, 158, 184,
    203–4, 207, 212
New Testament 180
new theater. See comedia nueva
New World 24, 69, 95, 103, 144, 190–1,
    193, 238 n.15
new world baroque 193, 238 n.15
New World Discovered by Christopher
    Columbus (Vega y Carpio) 103
new world order 95
New York City 104, 107, 108, 197
New Yorker 197, 212
"New York (Office and Denunciation)"
    (Lorca) 108–9
New York Times 9, 30, 182, 183, 229 n.13
niches 92
Nicole, Pierre 23
Nietzsche, Friedrich 129
Night Eternal, The (del Toro and Hogan)
    131

Night of the Dead of 38 (Martín) 146
Night of the Living Dead, The (Dir. George
    Romero) 133, 145, 149, 150
9/11 attacks 13, 69, 135, 199
9/11 Memorial Museum 197–8, 200
nocturnal horror 122–3
None Beneath the King (Zorrilla) 99
non-places 38, 202, 205, 228–9 n.6
North, John 227 n.5
nuclear disasters 60, 135, 155

Obama, Barack 73, 214–15
objects/objectification 1, 3, 10, 24, 36, 41,
    43, 54, 59, 74, 99, 112, 125, 126,
    131, 142, 146, 159, 170, 173, 179,
    180, 181, 184, 185, 187, 189, 200,
    202, 209, 219, 224, 226 n.1
oblique perspective 32
obscene 123, 168, 222
Ocampo, Florián de 65
"Occidental Tourist: *Dracula* and the
    Anxiety of Reverse Colonization,
    The" (Arata) 130
occult 126
Occupy movements 167, 201–5
Occupy Wall Street 147
Odyssey 185
okupas 201–5, 219–20
Old Testament 143
oligarchy 54, 153–4, 210
One, Great, and Zombie (Migoya) 144–6
online community 211–12, 213
online sources 171
online transaction 53
opera 43
operational doubles 38, 228 n.3
oppression 15, 213
optics/optical illusion 6, 18, 19–22, 181
Order of Things, The (Foucault) 22, 24
Oregon landscape 105–6
O'Reilly, Bill 63
Orient, the 50
Oriental 130
original *vs.* copy 2–3, 200, 224–5
ornamentation, baroque 191
Oscar Awards 169, 170
Osnos, Evan 214

otherness 32, 33, 62, 130
ownership 153, 202, 224
Oxford University 185

Packer, George 213
painting 1, 3, 10, 11–12, 17, 18–23, 45, 50,
    67, 80, 122, 142, 154, 178–81, 190,
    199, 222, 224–5, 227 n.5
Palin, Sarah 214
Panofsky, Erwin 227 n.4
Paris 107, 213
    attacks (2015) 215
    occupy movements 201
Paris Agreement (2015) 236 n.6
Pariser, Eli 5
Park Güell, Barcelona 204, 205
parody 62, 136, 141, 144, 184, 185, 207,
    228 n.3
Parra, Elena del Río 125
Parsley, Rod 69
participants/participation 27, 32, 37–8,
    45, 61, 108, 127, 145, 174, 181, 183,
    204, 225
passions 28, 41, 44, 132, 189, 200
pastiches 136, 141, 144, 224, 225
Patterson, James 158
pegma 92
Peisner, David 146
Pepperell, Robert 235 n.16
perfected nature 40
performatives 55, 95
Pericoli, Matteo 107
"Perils of Perfection, The" (Morozov) 121
Perry, Rick 62–3
Persiles (Cervantes) 67
persona 4, 44, 55, 77, 160
perspectives, rise of 17–25
    in architecture 21–2
    in literature 17–18, 22
    in painting 18–23, 45, 199
    in theater 19, 23, 199
Petrarch 18, 45
Pfeifer, Michelle 44
Philip II 3, 66
Philip III 66, 68
Philip IV 22
photography 35, 179–80, 224

picaresque 12, 144, 177–8
Pinker, Steven 155
Plato 3, 4, 169, 199
Platoon (Dir. Oliver Stone) 13
Plaza Janés 141
plurality 200
Pocahontas (Disney film) 101, 103–4,
    105–6
Pocket Oracle and Art of Prudence
    (Gracián) 4, 5, 78
poetic justice 93, 99
Poetics (Aristotle) 169
poetry 12, 44–5, 108, 125, 169, 170
point of view 1, 18
police procedural 97
political culture 71, 149, 158
political economy 41, 150
political parties 203
political theater 91–8
politics 2, 6, 9, 55–6, 61–2, 65, 69, 75, 76,
    133, 160, 168, 184, 190, 207, 214
popular culture 9, 13, 79, 127, 128, 134,
    145, 149, 158
portraiture 19–21, 20f, 21f, 100, 178–9
Port-Royal Logic (Arnauld and Nicole) 23
post-apocalyptic fantasies 60, 123, 136–8,
    143
postcolonialism/postcolonial age 104, 124,
    130, 131, 135, 238 n.15
posthumanism 6, 235 n.16
postmodernism 27, 39, 40, 53, 142, 146,
    156, 223, 229 n.13
pound sterling 52
poverty 108, 155, 193
Powers, Scott 35
power structure 5, 15, 31, 165, 194, 210
pragmatism 50, 83
Pride and Prejudice and Zombies
    (Grahame-Smith) 136
Prince, The (Machiavelli) 5
print culture 1, 4, 5, 11, 121, 134
proscenium stage 190
proscriptions 159
prose 12, 18, 22
public art 199, 203
public gaze 28, 29
Pueyo, Rivilla Bonet y 125

Pulitzer Prize 123
Puppet Show of Marvels, The (Cervantes)
    31
purchasing power 10, 74
purity 46, 166

Question Concerning Technology, The
    (Heidegger) 187–8
Quevedo, Francisco de 12
Quijote Z (González) 144
Quiroga, Vasco de 190

race 31, 68, 75, 116, 128, 136, 143, 148,
    150, 158, 184, 214
racism 10, 31, 36, 62, 68, 123, 132, 161,
    212
radicalization 213, 219
radio 2, 29
Rage of the Just, The (Loureiro) 141
Rainey, Reuben 106
Ramanna, Karthik 210
Rawlings, Hunter 114–15
Reagan, Ronald 70
realism 187
reality, notions of
    and appearance 27, 30, 221
    and dreams 28
    efforts and desires 54, 215, 216
    fiction and 145
    first age 10
    ideal form 3
    knowledge and 1
    and new medialogy 209–10
    reframing of 11
    and representation 3, 9, 29, 178, 180,
        220–1, 225
reality-altering technologies 121
reality-based community 9, 182
reality bleed 27, 31, 32, 181
reality-entitlement 158
reality hunger 3
reality literacy 221, 225
reality TV shows 5, 173
rebirth 138, 143
redemption 60, 82, 192, 195
redoubling 24, 25
Reeves, Keanu 212

reflexivity 24
Reformation, the 4
Reilly, Dave 150–1, 153
relativism 207–9, 215
religious orthodoxy 10
Remains of Being: Verwindung (Zabala)
      194
Renaissance 22, 125, 126, 170, 172
repetition 75, 146, 151
representation
      artistic 100, 178
      graphic 133
      media 9, 184, 199
      modes of 192, 221
      political 167, 184
      and reality 3, 9, 29, 178, 180, 220–1,
         225
      scope of 1
      of the world 1, 23, 174, 184
reproductions 3, 5, 147, 200, 208, 225
Republic, The (Plato) 169
resemblances 24, 174
resistance 30, 48, 66, 165, 167, 179, 193,
      201–5
revenge fantasies 144, 212
reverse colonization 130–1
Revolution (TV series) 137
Rice, Anne 128
Richardson, Kathleen 47
righteous suffering 82
right-wing politics 183, 210, 211, 214
Ring, The (Dir. Gore Verbinski) 27
Ringu (Dir. Hideo Nakata) 27
Rio de Janeiro 107
Riolan, Jean 125
*Rise of the Robots: Technology and the
      Threat of a Jobless Future* (Ford)
      151
ritual 18, 28, 45, 61, 66, 132, 198
Road, The (McCarthy) 123
Roberts, Justice John 171–2, 173
Robertson, Pat 69
robots 47–9
Rojas Zorrilla, Francisco de 99
Rolling Stone 146
Roman Empire, fall of 50, 143
Rome 107

Romero, George 127, 133–4, 135, 136–8,
      141, 145, 149
Romney, Mitt 183–4
Roth, Veronica 137, 138
Rousseau 208
Rove, Karl 9, 73, 74, 182
Roxxy 47–8
Rubin, Jennifer 62
Russell, Chuck 29
Russell, P. E. 185

sacred 44, 46, 67, 122, 198
Saint Augustine 124
Saint Genesius 29
Sandel, Michael 74, 112
Sanders, Bernie 214
San Francisco 107
Sant Antoni 204
Sao Paolo 107
Sarduy, Severo 193, 194, 238 n.15
satire 14, 63, 70
Scandinavia 36
scenarios 81, 113, 151, 154, 157, 158, 178
scenery 100
scenographies 81
Schama, Simon 105
Schmid, David 112, 135, 149–50
sci-fi movies 35, 47, 134
Scream (Dir. Wes Craven) 9
sculpture 70, 199, 222
sea-level rise 217
Secada, Jon 104
Second World War 46
secularism 59
seducer/seduction 43–4, 54, 56, 214
see/seeing 31–2
Segal, Steven 139
self, the 4
self-aggrandizement 19
self-alienation 126
self-consciousness 106, 136, 142, 144
self-destructive 135, 160, 217
self-directed suffering 87–8, 88f
self-mutilation 61
self-portraits 19, 20f
self-representation 40
self-sacrifice 87

sensation 126, 152
Seville 93
sex/sexuality 10, 28, 30, 43, 47, 54, 113,
        123, 124, 125, 127, 132, 144
sex robots 47–9
Sexton, John 60
Shakespeare 127
Shanice 104
shared space 23
shared symbols and practices 208
Shelton, Donald 80
Sherwin, Richard 6, 13, 81, 98, 221, 225
Shields, David 3
shoot-them-up movies 131
Sidney Opera House 107
Siemens 36
signs 22, 23, 36, 71, 97, 124, 228 n.3
Silent No More (Parsley) 69
Silicon Valley 121
Silva Curiosa (Medrano) 122, 126, 145
silver 50–3
Simon, Julian 160
simulacrum/simulation 3, 36–7, 38, 39,
        48, 81, 145, 205, 228 n.3
Siri 49
Sisí, Carlos 141
skepticism 158, 173
Skin I Live in, The (Almodóvar) 29–30
skull, symbolism of 221–2, 225
'Skyline of the World' 107–8
skylines 104, 107–8
slavery 36, 129, 130–1, 132, 153, 202
Sloterdijk 31
Smith, Adam 74
social identity 31, 32, 33
social media 4, 167
society of the spectacle 39, 40–1, 220
Society of the Spectacle (Debord) 220
Socrates 169
solipsism 48, 173–4
Sophocles 128
soul 44–5, 46–7, 51, 81, 83, 91, 122, 135,
        159, 165, 186, 200
sovereignty 2, 22, 76, 82, 83, 87, 95, 97,
        107, 184, 208
Soviet Union 101
space 1–2, 10, 17, 23, 25, 30

closed 39, 229 n.8
commoditized 205, 219–20
liberated 203
occupation and communal use of
        201–5
production and regulation of 201
public/private 201–5
sacred 46
shared 23
"survival" 152
theatrical 41, 45, 92, 100, 181, 190
time and 2, 36, 45, 105, 187
urban 203
virtual 211–13
Spacey, Kevin 78
Spadaccini, Nicholas 177–8, 229 n.13
Spain
    anti-intellectualism 62
    Counterreformation 62
    Golden Age classics 144, 229 n.13
    imperial era 5, 14, 31, 52, 65–71, 99–
        101, 124, 126, 133, 141–2, 144, 193
    Indignados movement 167
    justice system 79–80, 83
    mass-oriented theater 5
    morisco expulsion 66, 68
    Nebrija's work on grammar 65–6
    okupa movement 201–5, 205f, 219–20
    royal seal 3
    the state 65, 79–80, 92, 98, 101, 183,
        214, 229 n.13
spectacle 6, 13, 31, 45, 101, 105, 106, 152,
        192, 193
    commodity- 35–41
    -resources 220
    topophilic 104
spectators/spectatorship 27, 28, 30, 31,
        32, 33, 36, 38, 39, 41, 50, 55, 82, 92,
        104, 105, 107, 108, 137, 152, 174,
        178, 181, 192, 222, 224–5
speech act theory 95
Spielberg, Stephen 169, 170
Sprint 74
St. John 156
stability 194, 210
Stage of Wonders, The (Cervantes) 31–2,
        55, 166, 178, 193, 225

stage (theatre) 30, 31, 50, 51, 60, 61, 81, 92, 187–95, 199
  architecture 92, 190
  baroque aesthetics 179–80, 191–2
  classical 189–90
  designers 19
  diagetic space 190
  framing of 180, 181, 190
  Heidegger's concept of *Gestell* 187–9
  hermeneutic strategies 192–3
  machinery 92
  modern 190–1
  new world 191, 193
  proscenium 190
Stallone, Sylvester 139
Standage, Tom 4
Stanford 113, 212
Starry Messenger (Galileo) 122
state, the 66, 75, 79, 80, 98, 101, 106, 128, 155, 209, 210
stereotypes 13, 184
Stewart, Jon 63
Still Life (Conde) 142–4
St John of the Cross 44–5
Stoker, Bram 129–32
stone 100, 199
storytelling 146, 177–8
subjectivity 50, 76, 189, 201
subjects 5, 12, 19, 24, 29, 41, 48, 59, 75, 77, 93, 99, 132, 136, 168, 175, 180, 192, 201
suffering 36, 82, 83, 87, 90, 95, 97, 108, 109, 116, 122, 150, 151, 173–4, 207, 223
supermodernity 229 n.6
surrealism 108
Suskind, Ron 9, 182
sustainability 159–60
symbolism 13, 15, 17, 77, 106, 127, 128, 142, 143, 160, 165, 190, 204, 208, 210, 221–2
synchronization 4–5
Syriana (Dir. Stephen Gaghan) 13

tableaus 31–3, 55, 91, 92, 178
Taibbi, Matt 129
Talens, Jenaro 178, 229 n.13
Tanah 61

Techne 188
technology 1, 2, 5, 6, 35, 36, 38, 40, 46, 121, 133, 147, 151, 153, 155, 158, 167, 187, 188, 217
telegraph/telegram 1, 2, 53
television 5, 13, 60, 115, 173, 176, 212
Terminator, The (Dir. James Cameron) 133–4
terrorism 13, 68–9, 73, 123, 129, 133, 135, 146, 151–2, 167, 205, 210, 211–15, 220
Tesoro de la lengua castellana o española (Covarrubias) 92, 125
text, meaning of 51, 172
theater 1, 3–5, 10–14, 19, 23, 27–33, 40–1, 45, 55–6, 80, 82, 91–8, 100, 105, 111, 132, 145, 166, 168, 170, 173–5, 178–82, 189–90, 192–3, 199, 201, 203
theater of marvels 31, 32, 55, 56, 182
theaters of heroism 41
theaters of reputation 40, 41
theology 3, 46, 59, 68, 69, 123, 192, 193, 211
theory of fictionality 237 n.10
theory of the sublime 151–2
think tanks 158
This Changes Everything (Klein) 156
time 24
  degeneration of 127
  end of 147, 156
  of judgment 192
  and loss 198, 199
  and space 2, 36, 45, 105, 171, 187
Times 207, 210
Tirso de Molina 43
"Tlön, Uqbar, Orbis Tertius" (Borges) 188
Tokyo 107
tolerance 69
Tony Awards 170
Topophilia: A Study of Environmental Perception, Attitude and Values (Tuan) 100
topophilic mythology 104–5
topos 62, 101
Torah 61
Tormes, Lázaro González Pérez de 144
Toronto City Hall 107

Torquemada, Antonio de 126
Torre, Francisco de la 87, 87f
tourist industry 61, 204–5, 219–20
trade 50–1, 61, 65, 73, 74, 210–11
tragedy 27, 48, 69, 212
transcendentalism 75, 93, 160, 208
transformation 31, 36, 100, 168, 203
trans-historical 13, 14, 70, 105
transparency 46, 55, 76, 180
trauma 93, 101, 200
travesty 73, 80
Treaty of Versailles 52
tribalism 10, 161
trompe l'oeil 21–2, 191
tropes 11, 12, 44–5, 62, 82, 136, 172, 186,
     191, 194
Troyes, Chrétien de 17
True Blood (TV series) 124, 128, 129
True Companion 47–8, 50
True History (Luna) 67
True Pretense (Vega y Carpio) 29, 31
Truman Show, The (Dir. Peter Weir) 27, 36
Truman Show Syndrome 173–6
Trump, Donald 43, 54–5, 56, 73–4, 155,
     214
truth
     access to 209
     and authenticity 3–4
     denial 5, 137, 165–6
     education 114
     and fiction 170–1
     fundamental 59–60, 159, 165
     hidden 92
     historical 71, 169–70, 185
     and lies 177–86
     metaphysical 11
     philosophical 172, 188
     ultimate 3, 192
     unstable 168
"truthiness" 182, 207–8
Tuan, Yi-Fu 100
Turing, Alan 46–7
Turing test 46–7, 48
Turner Prize 221
Tuvalu 157
tweets 1, 73

Twilight (book and movie) 128
Tyndall Centre for Climate Change
     Research 157

UKIP 214
*Una era de monstruos: Representaciones de
     lo deforme en el Siglo de Oro español*
     (Parra) 125
uncanny 40, 68, 69, 108, 122, 128
uncertainty 22, 28, 135
undead 122, 126, 127, 136, 141–8, 152, 154
United Kingdom
  campaign against sex robots 47
  corporatization of universities 113
United Nations Climate Change
     Conference Paris 236 n.6
United States
     demographics 65
     economy 52
     extremist politics 214
     global warming impacts 157
     higher education in 111–13, 115
     invasion of Iraq 69–70, 167
     popular culture 127
     presidential campaigns 43, 54–5, 69,
          73, 155, 183–4, 207–8, 214
     school shootings 211, 212
universities, defunding and
     corporatization of 111–15
US Supreme Court 15, 171
utopianism 39, 75, 143, 148, 203

Valdés Leal, Juan de 222, 222f
values 13, 15, 31, 39, 59, 69, 75, 76, 100,
     105, 112, 137, 160, 165, 168, 172
vampires 124
     blood markets/blood culture 129–31
     "humanized" 128
     and humans 128–9, 234 n.4
     as metaphor 128–31, 135
     in popular culture 127–32
     and zombies, difference between
          235 n.17
Vampire Chronicles, The (book and movie)
     128
Vampire Diaries, The (TV series) 128

Van Dine, S. S. 97
Vanilla Sky (Dir. Cameron Crowe) 27
vanitas 133, 142, 222
Van Wert, William 36, 39
Vathek (Beckford) 125, 126
Vattimo, Gianni 14, 187
Vega y Carpio, Félix Lope de 12, 27, 29, 31, 71, 93, 95, 99, 101, 103, 106, 177, 178
Velázquez, Diego de 3, 22–3, 27, 178–82, 182f, 220, 221, 223–5, 223f
verwinden (surpass) 194–5
video games 134, 146
Vietnam war 13
violence 82–3, 87, 95, 97, 105, 127, 131, 138–9, 150, 156, 212
virtues 41, 44, 46, 47, 50, 51, 75, 79, 98, 169
Visigoth empire 67, 69
visiocracy 6, 80–3, 95, 98
visual arts 11, 18
visual culture 27, 80–2, 92, 93, 95, 98, 105, 221
Visualizing Law in the Age of the Digital Baroque (Sherwin) 6
volonté générale 208
von Hagens, Gunther 61
Vonnegut, Kurt 29

Waldman, Paul 54
Walker, Peter 198
Walkers (Sisí) 141
Walking Dead, The (comic book and TV series) 134, 137, 138, 139, 146
walking dead fantasies 132, 133–5, 138, 141. *See also* zombies
Wallerstein, Immanuel 1
Walpole, Horace 125
Walt Disney 14, 35–6, 38–9, 108. *See also* Epcot (Experimental Prototype Community of Tomorrow)
war on terror 68, 69, 73, 135
Washington Post 62, 114
wealth and power 43, 44, 50–4, 56, 222, 223
wealth of nations 2–3, 10, 159, 208
weapons of mass-destruction 167

Weatherford, Jack 51
werewolves 121, 129, 134
western culture 9, 124–5, 130, 191, 199
Western Europe 23, 51
What Money Can't Buy: The Moral Limits of Markets (Sandel) 74
White House Press Forum, 2006 166
Whiteread, Rachel 199
White Zombie (Dir. Halperin brothers) 132, 133
Wilde, Oscar 171
Winnie the Pooh (Milne) 14
Winthrop, John 70
wireless technology 2
witchcraft 126
witches 121, 122, 126, 156
women
    "free" 12
    objectification of 43–5, 54, 56
    rape of 93
    silent victimization of 133
    torture of 123, 211
    virtue of 44, 51
    whore house for 62
"Work of Art in the Age of Mechanical Reproduction, The" (Benjamin) 200
world, notion of
    character and actor 1, 11, 174–6
    as a city 106
    copy of 11, 15, 50, 61, 158, 160
    end of the 156
    fictional 184, 186
    illusion 100
    imaginary 35–41
    individual perspectives on 12, 15, 17–25, 98, 189
    knowledge of 4, 9, 22, 191
    as a picture 189
    as resource 157, 158, 159–61, 219, 221, 225
    theatrical framing of 99–109, 175–6
    truth and 60, 171
World Bank 155
world history 36
world population 155
world system 1

World Trade Center 13, 197
worldviews 12, 24, 100, 116, 177, 178, 219, 224
World War Z (book and movie) 134
Writing on the Wall (Standage) 4
WWCD mantra (what would
  Cervantes do?) 215
WWJD mantra (what would Jesus do?) 215

xenophobia 211

Yankah, Ekow N. 80

Zabala, Santiago 14, 187, 194
Zamora, Parkinson 238 n.15
Zayas, María de 12, 123–4, 132, 133
Zemeckis, Robert 62
Zero Dark Thirty (Dir. Kathryn Bigelow)
  169, 171

Zimmerman, George 80
Žižek, Slavoj 31, 53, 156, 215,
  235 n.17
zombies 127, 132–4
  African/Haitian 132, 134
  ancient Judeo-Christian motifs 143
  and global capitalism 147–8, 150–1,
    153–4
  limitations of symptomatic readings
    149–50
  as metaphor 135, 136, 149, 150–3
  in news cycles 134–5
  notion of global invasion 145
  in popular culture 134–9, 141–8
  "survival space" of 152
  and vampires, difference between
    235 n.17
Zoo (book and TV series) 158

www.ingramcontent.com/pod-product-compliance
Lightning Source LLC
Chambersburg PA
CBHW060155280326
41932CB00012B/1772